Special Education Re-formed

The term 'inclusion' has become part of the new official rhetoric of special needs education. Recent years have witnessed extraordinary debates concerning definition and ownership of the term. It is now time to move beyond this rhetoric in order to establish an evidence base for policy reform.

In this volume a respected group of researchers and practitioners, who share concerns for equity and excellence in education, write about their thoughts and concerns for the future of special needs education. They bring different perspectives on the value base which underpins current practice; they explore some of the pedagogic concerns which are raised by practices of inclusion; they reflect on different aspects of the processes of collaboration which may well be of considerable importance in the development of inclusive practice; and they consider the position of pressure groups in the promotion of inclusive practice.

The concept of the welfare state is undergoing scrutiny and questioning; there is a growth in the level of unease surrounding questions of effectiveness with respect to current equality of opportunity policy; there is international concern about the conditions and processes of social exclusion and the prospects for social cohesion. It seems timely and appropriate to ask searching questions about the material conditions which are likely to face children who get 'included' and the prospects for the creation of more inclusive schooling. This is a book that should be read by all those working within education, particularly those with a special interest in inclusive and special education.

This book is in the New Millennium Series which aims to make accessible, both for the lay reader and the professional, the complexities of education at all levels.

Harry Daniels is currently Professor of Special Education and Educational Psychology at the University of Birmingham, where he is also Deputy Head of School (Research). His research interests include gender and attainment in junior schools, peer support for teachers, emotional and behavioural difficulty, and mental health. He has taught in mainstream and special schools and is President of the Association of Workers for Children with Emotional and Behavioural Difficulties and the European Association for Special Education.

New Millennium Series

Special Education Re-formed

Beyond Rhetoric?

Edited by
Harry Daniels

FALMER PRESS
Taylor & Francis Group

London and New York

First published 2000
by Falmer Press
11 New Fetter Lane, London EC4P 4EE

Simultaneously published in the USA and Canada
by Falmer Press
Garland Inc., 19 Union Square West, New York, NY 10003

Falmer Press is an imprint of the Taylor & Francis Group

Typeset in Garamond by Taylor & Francis Books Ltd
Printed and bound in Great Britain by
Biddles Ltd, Guildford and King's Lynn

British Library Cataloguing in Publication Data
A catalogue record for this book is available from the British Library

Library of Congress Cataloging in Publication Data
Special education re-formed : beyond rhetoric? / [edited by] Harry
Daniels.
    p.   cm. – (New millennium series)
Includes bibliographical references and index.
1. Inclusive education – Great Britain. 2. Special education – Great
Britain. I. Daniels, Harry. II. Series.
LC1203.G7S72   1999
371.95'2–dc21   99–39366

ISBN   0–750–70893–X (hbk)
ISBN   0–750–70892–1 (pbk)

Contents

Figures and tables

Figures

Tables

Introduction

This book provides a platform for a respected group of researchers and practitioners who share concerns for equity and excellence in education. The term 'inclusion' has become part of the new official rhetoric of special needs education. Recent years have witnessed extraordinary debates concerning definition and ownership of the term. It is now time to move beyond this rhetoric in order to establish an evidence base for policy reform.

At present:

- the concept of the welfare state is undergoing scrutiny and questioning;
- there is a growth in the level of unease surrounding questions of effectiveness with respect to current equality of opportunity policy;
- there is international concern about the conditions and processes of social exclusion and the prospects for social cohesion.

It seems appropriate to ask searching questions about the material conditions which are likely to face children who get 'included' and the prospects for the creation of more inclusive schooling.

In a recent study of integration in Europe which made special reference to provision for pupils with special educational needs in fourteen countries, Cor Meijer gives us reason to feel some cause for concern. This publication by the European Agency for Development in Special Needs Education, which is funded by the European Commission, gives us reason to believe that while policies emphasize inclusion, practices still retain significant levels of segregation. Furthermore, the data suggests that current trends may be seen to favour the practice of segregation despite the international pressure for inclusion (Meijer, 1998).

This book is organized into four sections. In the first section there are three contributions which bring different perspectives on the value base which underpins current practice. In the second section five chapters explore some of the pedagogic concerns which are raised by practices of inclusion. As Slee (1998) reminds us in his chapter, 'High reliability organisations and liability students', to be found in the collection *School Effectiveness For Whom?*

(Slee 1998) the school effectiveness movement has tended to place little emphasis on both values and pedagogy. Writers such as Slee remind us of the importance of these matters.

In Section 3, four chapters explore different aspects of the processes of collaboration which may well be of considerable importance in the development of inclusive practice. The redressing of the balance between competition and collaboration in schools would seem to form an important part of the inclusive agenda.

Lastly, in Section 4, the position of pressure groups in the promotion of inclusive practice is explored by three authors. This collection of chapters was selected and combined with a view to promoting a debate that goes beyond rhetoric.

Harry Daniels

January 1999

References

Meijer, C. (1998) *Integration in Europe: Provision for Pupils with Special Educational Needs. Trends in Fourteen European countries*. Middlefart, Denmark: European Agency for Development in Special Needs Education on behalf of The European Commission Directorate General XXII.

Slee, R. (1998) 'High reliability organisations and liability students – the politics of recognition', in R. Slee, G. Weiner and S. Tomlinson (eds) *School Effectiveness for Whom? Challenges to the School Effectiveness and School Improvement Movements*. London: Falmer Press.

Section 1

Values

1   Inclusion in Education

From Concepts, Values and Critique to Practice

Brahm Norwich

Introduction

At one level it looks as though there are major changes going on within the field of educating students with disabilities and difficulties. There is a new government which has set education as its main focus for social policy, and the inclusion of students with disabilities and difficulties appears to be an important policy priority. At the time of writing we are waiting for policy developments following consultation over the Green Paper *Excellence for All Children* (DfEE, 1997). There have also been practical developments of innovatory practices and changing ways of thinking about the field over the last ten years, taking the introduction of the National Curriculum and the establishment of more autonomous school governance as the reference point. The term 'inclusion' has come into more common use than the term 'integration' in talking about increasing the involvement of students with disabilities and difficulties in the mainstream of education. There has also been an increasing interest in organizational and curriculum responses to diversity and a movement away from focusing on the individual student's deficits.

However, at another level, there has been a growth of exclusions for disciplinary reasons, and increasing pressures from mainstream schools for Statements in response to what are seen as the increasing demands made by students with difficulties and disabilities. These trends have come to be seen as systemic responses to the increasing pressures placed on schools to demonstrate increased accountability for their practices and learning outcomes. As many commentators anticipated in 1988, the impact of the introduction of market-style changes to schooling has been to reduce overall school tolerance for challenging behaviour and children deemed difficult to teach. But these trends have to be set next to countervailing trends towards a steady decline in the proportions of students in special schools and legislation to reinforce the responsibilities of mainstream schools for their special provision through the SEN Code of Practice. To understand the current context of special educational provision, we need therefore to recognize this interplay and changing balance of social processes and forces. This clearly places the disability education field or special needs education within a national political context, where legislation, funding and social policy orientations are major influences on what goes on within local areas and neighbourhood schools.

In this chapter I will discuss some of the current conceptions of inclusion which are found in policy positions and papers and expressed in academic debates about the nature of field and its place within education more generally. I will restate some of the arguments which I have developed elsewhere (Norwich, 1990, 1993, 1996, 1998) for understanding the significance of the multiplicity of values in education and special education, and how these imply the presence of basic value dilemmas. I will argue that these value dilemmas become policy and practice decision-making dilemmas at different levels within the system, for legislators, for local authorities, for school managers and even for class teachers. The main aim of this chapter, however, is to illustrate how recognizing basic dilemmas within the field can be a spur to more creative and optimal ways of educating students with disabilities and difficulties.

The chapter will begin with a brief analysis of some current policy and conceptual positions on inclusion. These will be set in the context of a discussion of some research findings about professional perspectives about inclusion. I will then discuss current government educational policy in terms of the compatibility of its mainstream and special educational policies. This will focus in particular on school target-setting and its impact on educating students with disabilities and difficulties. This leads into a more general commentary and analysis of what is involved in pursuing excellence and improving schools if the full diversity of students is taken into account. I then review the key points of the difference dilemma perspective and connect it with other conceptual perspectives on the field. In the next section I consider and evaluate different forms of school inclusion by comparison with some other current perspectives on making mainstream schools more effective for all. Finally, I discuss some current models for developing more inclusive mainstream schools. I conclude by showing how these reflect particular approaches to the compatibility and balancing of key values, and consider some possible options for the future of special schools.

Perspectives on Inclusion

I start by contrasting key principles from the SEN Code of Practice, as an expression of current government policy (DfE, 1994), and the widely referenced Statement on special education from the Salamanca UNESCO conference (UNESCO, 1994). Among the Code of Practice principles is one which states that:

> The needs of most pupils will be met in the mainstream and without statutory assessment or a Statement of SEN. Children with SEN, including those with Statements of SEN, should, where appropriate and

taking into account the wishes of their parents, be educated alongside their peers in mainstream schools.

(DfE, 1994: section 1.2, 2)

This expresses a conditional commitment to inclusion which is also expressed in the more recent SEN Green Paper (DfEE, 1997), in talking about 'inclusion of children with SEN within mainstream schooling wherever possible'. This shows continuity with the basic conditions set out in legislation from the original formulation in the Education Act 1981, which placed the onus on local education authorities (LEAs) to educate all children in the mainstream, subject to four key conditions:

1   that the child's special needs were being met,
2   that this did not interfere with the education of other children involved,
3   that it should be compatible with the 'efficient' use of resources, and
4   that it took account of parental wishes.

These conditions can be seen to represent the interests of those involved: the child with a disability or difficulty in learning, his or her peers, the parents and the LEA responsible for deciding about special provision. They set the commitment to inclusion as hanging on the relative weighting of these potentially contrary factors. Another feature of the current government policy is that the onus is for inclusion in mainstream schools, not necessarily mainstream classes.

Although the Green Paper expresses support for the UNESCO Salamanca Statement on special educational needs, it is clear this UNESCO Statement goes well beyond the conditional government commitment to inclusion:

Every child has a fundamental right to education and must be given the opportunity to achieve and maintain an acceptable level of learning;
Every child has unique characteristics, interests, abilities and learning needs;
Educational systems should be designed and educational programmes implemented to take account of the wide diversity of these characteristics and needs;
Those with special educational needs must have access to regular schools which should accommodate them within a child-centred pedagogy capable of meeting their needs;
Regular schools with this inclusive orientation are the most effective means of combating discriminatory attitudes, creating welcoming communities, building an inclusive society and achieving education for all; moreover they provide effective education for the majority of children and improve the efficiency and ultimately the effectiveness of the entire system.

(UNESCO, 1994: viii, section 2)

It is clear that there are different conceptions about inclusion which have a very significant bearing on the extent and nature of educational provision for students with disabilities and difficulties. Bailey (1998) from an Australian context outlines a definition which would reflect the perspectives of many in this country, too:

> Inclusion refers to being in an ordinary school with other students, following the same curriculum at the same time, in the same classrooms, with the full acceptance of all, and in a way which makes the student feel no different from other students.
>
> (Bailey, 1998: 173)

This definition focuses on two key aspects,

1 physically being in the same place and doing the same as other students, and
2 social acceptance and belonging.

'Inclusion' in this sense is usually contrasted with the now less used term *integration*, which is seen to reflect physical placement in the mainstream and the expectation that the student assimilates, as it is said, to the unchanged mainstream system. By contrast, in inclusion the mainstream school accommodates and restructures to respond to the needs of students (Ainscow, 1995). Whether integration was actually used to imply a lack of adaptation and response can be doubted, but it is clear that the force of the newer term 'inclusion' is to focus on systemic school adaptation and not just individuals separately.

However, Booth (1996) has criticized concepts of inclusion and inclusive education which purport to describe an ideal state or aim. He argues that reference to inclusive schools implies that inclusion is an attainable state and that good practice can be identified. Booth believes that there are few examples of inclusive schools which include all children from the neighbourhood, and therefore that it is better to think in terms of inclusion as an 'unending set of processes'. For Booth, inclusion:

> comprises two linked processes: it is the process of increasing the participation of students in the cultures and curricula of mainstream schools and communities; it is the process of reducing exclusion of students from mainstream cultures and communities
>
> (Booth, 1996: 96)

This definition takes a position on two of four dimensions of inclusion (inclusion as process and as connected to exclusion) which Booth and Ainscow (1998: 234) identify:

- as unending or as state;
- as linked or separate from exclusion;
- as limited to some taken-for-granted kinds of exclusion or applicable to all kinds of exclusion;
- as applied to limited groups (vulnerable, disabled) or to all students' participation.

For these authors, inclusion is not only an unending process connected to exclusion, but also applies to all kinds of exclusion and is not limited to students with disabilities and difficulties. In adopting this stance they are attempting to redefine the field of educating students with disabilities and difficulties – special education – in terms of the processes of inclusion and exclusion.

Booth is aware that this attempt to broaden the focus of inclusion – making schools responsive to all students, not just those with disabilities and difficulties – goes against positions within the disability movement to concentrate on inclusion and disability (Oliver, 1992). And he tries to detract from a focus on disability by suggesting that certain groups might not wish to have this term applied to them. However, the term 'disability' has changed over the last decade and is now used in legislation (Disability Discrimination Act) to include wider difficulties, while members of the disability movement have also come to adopt it. Though there may be differences between professionals and members of the disability movement about causal models of disability and there are areas of uncertainty about the range of disability, this does not undermine the importance of the disability focus and interest. I have chosen to use the reference 'disability and difficulties' in this chapter to talk about this focus. In doing so, I understand the connections between this focus and a focus on other disadvantaged and oppressed groups subject to discrimination, such as ethnic minorities and gender groups, and smaller groups such as travellers and pregnant teenage girls. It is also important to recognize that there are similar uncertainties about range, membership and identity for all these groups. This is relevant to attempts to undermine a disability focus and to incorporate it into a wider group defined in terms of the general processes of exclusion and inclusion.

This attempt to incorporate and even to dissolve a specific disability focus can be seen to reflect an interest in inclusion as a general social and political value. But as such, inclusion acts as a complex and abstract value, like equality or justice, which cannot be simply applied to the many areas and contexts of teaching and learning, let alone other areas of social life. This is because, like equality, there are different aspects and features of what is meant by inclusion and inclusiveness. Inclusion theorists, like those quoted above, imply that students have a right to be part of the mainstream but also a right to positive evaluation and respect. This is evident in the justifications for increasing participation and for reducing exclusion. But in addition to the right to participate and the right to respect, there is also an implied right to individually relevant learning. This emerges in the value placed on schools being 'responsive to differences between all students' (Booth et al., 1998: 224). If inclusive values are considered to underpin these three broad kinds of rights for all, then it becomes clear that inclusion – and, by implication, exclusion – are complex values over which there will be uncertainties about their applicability. For example, if the right to be part of the mainstream means being in the same location as others and being respected, then any separate provision will be considered as exclusionary, whatever the level of respect.

But we also find an authoritative concept of inclusion which does not equate the same location with inclusion. In the Tomlinson Committee Report on post-school education of those with learning difficulties and disabilities (Tomlinson, 1997), inclusive learning is about a system which is inclusive and not necessarily in an integrated setting. Tomlinson states that: 'No apology is necessary for the paradox, as some have seen it, that the Committee's concept of inclusive learning is not necessarily coincident with total integration of the students into the "mainstream"' (Tomlinson, 1997: 193).

He then goes on to explain that:

> The Committee was asked to advise how matters could be improved assuming limited resources. Full integration implies a very well-resourced education system, if it is to do justice to all the students who would, as a matter of dogma, then always be taught in the same setting. The number of teachers and other experts that would need to be deployed, together with the range of technological help needed, would be more expensive than is now the case, where concentration of resources is achieved.
>
> (Tomlinson, 1997: 193)

The significance of Tomlinson's concept of inclusion is that participation operates at different levels: the education system as a whole, the institution and the teacher in a particular setting. The right to participate at one level might or might not be matched by participation at another level. Whether it is matched at each level depends on resourcing, but also on individual students' learning needs. As Tomlinson goes on to explain: 'Full integration as an aim should be retained, and when achieved, it will be coincident with inclusive learning' (Tomlinson, 1997: 193).

It is clear that we have quite divergent and incompatible concepts of inclusion – Bailey's that it is learning in the same place on the same curriculum as others, Tomlinson's that it relates to the system and not necessarily to the same place and curriculum, and Booth and Ainscow's that it is not a state at all, but an unending process of increasing participation. A further problem with the unending position is that it does not seem to specify steps towards this unattainable goal. So we do not know whether one form of provision is more inclusive than another. How does physical proximity to mainstream activities compare with social acceptance of students with disabilities and difficulties? Is greater physical proximity but low social acceptance more inclusive than less physical proximity but greater social acceptance? Without specifying steps or criteria for a complex value like inclusion, what can happen is that any educational practice which involves some but not pure inclusive features can come to be identified as exclusionary. For example, if a student with a disability or difficulty is content to have some individual teaching outside her mainstream class separate from her peers, this system could be dismissed as exclusionary, even when it has many of the features of inclusive practices. Inclusion as an unending process goes with thinking in terms of dichotomies, a kind of purist either/or thinking which condemns any form or degree of separate provision or distinct support system.

In this respect Low (1997) makes an interesting and provocative distinction between different kinds of inclusivists: hard, soft and stupid. Hard inclusivists believe, in his analysis, that all needs should be taken care of as part of the general social arrangements. Systems of education should in this view be designed to include the full diversity. Soft inclusivists believe in supporting systems which enable maximum independence for those with disabilities and difficulties and recognize that this requires special support and provision. For them, inclusion is about this provision and support being available as part of mainstream arrangements. Stupid inclusivists, according to Low, recognize the need for special provision and support in practice but do not like to call it 'special'. An example of this would be the avoidance of the word 'special' because this language was seen as 'retarding the development of thinking about inclusion' (Booth, 1996: 89). Low considers hard inclusivism as wrong in principle and practice, as it denies, in his view, that people with disabilities, although they share common needs with all others, also have distinct and specific needs: what he is willing to call special needs. It is not clear whether Low believes that hard inclusivists turn out in practice to recognize the need for special provision but do not like to call it special, and are therefore also, in his terms, stupid inclusivists. However, it is probably only someone like Low who, having a disability of sight, is in a position to use such a provocative description of certain kinds of inclusivists.

Professional Perspectives on Inclusion

There is a sense in which we are all inclusivists now, as there are few, if any, interested and involved in the education of students with disabilities and difficulties who do not now favour some form of participation in the mainstream. This is where Low's distinction between hard and soft versions is useful, in highlighting differences over the presence and function of separate and distinct systems in addition to any generally built-in adaptations to the mainstream system. That there are significant differences over inclusion is evident in policy debates and from any examination of the differing perspectives of parents and professionals. These differences can be illustrated by two studies which I conducted in the mid-1990s of professionals' views about inclusion. They were two postal surveys of teachers in mainstream and special schools, support services, educational psychologists and LEA officers involved in special needs education. The surveys were based on samples of 236 and 150 people, selected randomly from LEAs in two areas of England, the South East and the Midlands.

Although there were several parts to the studies, for the purposes of this chapter I will report responses to general and more specific statements about inclusion and placement. What was most striking about the results was the consistency of response between the two samples. In both samples, over 90 per cent agreed with the statements that 'Integration is a desirable educational practice', with about 60 per cent agreeing strongly. However, when the focus became more specific the degree of endorsement decreased. In response to the statement 'All have the right to be in ordinary classrooms', just under 70 per cent agreed and only about 30 per cent agreed strongly. Disagreement to this statement rose to over 20 per cent. In response to a statement about feasibility, agreement dropped more sharply. To the statement 'It is feasible to teach very able, average and intellectually impaired children in the same class most of the time', agreement was about 55 per cent and mainly at the moderate, not the strong, level. Disagreement rose to above the 30 per cent level. A similar balance of views was expressed to the statement 'Integration will be sufficiently successful to be a required practice'.

When asked about a range of different kinds of impairments and functional difficulties, these professionals showed a wide range of differences about appropriate placements depending on the kind and degree of functional difficulties. They were specifically asked to indicate a range of appropriate provision from:

1   ordinary class without support;
2   ordinary class full-time with support;
3   ordinary class part-time and special class/withdrawal part-time;
4   special class in ordinary school full-time; and
5   special school full-time.

However, most responded by giving only one kind of provision. They were also asked to make their judgements taking account of current and likely future levels of resourcing. To illustrate the kinds of views expressed in these studies, I will focus on responses to provision for children with motor impairment, severe intellectual difficulties and aggressive behaviours. It was found that for the milder kinds and degrees of functional difficulties the most favoured provision was ordinary class with support. For children with 'motor impairment who cannot move without help', it was found that the most favoured provision was also ordinary class full-time with support (about 45 per cent in both samples), with the next most favoured being ordinary class part-time and special class part-time (about 20–25 per cent). Less than 10 per cent favoured ordinary class with support or special class full-time, but about 15 per cent did favour special school full-time.

The difference in views about provision for motor and intellectual impairments is shown by considering views about provision for 'children with severe intellectual difficulties needing training in self-help and daily living skills'. Over 50 per cent in both studies favoured special school full-time for these children. About equal proportions favoured special class in ordinary schools full-time and ordinary class part-time / special class part-time (about 20 per cent each). Very few gave full-time ordinary class provision. However, the widest range of views about provision was expressed concerning children showing significant aggressive behaviours. For 'children who are verbally aggressive to peers and staff', the most favoured provision was ordinary class part-time / special class part-time (about 30 per cent in each study) with nearly that proportion favouring ordinary class full-time with support (about 25 per cent). However, there were notable proportions favouring special class and special school provision (10–15 per cent each). There was a similar pattern of views about 'children who cannot easily control their aggressive behaviour', but special class and school provision was more favoured than ordinary class full-time with support.

The studies also examined the relationships between these inclusion views and the professionals' political beliefs and professional positions in the education system. As was found in a similar previous study of professional views in England and the USA in the early 1990s (Norwich, 1994), there were systematic differences in inclusion views and whether the professionals were mainstream teachers or senior teachers, SEN support teachers, teachers or senior teachers in special schools, or outside professionals such as educational psychologists or education officers. These differences can be illustrated by comparing the views from the larger sample of mainstream primary and secondary class teachers with those of outside professionals about provision for 'children who cannot easily control their aggressive behaviour'. While the class teachers most favoured special schools or classes (about 47 per cent) and least favoured ordinary class full-time with support (about 22 per cent), the outside professionals most favoured ordinary class types of provision (about 49 per cent) and least favoured special school (about 27 per cent).

Studies like the three mentioned in this section have their weakness in terms of sampling and methods of identifying views about inclusion, and no doubt can be subjected to more radical criticisms in terms of their generalization and quantitative assumptions. However, they do indicate the complexity of professional perspectives in terms of the differences between positions about principles and ideals and positions about feasibility and

specific kinds of provision for different kinds and degree of functional difficulties. They show the overall tension between support for the ideals of
inclusion and the reluctance to take responsibility for the more challenging
forms of special needs. Such professional perspectives are clearly also subject
to other influences, such as the quality of experience with inclusion, relevant
professional development, school and LEA policies and practices. Professional
perspectives are also ultimately about individual children, with their unique
characteristics and circumstances. However, there are also commonalities
between individuals with disabilities about which professionals can make
rough generalizations. This needs to be recognized if the important role
which teachers play in policy moves towards greater inclusion is to be taken
into account.

Current Government Positions: The Place of the Green Paper

There is much to welcome in the commitments and practical initiatives
taken by the new government in this field as expressed in the SEN Green
Paper. But these have to be seen in the wider context of general school
policy geared to raising standards, especially in literacy and numeracy for
the majority of students. This priority on standards has been presented as
raising standards for more students, not just the few. An extension of raising
standards as an aim for all – in the phrase used in the Green Paper, 'excellence for all' – has a very plausible ring to it. But is it just a fine example of
political rhetoric, a 'soundbite', as journalists say? Is it a coherent position
on inclusion for students with disabilities and difficulties?

To start to answer this question it is useful to consider the National
Curriculum (NC) with respect to special needs, as this innovation ten years
ago illustrates how the system as a whole responded and still responds to the
diversity represented by students with disabilities and difficulties. When it
was introduced, little consideration had been given to the degree of diversity
of students. Yet it was supposed to provide everyone with an entitlement to
a common curriculum, as an expression of inclusive values. Since the Dearing
modifications and the loosening of the NC requirements, the NC has become
more adaptable to the needs of students with disabilities and difficulties.
However, even now there are inflexibilities and uncertainties about the
applicability and relevance of the NC to literally all children.

The government has stated in the Green Paper that: 'All policies for
schools will include an explicit assessment of the implications for children
with SEN' (DfEE, 1997: 7). Although this position is welcome, we must
avoid confusing a commitment to assessing implications with one to
ensuring that general policies are compatible with the needs of the minority
with disabilities and difficulties. We only have to consider the general
commitment to raising standards of literacy and numeracy at primary Key

Stage 2 and school target-setting to ask whether these policies support or undermine the moves towards greater inclusion in mainstream schooling. Special schools have been informed that they have to adapt the National Literacy strategy to their own needs. Target-setting will apply to special schools and will be based on current work by the Qualifications and Curriculum Authority (QCA) to extend and refine NC assessment criteria for students with disabilities and difficulties. This will enable teachers to assess the attainments below level 1 and between levels 1 and 3 of the NC assessment framework. However, what is most striking about this is that it has taken ten years for there to be a national initiative to develop relevant assessment criteria, despite calls for developments a decade ago.

When we turn to school target-setting, we find that there is a similar gap for students with disabilities and difficulties. What targets are schools supp-osed to set for students with disabilities and difficulties in the mainstream, who we can assume will make up most of the 20 per cent not expected to reach level 4 in literacy by the year 2002? Will their attainments and progress be counted when schools are judged to have improved their literacy and numeracy standards, or not? The answer so far seems to be no, which can be taken to mean that the current system of setting a uniform national target is excluding 1 child in 5. It is not hard to understand the attractions of setting a single and simple national target. It is simple to communicate, politically convenient and relatively straightforward to administer. But, although having a high proportion like 80 or 75 per cent of children included is better than a lower proportion like 50 per cent, it is clearly not in accordance with a policy of excellence for all.

The general risks of using uniform and crude national targets are evident in the recent economic history of problems in the Soviet Union's command economy, where there were abuses from imposed and unsuitable production targets. Parallel problems can be anticipated with school target-setting in this country, in a narrowing of the curriculum and teaching and a concentra-tion on test results and not the wider quality of learning. From a special needs perspective, there is the risk that schools will apply their resources and efforts to bringing students near level 4 up to target by 2002. This could be at the expense of those less likely to reach level 4, who could then become less important to the schools. What we might find as a result of this process of selective effort is that the majority might reach the target but the varia-tion between the highest and lowest attainers in schools might widen.

One option is to change the way in which targets are set, from a threshold percentage figure to one which includes the attainments of all through a points system. All pupils' attainment levels would be counted, whatever their level of attainment. This has been recommended by one of the govern-ment's advisers (Brighouse, quoted in *The Times Educational Supplement*, 1998). This option would mean that simple uniform targets could not be set, but mean scores could be estimated and these could be compared with norms based on attainments in comparable schools. The variation in attainments between high and low attainers could also be estimated and monitored. But there is also another option, which relies less on central prescription. In this more school-centred option there would be a less centralized and command style of planning. Schools could be required to set realistic and challenging attainment targets which were relevant to their students and local circumstances. Central guidance and professional training could be provided for schools on how to go about this kind of planning, and they could be held to account for both the planning and the resulting attainment levels.

Excellence and Effective Schools

Despite contemporary interest in developing effective schools, there is entrenched muddle over concepts and values included in policy talk about improving schools and making them more effective. There are some commentators who advocate a form of effective school which is geared to responding to the full diversity of student needs (Ainscow, 1995). In this view, what is effective for the minority is taken to be effective for the majority. But, as Reynolds (1995) in this country and Gerber (1996) in the USA have argued, schools and practices which are associated with high attainments for students with disabilities and difficulties are not necessarily associated with high attainments for the modal or average student. Gerber explains that it is often overlooked that there is a conflict between public education geared to universal education and special education. This comes from: 'the insistence that design and deployment of instructional effort within schools could and should be modified to accommodate individual differences rather than expectations for modal students' (Gerber, 1996: 170).

Applied to the current context in this country, this leads us to ask whether what we commonly call an effective school can also be assumed to be an inclusive one, in terms not only of participation but also of substantial opportunities for optimal attainments. The answer depends on what counts as effective and what counts as inclusive. If we take a definition from Stoll and Mortimore (1997) of an effective school as 'one in which pupils progress further than might be expected from consideration of its intake' (p. 10), then it is clear that there is no explicit reference to either the modal or lowest attaining students. But the methods of research and assumptions of most school effectiveness and value-added research do show that it is the modal student who is the focus of interest. Schools are not identified as effective when their lowest attaining students show significant attainment gains. This is also demonstrated in government target-setting policies for raising standards. However, if the effective school is the one with consistently high A–C GCSE or level 4 literacy and numeracy results, then this excludes a significant minority with lower attainments from the operational concept of effectiveness.

Nevertheless, there are problems which arise in planning provision and setting standards in a genuinely inclusive way. They are problems which are associated with historical and continuing uncertainties about equality as a guiding educational value. Do we set standards in terms of attainment levels irrespective of individual differences in the starting levels and material and human resources for learning? If we do, as the current government has for literacy and numeracy at Key Stage 2, then we have to consider the relevance of these standards for those distant from the modal standard. As a second option, we could abandon a concept of equality defined in terms of the same or minimum outcomes for all because of individual differences. We could then interpret equality in terms of similar gains from different starting levels. This would mean legitimizing different outcomes, which might be seen to undermine a commitment to equality. It would also raise technical assessment questions about being able to compare gains across different levels of attainment. It might also require that additional instructional resources be applied to lower attainers to reach similar learning gains to the higher attainers. In a third option, we could abandon common standards for all, whether defined in terms of common outcomes or as gains for all. In this option, we could refuse to have any common standards at all, and opt for individually set standards. This would present a massive technical and practical problem, on one hand, and would relinquish any prospect of interpreting the value of equality in terms of comparability to general standards. Another alternative within this third option would be to have different standards for different groups, and aim to reduce the differences between these standards. This option retains common standards but diversified ones for students with different starting levels and resources for learning. It gives up equality in its simple interpretation in the first two options and replaces it with the value of reducing inequalities. But it also has the problem of how to decide which standards are relevant to which individual and groups. This move from options 1 and 2 to option 3 represents what Walzer (1983) has advocated in moving from 'simple equality' to 'complex equality'. In simple equality everyone gets access to the same thing, whereas in complex equality distribution varies according to different criteria. Ideas of complex equality are relevant to the contemporary interest in differences and what has come to be called the politics of difference. But, as Walzer recognizes, this raises the question of how to decide what is a 'relevant difference' for different treatments, which is another way of putting the problem associated with option 3 that I have just mentioned.

Multiple Values and Policy Dilemmas about Difference

I contend that there are problems and uncertainties about inclusion and effectiveness in education because we do not have simple and single ideas and values about educational excellence. As with equality, we cannot avoid complex ideas about inclusion and effectiveness. This arises in part from contradictions or dilemmas about educational values themselves and in part from limitations of our current capabilities to resolve problems in education and the wider society. We have multiple values in education which cannot be assumed to be mutually compatible in full. As I explained above, inclusion theorists take students to have a right to participate in the mainstream, but also to have a right to positive evaluation and respect. In addition, it is widely assumed that students have a right to individually relevant learning. There are also other rights which are invoked, such as to have some choice about the institution of learning and to achieve a basic minimum in terms of either outcomes or genuine opportunity. Analysis shows that not all these rights or entitlements are compatible with each other. This arises partly because if rights are extended to some, then they apply to all. This means that there is the continuing risk and the actual reality that minorities, such as those with disabilities and difficulties, are subject to majority interests which do not necessarily take the interests of the disabled, let alone their rights, into account. For example, this incompatibility of rights can arise from the potential tension between the minority's right to participate and the majority's right to individually relevant learning and choice about institution of learning. Unless some rights are given priority over others and backed by legislative systems, minorities are prone to dominance and exclusion by the majority. But there can also be a tension between the right to choose a separate institution of learning by some parents of students with disabilities and by these students themselves, on one hand, and the right of other students with disabilities to participate in mainstream institutions, on the other.

It should not be surprising that there can be clashes between different rights and entitlements, as one person's or agency's entitlement places a potential requirement or constraint on another person or agency. Rights and entitlement require resourcing and others' acceptance or tolerance of compliance. The implications of this position are that we take seriously the multiple values and associated rights or entitlements which are adopted in the educational field, and understand the implicit social conflicts and inter-relationships between mass school education and 'special' education. Much is heard about conflicts and contradictions from critical perspectives on special education which reveal oppression and unmask concealed dominant interests in current and historical policy and practice. This is done from an approach to theory and inquiry in which certain values and principles are assumed without detailed conceptual and empirical grounding (Clark et al., 1998). Policy and practice is interpreted in terms of idealized models and ideal types of provision, rather than in terms of more complex ideals and the range of realities experienced by participants in the educational endeavour. Less is heard about the tensions within individuals and agencies about aiming to increase participation in mainstream settings while aiming to increase teaching and learning opportunities for those with disabilities and difficulties. These tensions represent dilemmas between providing optimally for individual learning needs and participation and acceptance in the mainstream. These dilemmas, which have been called *dilemmas of difference*, take the form: if you include and treat in the same way as most others, individually relevant learning opportunities could be denied, but if you treat in individually relevant ways, some separation could be required and devaluation could result. On the basis of this model of social and political values, I have argued that there are basic dilemmas in education, and in particular the field of educating students with disabilities and difficulties (Norwich, 1993). These dilemmas are found in:

1   the identification of students as having some distinctive kind of characteristics or needs, such as special educational needs,
2   a common curriculum for all, including students with significant disabilities and difficulties, and
3   the organization of education services into common schools and classes for all or specialized to some students.

Clark et al. (1995, 1997 and 1998) have also found it useful to consider policy and practice in this field in terms of dilemmas in very similar terms.

These dilemmas of difference arise from trying to match the full range of individual needs into a common system while dealing with further dilemmas about choice and inclusion. When facing these dilemmas, individuals and agencies, whether government and its educational agencies, local authorities or schools, either adopt established ways of resolving these tensions or construct their own strategies. There are certain established ways of finding some compatibility between these values and ideals, in which resources of finance, staffing, facilities, equipment and human capabilities all play a significant contribution. But, unlike other perspectives on the education of students with disabilities and difficulties, this dilemmatic model does not assume that the tensions are basically resolvable. It might be possible under changed social and economic circumstances to reduce the sting in these tensions, so nurturing the hope that they will in time dissolve. But this does not eradicate the possibility of tensions in balancing potentially contrary values and goals. What is presented, therefore, is a model of educating students with disabilities and difficulties which recognizes that education involves interactions within and between multiple levels (macro, micro, meso and individual levels) and that decisions and actions at these levels are best understood in terms of the resolution of multiple and potentially incompatible values and goals. Such a model has key implications for policy formation and practice. Policies will therefore be seen to seek the optimal realization of multiple values and goals. Optimal compatibility will depend on an acceptance that full realization of values and principles calls for balancing and trading off. I have suggested elsewhere that this balancing requires an acceptance of ideological impurity in this area of education (Norwich, 1996).

This perspective differs from the perspectives of others who are critical of special education in terms of single ideals and principles. This can be understood by examining how Ainscow (1995) approaches the field. He is critical of the individual deficit focus and the lack of interest in systemic accommodation and response to diversity. Drawing on the work of others, especially Skrtic (1991), he uses the notion of organizational problem-solving as the way to develop new responses to student diversity. Practitioners' problems are taken in this view to be soluble only if they are enabled to collaborate in a problem-solving mode and can escape their preconceptions through critical reflections.

> I have come to the view that progress towards the creation of schools that can foster the learning of all children will only occur where teachers become more reflective and critical practitioners, capable of and empowered to investigate aspects of their practice with a view to making improvements. Only in this way can they overcome the limitations and dangers of deficit thinking, only in this way can we be sure that pupils who experience difficulties in learning can be treated with respect and viewed as potentially active and capable learners.
>
> (Ainscow, 1998: 12)

A common response to this would be: if it were only so straightforward as this. Linguard (1996), as an ex-SEN co-ordinator, probably represents the thinking of many directly and practically involved in the field, when he opposes it by arguing that it is: 'as realistic and helpful as arguing that all teachers could become millionaires if only they were to get together and work out ways of doing it' (Linguard, 1996: 40).

Clark et al. (1998) support this criticism by explaining that, in not accepting general categories of difference and difficulties in learning, commentators like Ainscow are unable to develop and accumulate pedagogical knowledge. Even trying to accumulate such knowledge would be to adopt aspects of what he criticizes as a positivist and technicist approach. Linguard is openly critical of this approach, which he presents as 'eloquent, but impractical and utopian', an approach which he considers to inhibit rather than encourage effective innovation. Clark et al. (1998) take a similar but less overtly critical and more moderated position by asking rhetorically whether such approaches become 'too unproblematically and unidimensionally millennialist'. Gerber (1996), from his US perspective, echoes a similar concern about 'these radical proposals as misguided zealotry' (p. 159). From his analysis, the demand to define educational opportunity for all disabled students in terms of location is seriously misguided: 'It is therefore unfortunate that contemporary reformers who urge "inclusion" have emphasized place over instructional substance and confused "participation" with real opportunity' (p. 158).

Models of Inclusion

There is the risk that, in trying to moderate the excesses of a simple concept of inclusion or any other value, we take up an opposite position and adopt an equally simple conception of individuality. I have been arguing for a model which while recognizing the tensions between pure versions of such positions also seeks constructively to find compatibilities. I recognize the benefits that come from past critiques of concepts and practices of separate special education and from current critiques of mainstream placements which are far from inclusive ideals. These perspectives continue to offer us essential ways of exploring what underlies the system and what is not working. But the critical mode is not enough, and the risks are that commentators can get stuck into the deconstructive mode and find neither time nor inclination to address constructive approaches to policy and practice. For example, Slee (1996) refers critically to the inclusion policies of education authorities as attempts to combine the incompatible discourses of social justice with deficit models. He then writes that it is unsurprising that such policy represents 'attempts to manage contests and orchestrate compromises' (p. 105). By contrast with the perspective advocated in this paper, Slee shows an unease often found among other critical proponents by portraying balancing and resolving tensions only in negative terms. What seems to underlie this unease is a concern that inclusion should not be about allocating further resources for students with disabilities, but about a 'challenge to the structure and culture of schooling' (p. 105). The position which I advocate in this chapter is that inclusion is neither exclusively about additional resourcing or different systems nor only about challenging current schooling. Too much focus on challenge assumes that there are certainties about what is wrong and therefore what needs to be done. This is contrary to the basic position in this chapter that there are multiple values and basic uncertainties about resolving value incompatibilities. In other words, educating students with disabilities is not only about inclusion. Inclusion can be justified as both an educational means, if it enhances access and opportunities for learning, and as a goal, through learning to collaborate with others and enhancing a sense of belonging and self-respect. But it is not the only value in education, and does not necessarily promote opportunities for learning.

In this section I will consider several schematic models of inclusion in order to illustrate the kind of differences we can expect from different ways of balancing the value of participating in mainstream curricula and schooling (inclusion) and the value of promoting individually relevant

21

learning (individuality). Inclusiveness is represented in Table 1.1 at four levels in the system: national legislation and systems; LEA policy and practices; school policy and practices; and classroom practices. Certain key aspects of provision are identified for each level. These are concerned with whether additional or different features are used at each level. For national legislation and systems, this is about whether legislation covering the needs of students with disabilities is additional to general coverage or considered to be included in general coverage. It is about whether there are special parts to the differentiation of the National Curriculum or no special differentiation for the disabled. It is also about whether the duty to include is unconditional or conditional on particular factors, such as parental wishes. For LEAs, this is about whether there are any special schools, any additionally SEN-resourced mainstream schools and any external SEN support services for schools. For schools, this is about having a learning support base for withdrawal teaching, ability grouping which includes those with disabilities and difficulties, and a system of in-class support for regular classes. For classrooms, this is about whether there is group and individual teaching as part of class teaching approaches and the use of support and team teaching.

In identifying four distinct versions of inclusiveness I am merely trying to illustrate some of the key differences between different ways of balancing inclusiveness and differentiation–individualization. This is not intended to be a definitive model of options. The first version is called *full non-exclusionary inclusion*, as it covers the full diversity of individual needs without additional legislation, curricula, special schools, different support services, separate classes or bases. In this version there is an unconditional duty to include in neighbourhood mainstream schools and classes. This means that adaptive responses to diversity are solely located at classroom level with different grouping and teaching variations without additional, different or special systems, curricula or staffing. In my assessment, this version raises serious problems of principle and practice, as it would involve prescriptive national legislation which would probably be opposed on democratic grounds that it restricted parental choice. And, if its fixation that inclusion is about place were enforceable, there would be problems over the grouping of students. If grouping represented the full range of diversity in the community, there would be concerns about finding practical and inclusive teaching methods which responded to the full diversity of individual needs.

The difference between the first and the second version, called *focus on participating in same place*, (compare columns 1 and 2 in Table 1.1) is in the acceptance of some additional and different systems to support participation in mainstream classes. In the second version, there is special legislation protecting the needs of students with disabilities and difficulties and a National Curriculum with special differentiation for disabled students. Inclusion in mainstream schools is conditional, as only some schools are additionally resourced for the needs of students with significant disabilities

Table 1.1 *Different versions of inclusiveness across different levels in the school education system*

Levels in system		System			
		1 Full non-exclusionary inclusion	2 Focus on participating in same place	3 Focus on individual needs	4 Choice-limited inclusion
National legislation and systems	Needs of disabled protected as part of provision for all; unconditional duty to include in mainstream schools and classes; no special differentiation of national common curriculum	yes yes	no	no	no
	Special protection of needs of disabled; conditional duty to include in mainstream settings; special differentiation of national common curriculum	no	yes yes	yes yes	yes yes
LEA policy and practices	Use of special schools	no	no	yes	yes yes
	Use of additionally resourced mainstream schools	no	yes yes	yes yes	yes
	External support services	no	yes yes	yes yes	yes yes
School policy and practices	Learning support base for withdrawal teaching	no	no	yes	yes yes
	Ability grouping	no	no	yes	yes yes
	Internal support system for regular classes	no	yes yes	yes yes	yes
Classroom practices	Group and individual teaching	yes yes	yes yes	yes yes	yes
	Team and support teaching	yes yes	yes yes	yes yes	yes

Notes:
no denotes not used/absent
yes denotes used to some degree
yes yes denotes used fully

and difficulties. In this version, 'special' is what supports participation in the mainstream, not what is apart from it. There are no separate special schools, separate classes or resource bases, there are only special external and internal support services to support additionally resourced schools and regular classes. What this version shares with the full non-exclusionary inclusion is therefore the focus on participation in mainstream learning settings; both versions reject any degree of separated learning as exclusionary. Though there are SEN specialized mainstream schools and support systems for regular classes, there is still the continuing issue of whether the full diversity of needs can be met even with this degree of additional support. The problem is less acute than for the first version, but there would still be questions about meeting the full diversity of needs within regular class groupings, even with group and individual teaching and team teaching. There would also be continuing issues over potential restrictions to parental choice.

Version 3, *focus on individual needs*, compared to version 2 accepts the limited use of special schools and learning support bases for withdrawal teaching. It would also accept a limited use of ability grouping for regular classes. As in version 2, the onus is on the mainstream to accept and accommodate systemically as far as possible. The use of special settings would depend on continuing connections between staff and students in mainstream and separate settings. Limited period and part-time placements would be used as far as possible. The key criterion for decision-making about educational provision would be individual needs, not place as in version 2. Limited separate provision would be justified if mainstream placement harmed the education of others or if special programmes promoted longer-term inclusion. This version goes well towards reducing the diversity of students in mainstream classes compared to version 2, but may still not take enough account of some parents' wishes about the need for specialized programmes in separate settings. Neither might it take enough account of policy-makers' concerns about the efficient use of scarce funding, given the need for dispersed special provision. The acceptance of even limited separate provision could also raise questions about denying opportunities to those who are withdrawn from the mainstream settings and about stigma and devaluation.

Version 4, *choice-limited inclusion*, goes even further down the route of justifying separate provision, while maintaining some rights to participation in mainstream schools and classes. This could be done in terms of parental wishes on one hand and school specialization on the other. Parents would have their preference for mainstream or special school provision respected as far as possible, thus leaving it open for some to opt for separate settings and programmes. Schools could also relinquish responsibility for certain students with disabilities, were they granted some discretion about entry on grounds of curriculum or programme specialization. Provision decisions would in principle be based on judgements about the individual student's needs, but in this version parents' perspectives would count. Were parents and schools to take up a more selective perspective, this would depend on support from the wider social and policy context in education. This was, for example, the kind of context established by the previous Conservative government, which operated a policy of school diversity and parental preferences. Applied to provision for students with disabilities and difficulties, this – at least in principle – shifted the balance of decision-making about participation in the mainstream and meeting individual needs from professional to parents.

The kind of separate provision found in the last two versions is usually justified in terms of preferences for teaching programmes which focus on students' difficulties. This is either in learning how to circumvent difficulties, such as learning Braille or sign systems, or learning to overcome and reduce the difficulties, such as in learning cognitive or self-control strategies. There is continuing debate about appropriate goals for these students, whether and to what extent programmes should be distinct and focus on and recognize their difficulties or whether they should take part in common programmes which are adapted to their individual needs. Of course, separate programmes and settings have historically also been shown to benefit the mainstream by removing students who were difficult-to-teach. But that has not been and cannot be a legitimate reason for separate settings. This places the onus on demonstrating the benefits of programmes focused on difficulties. Empirical evidence therefore places a key role here. I do not intend to discuss this issue further in this chapter, other than to make the point that policy decisions about the most appropriate of these different versions of inclusion do depend partly on such evidence and its use by those involved in decision-making about policy and individual educational needs. If and where it can be shown that longer-term participation in the mainstream can be enhanced by short-term separation, then some degree of withdrawal, whether internally to resource base, or externally to a special school, can be justified. This is a point which Booth and Ainscow (1998) accept in principle in relation to Reading Recovery withdrawal programmes (p. 100), though this puts the onus on making the empirical case and setting up programmes of evaluative research.

The Challenge for the Future

In setting out these four versions of inclusion I have tried to identify key aspects which illustrate different balances between inclusiveness, individualization and choice. I argued that there would be significant political and practical educational problems with the full non-exclusionary inclusion version. This is the version where inclusiveness, in my view, is predominant and where ideological purity can come to clash with democratic choice and individuality. I have also argued that the choice-limited inclusion version can perpetuate a system where unsubstantiated claims for the efficacy of specialist programmes can collude with a denial of mainstream opportunities and social acceptance. In this version, students could be in double jeopardy, denied access to mainstream while not benefiting from specialist programmes. This leaves the two middle versions, which involve a more even balance between inclusiveness, individualization and choice. From my perspective, this is where the current debate about the future should be centred. Version 3, with its focus on individual needs, represents elements of the current system. Version 2 represents a more inclusive system in which place is central. There are, of course, many variations between these schematic idealized versions around which there needs to be more debate, development and systematically evaluated trials.

In acknowledging that there needs to be some balancing and trading off between multiple values, I believe that this opens up the challenge to designing novel and practical arrangements which can better meet the needs of students with disabilities and difficulties. I have set out in the above scheme some of the options between retaining the number of many special schools we have now as separate institutions and having fully inclusive classrooms literally for all. The by now familiar strategy is the additionally resourced mainstream school, or what has also been called the mainstream special school. There is another option, elements of which have been developed: the cluster of mainstream primary and secondary schools attached to a special school. This could be a general cluster relevant to general matters concerned with professional development or sharing of resources, or it could be a specialized cluster relevant to disability inclusion. The special school can provide staffing and materials for mainstream schools in the cluster, and it can arrange for part-time or time-limited placements in mainstream. But there are still other options, such as when a mainstream cluster completely takes over the functions of a special school by dispersing these across the mainstream schools. Figure 1.1 shows how the functions of an all-age special school for students with physical disabilities can be dispersed into a cluster of mainstream schools. For illustrative purposes, this cluster consists of two infant/junior schools and one secondary school. Three types of provision are involved: mainstream class with general support; specialist teaching support from a cross-school support service; and separate resource base for complex difficulties. In this model, one primary school is additionally resourced for mainstream class placements with general support and for specialist teaching support from the cross-school support service. The other primary school has these two kinds of provision and also a resource base which is closely linked into the mainstream classes and their activities. The secondary school too has all three kinds of provision. The full-time teachers in the primary and secondary bases would also be involved in support work in mainstream classes like the specialist teachers from the support service. The additional provision dispersed in these three schools would be managed by a cluster management committee which takes over the modified responsibilities of the governing body of the closed down special school. The three mainstream schools and the LEA would be included in the governing body of the physical disabilities cluster. I am not aware of any examples of a cluster like this which takes over the operation of special provision in mainstream settings, but I consider that this example illustrates how we can construct creative ways of resolving the tension between meeting individual needs and participation in mainstream settings.

Figure 1.1   Mainstream cluster which takes over functions of special school

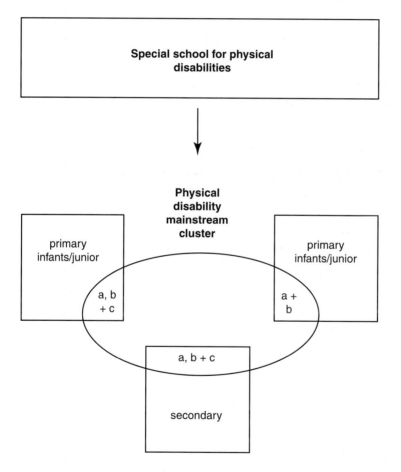

Notes:
a = mainstream class with support
b = cross-school specialist support service
c = resource base for complex difficulties

Concluding Comments

In this chapter I have advocated a position that recognizes and works with multiple policy values, that seeks their compatibility but recognizes that the full realization of ideals and values leads to tensions. This calls for balancing and trading off, which inescapably means the acceptance of some ideological impurity. When applied to the inclusion of students with disabilities and difficulties, inclusive values mean fewer – perhaps no – special schools and more mainstream schools which accommodate these students as part of the general response to the diversity of needs. But embracing inclusive values is in the context of embracing other values and the need for striking a balance between these values. And given the complexity and tensions between these values, we would expect to find different ways of doing so. As I have argued above, this means that in principle separate or withdrawal provision can be justified in inclusive terms, if the short-term separation promotes enhanced longer-term participation. This setting of limits to the purity of values like inclusion, equality and individuality comes from the complexity of these values, not just from resources constraints. Funding can soften much of the sting of tensions and problems I have discussed. But it needs to be remembered that money cannot be translated simply into the means to achieve learning experiences and outcomes. That requires educational organization, adequate staffing, professional training, teaching knowledge and skills. Some of these resources are not readily available, while others still need to be developed.

There is clearly a critical need for government commitment to significant funding and support for inclusive developments that are consistent with their other educational policy developments. This is in the context of there having been no specific central funding of inclusive development since the first legislation placing a conditional duty for mainstream education, in the Education Act 1981. There is now a government with an expressed commitment to inclusive values. What is needed is that we ensure that this expressed commitment is followed through and not undermined by other key policy moves. But, perhaps more importantly, there is a continuing need for all of us involved in education to find areas of common ground about values and principles. I present the argument in this chapter as a contribution to this goal. I believe that there is more common ground than there might appear to be. Professional teaching associations play an important part in this endeavour. There are, for example, associations like the Association of Teachers and Lecturers (ATL) which continue to support the policy of including children with disabilities and difficulties into mainstream schools (*Report*, 1998). Reflecting what would probably be the perspective of other teachers and many parents of students without disabilities and difficulties, its Assembly considered that this policy has to be consistent with the interests of all students and that this means it would be inappropriate for some children to attend mainstream schools. There is much scope for working out ways of protecting the education of the majority who do not have disabilities and difficulties without undermining systems of providing for greater diversity in mainstream settings. It is relevant here that we know little in this country about the full range of positive and negative outcomes of increasing inclusion for non-disabled students. By contrast, from the perspectives of those who lobby for inclusive education, we find that inclusion does not always mean full-time participation in mainstream classrooms. Micheline Mason, a leading person in the Alliance for Inclusive Education, was quoted recently as saying: 'We are not saying that children do not need help and we admit that sometimes help must be given outside of the classroom, but we do not believe in permanent exclusion' (*Guardian*, 1998). This perspective does not condemn all withdrawal teaching and is consistent with looking for creative ways of combining inclusive practices with practices which genuinely address individual learning needs. This is the challenge for the future.

References

Ainscow, M. (1995) 'Education for all: making it happen'. Keynote Address. International Special Education Congress, Birmingham.

Ainscow, M. (1998) 'Would it work in theory? Arguments for practitioner research and theorising in the special needs field', in C. Clark, A. Dyson and A. Millward (eds) *Theorising special education*. London: Routledge.

Bailey, J. (1998) 'Australia: inclusion through categorisation', in T. Booth and M. Ainscow (eds) *From Them to Us: An International Study of Inclusion in Education*. London: Routledge.

Booth, T. (1996) 'A perspective on inclusion from England', *Cambridge Journal of Education*, 26, 1, 87–99.

Booth, T. and Ainscow, M. (eds) (1998) *From Them to Us: An International Study of Inclusion in Education*. London: Routledge.

Booth, T., Ainscow, M. and Dyson, A. (1998) 'England: inclusion in a competitive system', in T. Booth and M. Ainscow (eds) *From Them to Us: An International Study of Inclusion in Education*. London: Routledge.

Clark, C., Dyson, A. and Millward, A. (1995) *Towards Inclusive Schools*. London: David Fulton.

Clark, C., Dyson, A. and Millward, A. (1997) *New Directions in Special Needs: Innovations in Mainstream Schools*. London: Cassell.

Clark, C., Dyson, A. and Millward, A. (1998) 'Theorising special education', in C. Clark, A. Dyson and A. Millward (eds) *Theorising special education*. London: Routledge.

Department for Education (DfE) (1994) *Code of Practice on the Identification and Assessment of Special Educational Needs*. London: HMSO.

Department for Education and Employment (DfEE) (1997) *Excellence for All Children: Meeting Special Educational Needs*. London: The Stationery Office.

Gerber, M. (1996) 'Reforming special education: beyond inclusion', in C. Christensen and F. Rizvi (eds) *Disability and the Dilemmas of Education and Justice*. Buckingham: Open University Press.

Guardian (1998) 'A class of her own', *G2*, 27 May.

Linguard, T. (1996) 'Why our theoretical models of integration are inhibiting effective innovations', *Emotional and Behavioural Difficulties*, 1(2), 39–45.

Low, C. (1997) 'Is inclusivism possible?', *European Journal of Special Needs Education*, 12(1), 71–9.

Norwich, B. (1990) *Reappraising Special Needs Education*. London: Cassell.

Norwich, B. (1993) 'Ideological dilemmas in special needs education: practitioners' views', *Oxford Review of Education*, 19(4), 527–46.

Norwich, B. (1994) 'A US–English comparison of attitudes to integration', *European Journal of Special Needs Education*, 9(1), 91–106.

Norwich, B. (1996) 'Special needs education or education for all: connective specialisation and ideological impurity', *British Journal of Special Education*, 23(3), 100–104.

Norwich, B. (1998) 'Aims and principles', in SEN Policy Option Steering Group (ed.) *Future Policy for SEN: Responding to the Green Paper*. Tamworth: NASEN.

Oliver, M. (1992) 'Intellectual masturbation: a rejoinder to Soder and Booth, *European Journal of Special Needs Education*, 7(2), 20–8.

Report (1998) *Annual Assembly Resolutions*, May edition of ATL magazine.

Reynolds, D. (1995) 'Using school effectiveness knowledge for children with special needs – problems and possibilities', in C. Clark, A. Dyson and A. Millward (eds) *Towards Inclusive Schools*. London: David Fulton.

Skrtic, T.M. (1991) 'Students with special educational needs: artifacts of the traditional curriculum', in M. Ainscow (ed.) *Effective Schools for All*. London: David Fulton.

Slee, R. (1996) 'Disability, class and poverty: school structures and policing identities', in C. Christensen and F. Rizvi (eds) *Disability and the Dilemmas of Education and Justice*. Buckingham: Open University Press.

Stoll, L. and Mortimore, P. (1997) 'School effectiveness and school improvement', in J. White and M. Barber (eds) *Perspectives on School Effectiveness and School Improvement*, London: Bedford Way Papers.

Times Educational Supplement (1998) 'Primary targets threat to weaker pupils', 29 May, 3.

Tomlinson, J. (1997) 'Inclusive learning: the report of the Committee of Enquiry into post-school education of those with learning difficulties and disabilities in England 1996', *European Journal of Special Needs Education*, 12(3), 184–6.

UNESCO (1994) *The Salamanca Statement and Framework on Special Needs Education*. Paris: UNESCO.

Walzer, M. (1983) *Spheres of Justice*. Oxford: Blackwell.

2 In Search of a Working Concept of 'Quality'

Control and the Consumer

Jesper Holst

Throughout the last decade there has been a steadily increasing interest in Quality of Life research in connection with people with disabilities. Research focused in this way has been pursued for a variety of purposes, related to the different types of problem that research has addressed and attempted to solve.

An important aspect of Quality of Life research has been the attempt to develop instruments of measurement, QOL scales, to provide a tool to evaluate and monitor the development of the services and support arrangements offered by society in relation to people with various forms of disability. Another, more ethnomethodological and phenomenological aspect of Quality of Life research has focused on getting people with disabilities to formulate their own subjective understanding and experience of Quality of Life, in order to use this material to ensure that society and the support services it offers are moving in a direction commensurate with the wishes, needs and visions of the people concerned. Finally, we have seen the Quality of Life concept used as a conceptual tool in relation to the politics of disability, and employed along with other terms such as normalization, integration, inclusion and empowerment to influence attitudes to the politics of disability and the way in which social support services and support personnel, professional or otherwise, understand their task (Holm et al., 1994)

It is clear that in their own way each of these three approaches attempts to come to grips with the concept of quality. This article will attempt to outline a number of central issues within and across these three approaches to Quality of Life research in relation to disability.

Following the American Quality of Life debate (Taylor, 1994) the first approach outlined here will be called the 'QOL' approach, the second the 'Quality of Life' approach, and the last one the 'Good Life' approach.

QOL: In Search of an Evaluation Scale

A great deal of Quality of Life research has concentrated on the development of concepts and instruments of measurement to ensure control of the effectiveness and development of the services offered by society in various ways to people with disabilities.

The following headlines (Schalock, 1994) offer an insight into the central concepts and activities that characterize this approach:

- Quality of Life Indicators
  - Home and community living
  - Employment
  - Health functioning

- Quality of Life measurement
  - Objective
  - Subjective
  - Goodness-of-fit

- Quality of Life applications
  - Research
  - Quality enhancement
  - Quality assurance
  - Policy formulation

As an example of a definition of the Quality of Life concept and associated Quality of Life Indicators, two theories which have had considerable influence in Scandinavia will be briefly presented here, though I am well aware that such a brief presentation in no way offers an adequate picture of these theories.

The ideas and understanding of the Quality of Life concept as developed by Professor Erik Allardt from Finland can be illustrated by the following model (Holst et al., 1995):

WELFARE	HAPPINESS
The objective dimension	The subjective dimension
Living standard	Joy and well-being as experienced
To have	
Quality of life	
To love	
To be	

Like a number of other researchers, Erik Allardt works from the basic idea that Quality of Life has an objective side, which can be studied by registering the actual conditions of life, and a subjective side, which is the extent to which people themselves feel satisfied about their lives (Allardt, 1975).

The objective dimension rests on the assumption that there is a connection between the satisfaction of needs and Quality of Life, which means that the more people are able to have their needs satisfied, the more the conditions for a good life are present.

The 'To have' category indicates the satisfaction of material needs in the form of income, housing, work, health and education.

The 'To love' category indicates the satisfaction of emotional needs, which means to love and be loved, to have close friends, family relationships, etc.

Finally, the 'To be' category indicates the satisfaction of social needs in the form of influence, reputation and feeling significant in the social contexts one is involved in.

Erik Allardt uses the Quality of Life concept primarily in connection with the 'To love' and 'To be' categories, in which the satisfaction of needs is directly dependent on relationships with other people. As may be seen, Erik Allardt derives his Quality of Life Indicators from Maslow's Pyramid of Needs: material needs (To have), emotional needs (To love) and social needs (To be). This connection between the satisfaction of needs and Quality of Life is quite usual, but does it hold water?

Another Scandinavian Quality of Life researcher, Siri Næss, has objected to this connection, on the grounds that human needs are not constant but constantly develop and change depending on age, personality and the social and cultural situations in which people live (Kajandi, 1985). Siri Næss herself is of the opinion that Quality of Life is primarily a psychological phenomenon, and has constructed the following Quality of Life categories based on philosophical considerations and empirical investigations. (Næss, 1979).

A particular individual's Quality of Life is dependent on that person:

1   *Being active* This means that the individual is able to use her own drive and initiative to involve herself in the world around her; has the energy and power to carry out her plans by her own efforts; is able to use her abilities, potentialities and skills; and that she has the freedom and the opportunity to make choices that enable her to shape the course of her own life.

2   *Having satisfactory interpersonal relationships* This means that the individual has at least one lasting, reciprocal, near relationship to another person and that the individual feels a sense of belonging and group identity in relation to friends, family, colleagues, etc.

3   *Having a positive self-image* This means that the individual sees herself as competent, useful and of value, as a person who is able to cope with the tasks of everyday life, and who feels satisfied with her own efforts.

4   *Experiencing a basic feeling of joy* This means that the individual has intense experiences of beauty, or of feeling at one with nature, that she feels secure and experiences a sense of joy at the richness of life and what it has to offer.

Siri Næss uses these four categories to deduce the following eleven Quality of Life Indicators:

Activity	1	Involvement
	2	Effort, own power
	3	Self-actualization
	4	Freedom
Relationship to others	5	Close relationships
	6	Friendship and belonging
Self-concept	7	Self-assurance
	8	Self-acceptance
Basic feeling of joy	9	Experiences
	10	Security
	11	Happiness

As may be seen, the QOL approach is based on the idea that Quality of Life can and must be defined and be measurable. The question is: how? This question raises the first and very fundamental point of difference between the three approaches outlined in the introduction, namely whether it is possible to define Quality of Life, and to measure it in relation to particular sections of the population. On the one side, the intransigent positivist viewpoint is proposed, as for example in a review of a book entitled *Quality of Life for Persons with Disabilities – International Perspectives* (Goode, 1994). In his review, Laird W. Heal writes:

> One of Wolfenberger's many contributions to this volume is to point out this Achilles' heel of such undisciplined humanism. William James is credited with saying that if something exists it exists in some amount and can be measured. It is to the discredit of most of the authors of this book that they are oblivious to this important point of logic – all believe that Quality of Life exists, but only four discuss its measurement using publicly communicable indices. To deny an entity's assessment is to deny its existence.
>
> (Heal, 1996: 558)

On the other side, there are a number of humanist and ethical objections to defining and measuring Quality of Life.

In 1989, the Danish disability NGO, LEV, convened a large conference on the theme of Quality of Life. At this conference, Niels Bank-Mikkelsen, a former head of care for people with mental disabilities who is widely known for having formulated the concept of normalization in the 1950s, presented a paper drawing attention to his reservations concerning the concept of Quality of Life (Bank-Mikkelsen, 1989). He expressed a fear that 'well-heeled' government social experts and researchers, using their own definitions of Quality of Life, would set in motion a process of control never seen before, by attempting to shape the lives of the disabled along the lines of that understanding of 'the good life' held by the more fortunate sections of the population.

The same objection has been voiced by the American sociologists David

Goode (Goode, 1992) and Steve Taylor (Taylor, 1994), who have warned against the 'Tyranny of Quality'. Bank-Mikkelsen was, he said, certain that in the past even large, impersonal institutions had been set up on the basis of what experts at the time understood to be 'quality' for people with disabilities, and he emphasized that in the course of time there have been countless instances of people being wrongly treated by those who were certain that they knew what was best for others. Apart from this obvious objection – that the Quality of Life concept can lead to people being guided and controlled by experts as never before – a number of other objections have also been raised.

In the last few years we have witnessed an increasing interest in the health and social welfare sectors in the Quality of Life concept and the measurement of it, due to the fact that the modern health system is faced with a number of very difficult questions concerning priorities. How are the resources available to be distributed? Hip operations or heart transplants? An attempt is made to solve these problems rationally by according the highest priority to those measures that have the greatest utilitarian effect in terms of Quality of Life and length of life, and measuring instruments have been devised to aid the decision-making process. The question is whether what we are seeing here is not merely what has been called a 'technical fix' – that is, an attempt to solve ethical and political problems by applying technical rationality. In the deepest sense it is surely unethical to establish priorities that remove support and help from groups of people who need help (Bauman, 1994).

Even though some will maintain that the fear of what Quality of Life measurements can be used for is exaggerated, it is worth considering the consequences and dangers of linking Quality of Life measurement and medical guidance in connection with such matters as foetus diagnosis and abortion on the basis of genetic indications.

One example which may serve to illustrate this fear is the use made of intelligence tests. The first intelligence tests were developed in France at the behest of the Ministry of Education with the aim of improving the service offered by schools; the test was to be used to identify those children in need of special support, so that interventions could be made more effective by the creation of homogenous teaching groups. Before long, however, intelligence tests were being used to separate off children with serious learning problems. These children soon came to be regarded as of less value, and as unsuitable to receive teaching.

What began as an attempt to improve the quality of teaching became an instrument for separating off children on the basis of quality. At that time it was a question of a measuring instrument developed to measure one particular human quality, important though this was and fraught with questions of value. When we talk about the Quality of Life we are talking about the measurement of a person's total life situation, putting a price, as it were, on the value of their lives. The risk of a development similar to the above is no less in the case of such an objective.

(Söder, 1991: 20–1)

Yes to Quality of Life, but No to QOL

'Quality of life is a useful sensitizing concept; QOL is a reification.' This is the view of the American sociologist, Steve Taylor, and other ethnomethodologists concerning Quality of Life research (Taylor, 1994). Quality of Life can only be understood as something quite subjective and culture-related. This does not mean that we should stop working on or researching the Quality of Life concept, but it does mean that we have to abandon operational definitions of the concept and all attempts to develop objective Quality of Life Indicators.

Blumer (1969) distinguished between two forms of sociological concepts: what have been called 'heart' and 'head' concepts, or 'definitive' and 'sensitizing' concepts.

> A definitive concept refers precisely to what is common in a class of objects, by the aid of a clear definition in terms of attributes or fixed bench marks. This definition or the bench marks serve as a means of clearly identifying the individual instance of the class and the make-up of that instance that is covered by the concept. A sensitizing concept lacks the specification of attributes or bench marks and consequently it does not enable the user to move directly to the instance and its relevant content. Instead, it gives the user a general sense of reference and guidance in approaching empirical instances. Whereas definitive concepts provide prescriptions of what to see, sensitizing concepts merely suggest directions along which to look.
>
> (Blumer, 1969, cited in Goode, 1994: 261)

As a concept, Quality of Life is a 'heart' concept, like 'love', and 'caring', but it points us in a particular direction – at the way in which people with disabilities experience the quality of their daily lives. And it is precisely this focus on the way in which people with disabilities understand and experience their lives that makes the concept important, since this angle has been much ignored. Quality of Life research must attempt through dialogue to help people with disabilities to formulate their own visions, dreams and ideas about quality in their lives, and of course use these formulations to create the changes that are called for. Inspired by this idea, a few years ago a participant-controlled action research project was carried out in Denmark, called the 'Grindsted Project' or 'Sunday, Bloody Sunday'. (Holst et al., 1995; Holm, 1996).

The objectives of the project were:

- To test and evaluate different methods for entering into dialogue with persons with disabilities about their everyday lives, whether they have a spoken language or not. This investigation of methodology was motivated by a research interest.
- To ensure that the dialogue would have consequences, i.e. result in changes in the everyday lives of people with intellectual disabilities in accordance with their own wishes. This was motivated by a development interest.

Eight persons with intellectual disabilities from a mini-community in the Municipality of Grindsted wished to take part in this project, along with their professional support persons. It was decided to trial and evaluate four methods to create a dialogue with these eight persons about their daily lives.

The four methods to be trialled were:

The future workshop method
The video method
The picture method
The participant observation method

The Future Workshop Method

The future workshop method, developed by Robert Jungk (Jung and Müllert, 1984), is an approach used to release creative capacities in people with the aim of helping them shape their own future. The workshop has a fixed course with several stages.

The first phase allows the participants to present their criticism, frustrations and aggressions in relation to a particular topic or situation which has been chosen in advance. The criticism is summarized in a number of broader themes, and one or two of these are used in the second phase, in which the imagination is given free rein – why cannot we just do this or that instead? The suggestions that arise at this stage are again summarized as themes. In the third phase the participants formulate suggestions and action plans as to how some of these proposals can be realized in practice.

Two future workshops were carried out in Grindsted. The first one, which lasted two days, involved the eight residents but not the staff. These two days were very exciting and inspiring, and some of the central points of criticism formulated here were as follows:

- Work in the special workshop is monotonous and boring.

- We feel that it is wrong and degrading that we receive social security benefits instead of wages for our work.
- Sundays and holidays are boring.
- We lack friends in general, and boy friends and girl friends in particular.

Many exciting and creative ideas were put forward in the imagination session as solutions to the criticisms voiced here. However, problems arose in the realization phase. We were shocked to discover that the absence of the staff meant that the residents were not able to plan any real changes in their daily lives, as this could only be done in conjunction with the staff. As a result, we had to carry out a further future workshop, this time for both residents and staff. This workshop, too, was both exciting and inspiring, but the pattern of communication was different. Even though in Danish terms the staff in Grindsted are both competent and sensitive, the professionals – perhaps without intending to – took over the initiative and controlled all communication.

All in all, the future workshop proved to be an exciting and productive way of creating a dialogue with the residents about their daily lives.

The Video Method

This method involved producing a video of the daily lives of each of the residents. The residents helped to prepare the script and to choose those central aspects of their daily lives which would be filmed, and naturally they took part in the filming. Further, the sound-track of the video was to consist of the residents' own comments on the situations and episodes filmed, on the presumption that a visual presentation of situations from daily life would make them more open to comment, and that in this way we could hope to gain an impression of how the residents saw their lives and what their wishes were in this regard.

The method proved to be useful, and the preparation of the script and the filming turned out to be especially motivating in terms of a productive dialogue about everyday situations. Production of the sound-track on the basis of the residents' own comments was more complicated, however, as the residents wanted to say far more than the time allowed by the individual video sequences permitted.

The Picture Method

This method was tried out with residents who had either very little verbal communication or none at all. The idea was to collect a number of pictures from the daily lives of the residents, to provide them with a background for an 'interview' about their lives.

The pictures were produced in various ways:

- The residents borrowed a Polaroid camera and film. They were given the task of photographing, in the course of a few weeks, all the people, places and events which were important and central to their daily lives.
- An investigator shadowed each of the residents for a week and photographed central events and routines from their daily lives. These photos were collected in an album for each of the residents.
- Finally, a number of archetypal pictures were collected from newspapers, magazines, advertisements, etc.

All these various pictures were afterwards used in connection with an 'interview' with each of the residents about their daily lives, This usually consisted in the pointing out or choice of pictures, so that, for example, residents answered questions such as: 'What do you like best about your work?', by pointing out or selecting a picture. This method was complicated and difficult to use, but gave an impression of certain central preferences held by the residents as regards their daily lives.

The Participant Observation Method

Finally, a more systematic method of registering data was attempted, which consisted in a more systematic observation of the daily lives of the residents in terms of time, place, social relations and activities. This systematic observation was carried out by the residents' own social workers, and revealed a number of patterns in daily life and the influence the residents had on these patterns. In addition, the observations formed the basis of interviews with the residents about the daily, weekly and yearly rhythms of life.

This participant observation also proved to be an exciting method, which made it possible for support personnel to discover new aspects and patterns in the daily lives of the residents.

Taken together, the four methods and the dialogue they created presented a picture of the criticisms, needs, wishes and dreams of the residents with regard to their daily lives, and this dialogue was followed up by a number of changes or qualitative improvements, including:

- Measures were taken to make Sundays and holidays less boring.
- Gitte was given a new job.
- New social relationships were created.
- Anna was put in contact with a family who visited her.
- The Municipality of Grindsted set up a culture and activity centre.

It is possible to enter into a dialogue with persons with intellectual disabilities themselves regarding what they consider as quality, and despite all our good intentions this dialogue is necessary if we want to avoid manipulation and paternalism. Even so, the approach to Quality of Life which emphasizes the subjective side of the concept with the aim of improving quality also has its problems and its critics. It is undoubtedly correct that Quality of Life does have a subjective aspect, and that one cannot imagine research into the quality of people's lives without entering into a close dialogue with the people involved.

But is this enough? Does this type of Quality of Life research not lead to a particular problem? If we imagine a group of researchers fifty years ago visiting one of the eleven large institutions for the mentally disabled that existed in Denmark at that time, and entering into a dialogue with the inmates about the quality of their lives, they would probably have reached the conclusion that the inmates were in the main quite satisfied. Was it therefore wrong to close these institutions and attempt to 'normalize' the lives of the inmates? Was it wrong to break down the fences that surrounded them? Was it wrong to have attempted to alter the conditions of life of the inmates?

In this connection the story is told of a boy with disabilities whose parents had kept him shut up in a little room, barely more than a broom cupboard, cut off from any contact with the world outside. At some point the child was discovered by the social services, and naturally enough a psychologist was appointed to talk to him about his childhood. To the psychologist's great surprise, the boy said that he had had a good childhood. The point at issue here is that our experience, understanding and visions about Quality of Life are coloured by the culture and social environment of which we are a part. Daily life in an institution or in a broom cupboard might seem so natural that a person might have difficulty imagining that things could be radically different. In terms of visions and ideas about Quality of Life, we are all limited by the natural inevitability of the world created by the social and cultural environments we form part of throughout our lives.

Some will perhaps maintain that with the development of modernity and the increasing contingency of values we are becoming increasingly more liberated from the world of inevitability. This is perhaps true in a number of western societies, but still does not solve the problem that in terms of our choices and our understanding of Quality of Life we are still dependent on what is familiar to us, which we regard as natural and inevitable.

Apart from setting up a dialogue with those who use the social services concerning their subjective view of Quality of Life, it is also incumbent on us to contribute to the politics of disability by discussing and formulating ethical criteria and human rights which, apart from the subjective views of these users, can help to develop the way society regards its most vulnerable citizens.

'The Good Life' as an Aim in the Politics of the Disabled

The formulation of the normalization objective at the end of the 1950s launched a progressive and innovative ideology within the politics of disability which in many ways revolutionized living conditions for people with mental disabilities. The normalization programme, which was and still is guided by the call for equality under the slogan: 'A life as close to the normal as possible', had the following consequences:

- Persons with intellectual disabilities were moved out of large centralized institutions to small groups or communities, more like normal homes, in their own municipalities.
- The dominant system of medicinal care and treatment was replaced by an educational approach based on development and training.
- The idea that some people could not be taught was replaced by the right to receive instruction and by efforts to integrate disabled children into normal kindergartens and schools.

There is no doubt whatsoever that the normalization programme improved the living conditions and opportunities of the mentally disabled in many ways. In an investigation carried out in the middle of the 1980s, forty mentally disabled people who had been moved out of a large central institution (Ribelund) on to an ordinary housing estate were asked to evaluate the changes in their living conditions (Jessen et al., 1985). Only two of them wanted to go back to the large institution, whereas the other thirty-eight felt that their lives had been improved. Yet, despite the fact that users feel that the quality of their lives has improved, in the course of the past decade criticism has been raised of the educational and administrative measures which the ideology of normalization has led to. The main points of this criticism can be expressed as follows.

The Skeletons are Still in the Cupboard

There is a tendency for the heavily planned and organized life of the large institution to be reproduced in municipal mini-communities and small institutions (Sletved and Haubro, 1985). One particularly glaring example of this is the following daily schedule for a municipal mini-community with eight residents:

07.30	Awake residents
08.15	Breakfast with all the residents (medicine)
09.00	Out for a walk, in all weathers
10.00	Morning coffee in the activity groups
10.15	Sing, play instruments in the activity groups
11.30	Lunch (medicine)

12.00	Toilet training
12.15	Siesta
14.00	Go to the toilet
14.30	Afternoon tea/coffee
16.00	Footbath
16.45	Free
17.30	Evening meal (medicine)
18.00	Toilet training
18.30	Change into pyjamas or tracksuits
20.30	Evening coffee (medicine)
21.15	Go to the toilet, personal hygiene
21.30	Bedtime

In addition, we may read:

> The above applies in general to all residents. The schedule can also be
> seen on the activity plan on the notice board. In addition, charts for
> bowel movement, weight and menstruation are to be found in the card
> index.

(Holst, 1991)

It cannot simply be a question of integrating the mentally disabled into
ordinary accommodation and learning environments. Both in mini-
communities and in schools, it must also be a question of deinstitutionaliza-
tion, so that the mentally disabled, through communication, can be
involved in the running of their own lives.

The Training of Functions, Independence and Taking Away People's Time

Anna is 80 years old. A few years ago she was moved out of a large, centralized institution, and now lives alone in a little terraced house. She is visited
every day by her social worker, who has naturally drawn up an individual
development plan for her. She has done this partly because it is her job, and
partly because she feels it is her professional duty to ensure Anna's continued
development in the form of increased mastery of the small tasks of daily life,
such as personal hygiene, eating, shopping, washing and cooking. Starting
from the idea that it is good for people to be independent, professional social
workers, trainers and teachers draw up individual action and development
programmes. They know what kinds of competence it is important to
develop; they know what is required to live an ordinary life.

Anna has lived for years in constant contact with professional support
persons who know what is good for her, who have more or less laid down the
objectives to be pursued and have defined her needs, so it is not surprising

that she does not express her own needs and desires and that the idea of making choices herself, of managing her own life, is foreign to her. In meta-cognitive terms, therefore, what the users surely learn from all these peda-gogical action plans is something like the following: 'The staff know what is best for me. They know my needs even better that I do myself, so why should I make any choices, why should I try to put my wishes into words?'

The normalization ideology has spawned a tendency to take away some-thing very precious from mentally disabled people – their time! Their days are filled up with work, various occupations, instruction and training, all planned and controlled by others than themselves. When planning teaching and living environments for children, young people and adults with disabili-ties, much more attention must be paid to allowing time for activities and social interactions determined by the wishes and choices of the users them-selves.

Loneliness and Isolation

The integration of mentally disabled people in the 1980s into more normal living environments and institutions often led to problems of loneliness and social isolation for those who were, on formal terms, integrated into society.

In modern society, people choose and maintain their social relations themselves, but it is often the case that the social relationships of supposedly integrated mentally disabled people often consist of other mentally disabled people, professional support staff, and possibly their families. (Gustavsson, 1992). The core problem here is that it is relatively easy – in theory – to integrate persons with intellectual disabilities into the ordinary situations of life, but real social integration is more difficult, and in recent years in Denmark this problem has led to a number of apparently contradictory views concerning the integration process.

On the one hand, it has been maintained that people with disabilities form a subculture, and that they need places to meet, a social arena, where this subculture can develop along its own lines. To this end, cafés, meeting and activity centres have been set up, and festivals of music and culture have been arranged. These 'subcultural' activities have created the basis for an incipient common political consciousness. In the wake of these cultural activities, therefore, we have witnessed the first strikes at sheltered work-shops and the creation of the ULF, which is an NGO specially for the mentally disabled themselves.

On the other hand, another problem has arisen: in the course of the last decade not only has the integration of disabled children into ordinary schools stagnated, but segregation into special schools and other special arrangements has gradually increased. This means that the debate about inclusion, focusing on a more open and accepting type of school, institution and indeed society in general, looks like becoming a central point of discussion within education and social pedagogy in the years to come, also in Denmark.

Normality as the Starting Point

Even though the normalization programme was basically a question of providing people with disabilities with the same rights and opportunities as other people in society, in many respects the programme was managed by administrators and educationalists, so that normality became the norm governing the way in which the lives of the mentally disabled were organized. Ordinary people (in Denmark) prefer to live on housing estates, preferably on the outskirts of large towns, and for this reason small institutions and mini-communities for the mentally disabled were set up in such areas. Ordinary people furnish their houses with sofas, televisions, bookcases and chairs in certain standard ways; therefore, accommodation for the mentally disabled should be furnished in the same way. Yet taking the generality, a statistically normal life, as the basis for planning living and learning environments for people with disabilities raises a number of problems. In the first place, it may be asked where 'ordinary life' exists other than in the statistics and in our imaginations. Social research indicates that we live our lives in a variety of ways. There is a variety of different lifestyles in accordance with which we organize our daily lives in connection with work and leisure. We live in a pluralist society, each with our own values and conceptions of what is 'the good life'.

In the second place, it may be asked whether 'ordinary life' can be prescriptive for the planning and management of the lives and opportunities of particular sections of the population. Are we not dangerously close to the naturalistic fallacy here – concluding from the way things normally are to the way they ought to be for a particular group?

Finally, in the third place, we may ask whether the objective of equality might not lead to a kind of 'tyranny of the normal'. If there is even some truth in the assertion that ordinary people in high-powered industrial societies live pretty stressful, alienated, rootless and divided lives, is it at all meaningful (anything visionary is out of the question) that planners and educators use the concept of a normal life as the yardstick for the management of a framework for the daily lives of disabled people? In this context it is essential that the normalization programme is not just based on a conception of 'ordinary life'; we must open up conceptions of 'the good life', creating conditions that will enable people themselves to develop quality in their own lives (Holm et al., 1994). 'The good life', or Quality of Life, will thus be the concept which, in the wake of criticism of the normalization programme, will point the way to new ideas in connection with the politics of disability.

In this chapter, the search for a viable concept of quality has led us into a discussion about different ways of approaching an understanding of the Quality of Life concept. In the last analysis, the aim of all the measures we take, and of our social-educational efforts to create a better framework and conditions for people with disabilities, must be that they can create a 'good life' for themselves.

A viable concept of quality in social-educational work with people with disabilities must be found, and constantly refined, through a dialogue with those who use the system coupled with a constantly critical attitude to dominant trends and developments within the politics of disability.

References

Allardt, Erik (1975) *Att ha, att älska, att vära – om välfärd i Norden*. Lund: Argos Förlag.

Bank-Mikkelsen, Niels Erik (1989) 'Historisk udvikling –.og en fremtid med perspektiver', *LEV*, 7, 21–7.

Bauman, Zygmunt (1994) *Modernitet og holocaust*. Copenhagen: Hans Reitzels Forlag.

Blumer, H. (1969) *Symbolic Interactionism – Perspective and Method*. Englewood Cliffs: Prentice Hall.

Goode, David A. (1992) 'Quality of life policy: Some issues and implications of a generic social policy concept for people with development disabilities'. Paper presented at the Annual Meeting of the American Association on Mental Retardation, New Orleans.

Goode, David A. (ed.) (1994) *Quality of Life for Persons with Disabilities. International Perspectives and Issues*. Cambridge, Mass.: Brookline Books, 266–84.

Gustavsson, Anders (1992) 'Livet i "Integrationssamfundet" – en analyse av nærhetens sosiale betydning', in J.T. Sandvin (ed.) *Mot normalt? Omsorgsideologier i forandring*. Oslo: Kommuneforlaget.

Heal, Laird W. (1996) 'Review of Goode, David (ed.) *Quality of Life for Persons with Disabilities. International Perspectives and Issues*', *American Journal on Mental Retardation*, 100(5), 557–60.

Holm, P., Holst, J., Olsen, S.B. and Perlt, B. (eds) (1994) *Liv og kvalitet i omsorg og pædagogik*. Århus: Systime.

Holm, P., Holst, J., Olsen, S.B. and Perlt, B. (1996) 'Quality of everyday life: the Danish approach', in J. Tøssebro, A. Gustavsson and G. Dyrendahl (eds) *Intellectual Disabilities in the Nordic Welfare States – Policies and Everyday Life*. Kristiansand: HøyskoleForlaget, 196–213.

Holst, J. (ed.) (1991) *Samvær Kommunikation Samarbejde*. Copenhagen: LEV´s Forlag.

Holst, J., Meyer, H., Kelstrup, F., Knudsen, A., Larsen, T. and Petersen, K. (eds) (1995) *Søndag er træls – Et projekt om udviklingshæmmedes livskvalitet*. Copenhagen: Forlaget LEV.

Jessen, K.E., Henriksen, E., Olesen, O.G., Frosch, H., Thomsen, K., Meyer, H., Jensen, J.K., Jensen, F.B., Bertelsen, M. and Holst, J. (1985) *Et integreret liv*. Copenhagen: Socialstyrelsen.

Jungk, Robert, and Müllert, Norbert (1984) *Håndbog i fremtidsværksteder*. Copenhagen: Politisk Revy.

Jesper Holst

Kajandi, Madis (1985) *Livskvalitet – en litteraturstudie av livskvalitet som beteende veten-skapligt begrepp samt ett förslag till definition.* Uppsala: Forskningsklinikken Ullråker sjukhus.

Næss, S. (1979) *Livskvalitet – Om at ha det godt i byen og på landet.* Oslo: INAS – rapport, Institutt for socialforskning.

Schalock, Robert L. (1994) 'The concept of Quality of Life and its current applications in the field of mental retardation/developmental disabilities', in David Goode (ed.) *Quality of Life for Persons with Disabilities. International Perspectives and Issues.*Cambridge, Mass.: Brookline Books, 266–84.

Sletved, Henning and Haubro, Henrik (1985) *Hvad er der galt med institutionerne? – en analyse af institutionskulturen og åndssvages muligheder for at leve en almindelig tilværelse.* Esbjerg: Sydjysk Universitetsforlag.

Söder, Morten (1991) 'Livskvalitet og handicap', *Social Kritik*, 16, 15–21.

Taylor, Steven J. (1994) 'In support of research on Quality of Life, but against QOL', in David Goode (ed.) *Quality of Life for Persons with Disabilities. International Perspectives and Issues.* Cambridge, Mass.: Brookline Books, 260–5.

3 Issues of Equity in Special Needs Education as Seen From the Perspective of Gender

Harry Daniels, Valerie Hey, Diana Leonard and Marjorie Smith

Introduction

For many years the analysis of a broad range of social phenomena has been influenced by a general concern for equality of opportunity. This chapter will explore some of the ways in which categories of analysis in education function, and illustrate the way in which focusing on gender casts light on the processes of identification of need, and on resource allocation in special needs provision in mainstream schools.

Davies and Burton (1996) note that there has been a significant shift in thinking about gender issues from a concern with the 'underachievement' of girls to a focus on gender relations and the way both female and male identities are constructed or mediated in schools. In the UK there is an increasing concern about the underachievement of boys, specifically from the working-class. For example, a recent OFSTED (1996) report drew attention to some of the ways in which gender is seen to affect performance in schools:

- Girls achieve better than boys in English from the age of seven.
- Girls are more successful than boys at every level in GCSE.
- Boys gain very low or very high point scores at A-level and Advanced Supplementary level more often than girls.
- Post-16 girls turn away from maths and science, subjects which could lead them to careers in such fields as engineering and technology.
- Schools are less likely to be able to deal with the behavioural problems of boys: they are four times as likely to be excluded from school – frequently because of aggressive behaviour.
- Girls tend to be more conscientious in doing their homework at primary school.
- Girls and boys often have different approaches to planning and organizing their work. Girls are more likely to bring the correct equipment to lessons and to respond to teachers' comments about their work.

It would seem reasonable to suggest that boys are increasingly seen to be more likely than girls to get into difficulty in schools. In the UK there has been a long-term concern for refining concepts of educational difficulty. These tend not to be informed by the perspective of gender. Concepts of educational difficulty have evolved from their origins in concepts of disability and deficiency. One of the key recommendations of the Warnock Report (DES, 1978) was that categories of handicap in education should be abolished and replaced with a concept of special educational need.

> We wish to see a more positive approach, and we have adopted the concept of SPECIAL EDUCATIONAL NEED, seen not in terms of a particular disability which a child may be judged to have, but in relation to everything about him, his abilities as well as his disabilities – indeed all the factors which have a bearing on his educational progress.
>
> (DES, 1978: para. 3.6, p. 37 [stress in original])

The Education Act of 1981 was heavily influenced by the Warnock report, and one of its key aspects was a change in the definition of SEN. Instead of practitioners allocating children to fixed categories of existing special needs provision, they were to formulate children's needs in terms of the provision required to help an individual to make progress, and school governors were required to ensure their pupils' specific needs were identified and met (Section 2 (5)). Much of the subsequent development in SEN provision took the form of LEA-provided resources and support services, including support within mainstream classrooms, together with schools' development of their own special needs policies and practices.

Norwich argued that

> behind the Warnock rhetoric of abolishing categories lie complex issues which need to be explored ... the central importance of values in education is evident in an educational perspective on disability and in the social movement towards educating children with special educational need in ordinary schools.
>
> (Norwich, 1990: 17)

At a very general level it would seem reasonable to suggest that many of those who to seek to analyse matters of gender, race and special educational need do so on the basis of at least some common values, albeit from somewhat different perspectives. A series of statements from international bodies have helped to create the climate in which political pressure is building on state-run agencies to at least accede to the notion of special needs as a human rights issue, while the inclusionist, 'schooling for diversity' or 'school for all' movement (e.g. the United Nations *Standard Rules on the Equalization of Opportunities for People with Disabilities* of 1993; the UNESCO Salamanca Statement of 1994) seeks to unite many practitioners and academics in the common purpose of creating an educational system that ensures equality of opportunity, equity and a humanitarian concept of effectiveness.

The rhetoric of integration is also witnessed in the Special Educational Needs Code of Practice, which, following the 1993 Education Act, provides practical guidance to LEAs and school governing bodies on their responsibilities towards pupils with special educational needs. Schools and LEAs have been required to have regard to its recommendations from September 1994. The Department for Education (1994a) also issued Circular 6/94 on 'The Organization of Special Educational Provision' which provided suggestions as to how schools should manage their provision alongside that made by other local schools. These documents embody the twin strategies of individual pupil support and whole school development, although many commentators have noted the somewhat over-individualizing impact of the Code. Thus Booth (1996), Lewis et al. (1996) and OFSTED (1996) all report on the implementation of the Code and note that there is still much to be done in ensuring that a system (designed to introduce some sense of regularity into a context in which there were tremendous disparities between schools and LEAs) is implemented and developed into a realistic and effective working tool. This problem has also been recognized in the recent Green Paper *Excellence for All Children*, which seeks to promote the development of more sophisticated and comprehensive forms of regional and local planning (DfEE, 1997).

Despite this torrent of legislation and recommendation there remain a number of key concerns, such as:

- the extent to which SEN are seen as a matter for analysis at the level of the individual – whether this be in terms of causation or intervention; and
- the extent to which individual needs are met by provision rather than individual need being reformulated in the light of the provision that is available.

Equality, Sameness and Difference

Moreover, the wish to respond to individual need may conflict with principles of equity and equality where these are of concern in the development of bureaucratic systems. For example, it is possible to apply a principle of equality of opportunity that boys and girls should be given equal access to SEN support. If provision is looked at from this perspective, stark inequalities are revealed. Data from the USA suggest an over-referral of males, especially African Americans (Haigh and Malever, 1993–4; Weinstein, 1993–4); while the National Longitudinal Transition Study of Special Education Students (NLTS) reports that although girls are under-represented, those who are certified are more seriously impaired:

> Females in secondary special education represented a different combination of abilities and disabilities than males. As a group, females were more seriously impaired; even among males and females with the same disability category, females had marginally greater functional deficits than males.
>
> (Wagner, 1992: 33–4)

We also know that there has been marked disparity of provision for boys and girls in access to many special schools in the UK. This has recently been confirmed by large-scale surveys (Cooper et al., 1991). But if boys and girls were treated equally, and equal numbers were sent to special schools, would this be equitable?

This tension has led White (1991) to propose the compromise strategy of developing solutions which are 'good enough' for individuals yet assure equity for all those 'in need'. This offers some way forward in a perennial dilemma. However, the strategy in and of itself tends to underplay the concept and reality of power relations. The categories which we use in practice owe their existence to the relations of power which serve to demarcate and maintain the boundaries which form categories. In the context of SEN practices, this is perhaps well illustrated by the boundary between the category Mental Retardation (MR) and Learning Disability (LD) in the USA. Entry into the more socially acceptable category (LD) is much more difficult to achieve than entry into the MR category, and so it is likely to be the educationally informed middle class who push to ensure the LD label for their children, especially their sons (Carrier, 1983).

The research reported here attempts to supplement the analytical tools which are brought to bear on this problem of reconciling concepts of need and equality in the context of power relations and the categories of gender and SEN. We know that different groupings within the research community have tended to be associated with different categories of social analysis, such as race, class, gender and SEN, and hence these categories have tended to remain conceptually and practically distinct, especially SEN from gender, race and class. We suggest that these boundaries are also witnessed in the actual practice of special needs education in schools.

Solstad (1994) suggests that the concept of equity may be embedded in two distinct set of referents. Equity may be referenced to equality, and the principle may be realized through centralized and centralizing actions by agencies such as the state. Alternatively, the principle of equity may be referenced to diversity, and realized in particular settings, regions and localities. Evans (1995) provides an extended discussion of this matter in the context of feminist theory. She contrasts the equality–difference controversy with a sameness–difference analysis.

We might then want to see 'equality', 'sameness', and 'difference' as forming not a continuum, but three corners of a triangle. Then the notion of 'equality in difference' enters in. (This is the idea that we merit equal though not identical treatment; equal in the sense of 'equally good, and appropriate to us'.) Though so does 'equality through difference', as opposed to 'equality through sameness'.

(Evans, 1995: 3)

Evans suggests that to treat people equally it is not necessary to treat them in exactly the same way. On the contrary, 'To treat people as equals may *require* that they not be treated the same way' (ibid.: 4). However, it is essential that they be treated fairly. The data suggest that girls and boys are not treated in the same way, in that more boys are sent to special schools. But this is not to say that more girls should be sent to special schools, nor to suggest that girls are being treated fairly, because in fact their needs may be being ignored (Haddock and Malcolm, 1992). If questions concerning equity are to be engaged with, then there is a requirement for appropriate tools or categories of analysis. These tools will need to be sufficiently sophisticated to encompass the complexity of issues surrounding the term 'equality'.

Categories as Tools of Analysis

Categories as tools of analysis may be thought of as relays of social priorities and assumptions in the way they enter the discourses and practices of resource allocation and management. For example, it is clear that monitoring systems, such as LEA SEN audits of need, take account of some groups and not of others. Many of the terms in popular use have highly situated meanings. This 'flakiness' of categories was all too apparent in the research discussed in this article. We found many examples of headteachers having access to information which wasn't available to special needs co-ordinators (SENCOs). We also found that descriptors applied to children and services were used in an inconsistent manner across the LEA. There was evidence of idiosyncratic use of services across schools and large differences in levels of statementing. It was also clear that the use of some categories implied permanency while others were suggestive of potential resolution (e.g. 'learning difficulty' and 'specific learning difficulty'). Categories formed by provision may also be used to formulate need (e.g. children who are cause for concern because of their behaviour may be referred to a literacy support service simply because there is no other service available). Above all, these categories are, as Norwich (1990) suggests, value laden.

In the two LEAs we considered in our own work,[1] gender and race were not monitored within the SEN Code of Practice and SEN register records. Difficulties in monitoring were compounded by general difficulty in collating systems of records within and between schools. (The variation between and within LEAs in the use of specific categories may, in part, be seen to depend on the quality and nature of the provision available within mainstream schools.) In addition, resource allocation devices seemed to generate categories into which data was forced. We may only speculate as to whether this actually results in the manipulation of perceptions into administrative categories at LEA level. Certainly there are complex relations between the language of description, with its categories and criteria, the administrative procedures and practices and the pedagogic reality. The very complexity and obscurity of these systems may allow for the relative autonomy of local ideologies. Our findings suggest that different schools interpret 'SEN' in very different ways, particularly in terms of implicit models of causality (e.g. societal, familial, individual) and response (e.g. whole class or individual; uniform or differentiated; outside the school or inside the school, etc.). The suggestion was prompted by the finding that there was no association between the level of SEN activity and resource allocation, and the Additional Educational Needs (AEN) budget for the schools we surveyed.

In an earlier small pilot study we had collected information on the gender ratios in special schools from several LEAs, and also looked in more detail in two mainstream primary schools, to see how they handled in-school SEN provision[2] to examine the interplay between two major sets of categories: SEN and gender. We found:

1   Significant gender differences exist in numbers of children receiving extra support irrespective of the identification procedure.
2   There were gender differences in the effective reasons for referral though reasons were rarely made explicit if referral was made to agencies outside the school or (in some cases) the classroom.
3   Boys were often given forms of support which were not designed to meet the needs identified (e.g. instruction in reading as a response to inappropriate behaviour).

These data supported the suggestion that constructs of SEN remain highly individualized and are tacitly associated with within-person accounts. It is therefore often seen as quite distinct from the social processes which bias resource allocation across gender and race boundaries, and so, in practice, provision is not 'answerable' to EO monitoring procedures (Daniels et al., 1995). We then explored this tentative suggestion about the interplay between categories in analysis, and practice was explored in a much larger ESRC-funded study. We aimed to test the hypothesis that significant gender differences exist in the allocation of special needs provision. We also sought to establish whether significant gender differences exist in the effective criteria used to identify need. That is, we were concerned to establish whether gender differences exist in the processes of matching different forms of provision to need, and to understand the consequences for pupils.

The first of the three phases of the ESRC project involved a broad survey of the allocation of the special provision made available in one local education authority (LEA) at Key Stage 2. This was followed by a series of in-depth studies of processes of identification, referral and allocation. Finally we conducted an evaluation of the consequences for pupils of inappropriate provision and/or over-representation, as well as lack of provision in the case of those under-represented.

The data we present here are mainly from phase one, which involved a broad survey of the allocation of the special provision made available at Key Stage 2 (KS2) in one LEA. This took place during the first year of the implementation of the Code of Practice (CoP).

Categories in Practice

The gender-ratio data we first collected aggregate for all the pupils in 35 schools out of the 42 schools we approached. The ratio of boys to girls receiving additional support was adjusted for the ratio of overall numbers of boys to girls in each school.[3] As Figure 3.1 shows, the mean ratio was 1.7 with a standard deviation of 1.71.

We then collected data on each pupil receiving additional support in 21 of the 35 schools, to give 358 pupil profiles.

The overall gender ratio here was then 1.84 (232 boys and 126 girls). See Figure 3.2. (However, when the ratios were calculated for each school on the basis of this second survey, the data did not concur with the school-based data of the first survey. The data are portrayed in Figure 3.3. The mean adjusted ratio for this data set was 2.5 with a standard deviation of 1.49, as shown in Figure 3.3.)

Comparison of adjusted ratios from the first (school-based) survey against the second (pupil-based) survey reveals that the greatest disparities are associated with the highest reported ratios. This suggests that there may be a relation between the quality and accuracy of school-based records and gendered inequalities in SEN resource allocation. We therefore decided to use only the pupil-based survey data in further analyses

Resource Allocation

It was with some surprise that we noted no discernible relation between the level of AEN[4] per head of pupil population and the level of SEN activity in the school. Many SEN co-ordinators and teachers in schools appeared to be unaware that an AEN budget existed, how much had been allocated, or who was responsible for the decisions about its use.

Schools do, however, seem to make a significant difference in the way that

Figure 3.1   Whole school returns on gender ratios

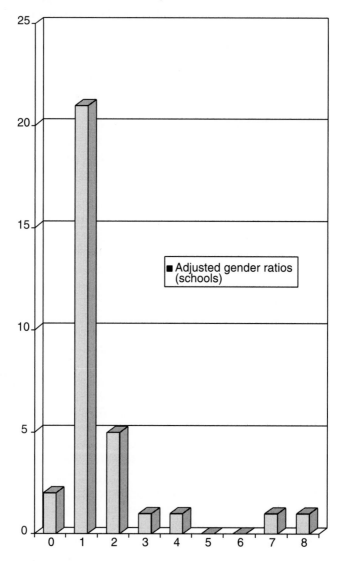

Note   *Mean = 1.7, SD = 1.7, N = 35*

Figure 3.2   Gender ratios based on all pupil returns

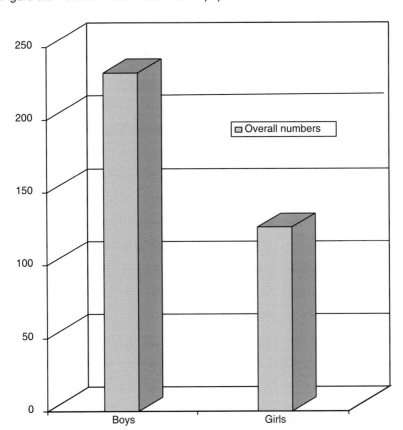

AEN budgets are spent, *and* to the extent to which boys are favoured in the distribution of this resource. To find one school working with a gender ratio of 1 (when adjusted for the overall numbers of boys and girls in the school) and another school working with an adjusted gender ratio of 8, in situations which appear remarkably similar within one LEA, must surely raise the eyebrows of those concerned with equity in resource allocation practices. These are significant school differences which appear to stand outside the gaze of current monitoring procedures. This variation *between* schools suggests that schools as institutions may exert considerable influence over local practice with respect to gender.

Within schools, gender differences were seen to vary as a function of the category of SEN[5] applied to the children. As can be seen in Figure 3.4, the most marked difference was revealed within the emotional and behavioural

Figure 3.3   Gender ratios collected from the pupil audit

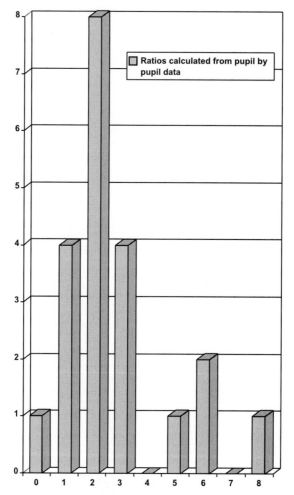

Note   *Mean adjusted ratio for this data set was 2.5 with a standard deviation of 1.49*

difficulty category, the least in the mild learning difficulty category (chi squared significance = 0.03, 22 DF).

Gender differences also appeared to vary as a function of ethnicity.[6] We experienced great difficulty in collecting these data since there was significant variation by school in the extent to which categories of ethnicity were applied and also variation in the actual categories used.

In Figure 3.5, the category 'black' is comprised of African Caribbean and 'black other', and the category 'white' is comprised of 'white English' and

Figure 3.4   Gender differences as a function of category of SEN

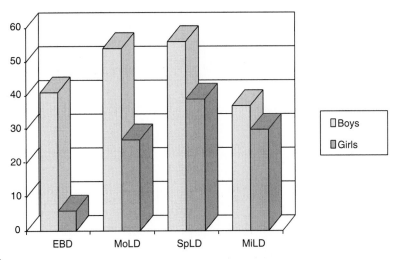

Notes:
EBD = emotional and behavioural difficulties
MoLD = moderate learning difficulties
SpLD = specific learning difficulties
MiLD = mild learning difficulties

Figure 3.5   Race by gender by SEN

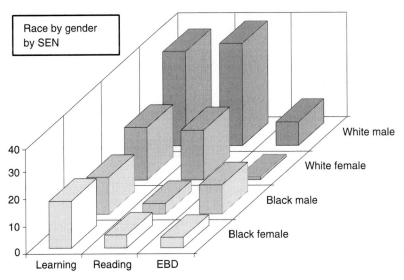

H. Daniels, V. Hey, D. Leonard, M. Smith

Figure 3.6   All pupils with SEN – number of hours support per week

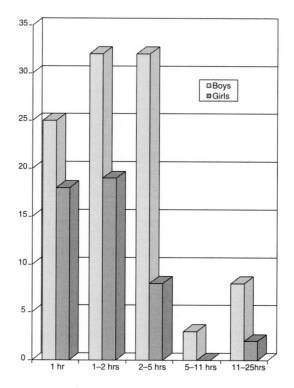

Figure 3.7   Gender differences in allocation of provision

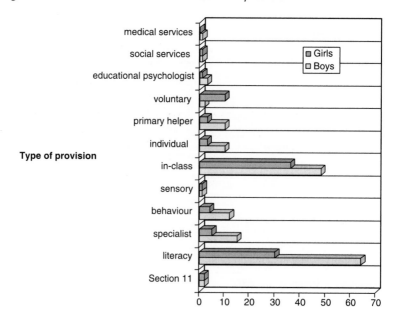

'white Irish'. Children who are in the process of acquiring English as a second language have been omitted from this analysis. The male/female ratio is close to 1.0 in the African Caribbean group and above 2.0 in the white English and Irish group.[7] When examined by ethnicity and gender, patterns of categorizations appear to vary significantly.

Within both 'black' and 'white' groups gender differences are greatest in the emotional and behaviour difficulty category; and gender differences are much greater in the 'white' group than the 'black' group. In addition, 'black' children appear to be more likely to be allocated to the category 'general learning difficulty' than 'reading difficulty' when compared with their 'white' peers. If we are concerned about equity for all, then we need to understand much more about SEN practices from the perspectives of both gender *and* race considered simultaneously.

Our data also suggest that not only are significantly more boys than girls allocated additional help in mainstream schools, but also they are given more in time, amount and quality. Figure 3.6 shows how the gender difference tends to increase as the allocation of hours of support increases, while Figure 3.7 suggests that boys are usually allocated the more prestigious and expensive forms of support. The trend to disproportionate allocation of support *time* appears to be more marked in the 'black' group (as shown in Figure 3.8).

We could find no overall relation between measures of attainment and gender ratios, apart from a slight positive association between poor performance in science SATs and increased gender ratios. In schools where overall performance in science SATs was poor, more boys tended to be allocated special help.

When the home background of pupils is considered, a first analysis suggests a strong association between children who live with a single-parent mother and all forms of SEN. This appears to be particularly marked in the case of pupils (referred to by teachers as) exhibiting emotional and behavioural difficulties (see Figure 3.9). However, when this same data set is analysed by an index of poverty, namely eligibility for free school meals, a very strong association between poverty and SEN is also suggested (see Figure 3.10). Subsequent analysis of the data (see Figure 3.11) suggests that many of the mothers living alone with their children are eligible for free school meals – which provides a good example of the dangers of confusing correlation with causation – a confusion which is politically labile.

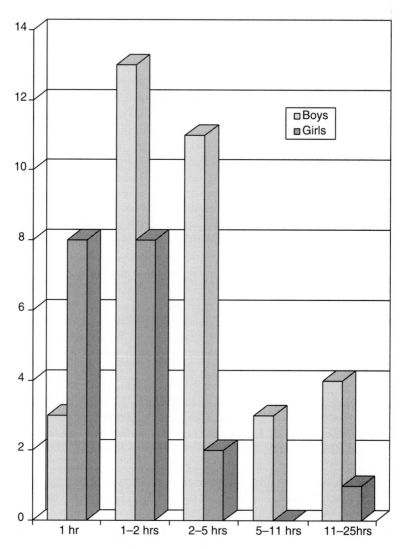

Figure 3.8   African Caribbean and black other – number of hours support per week

Figure 3.9   Home background and type of SEN

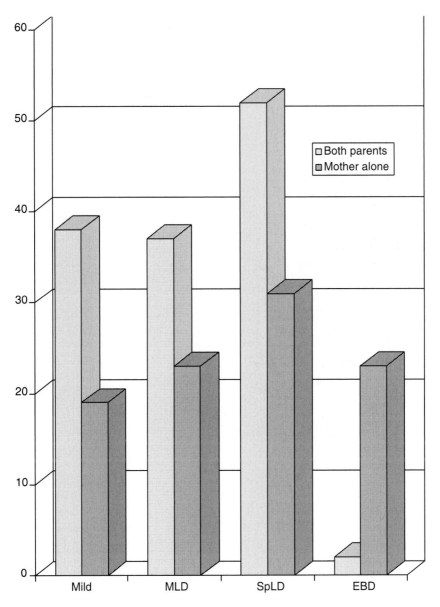

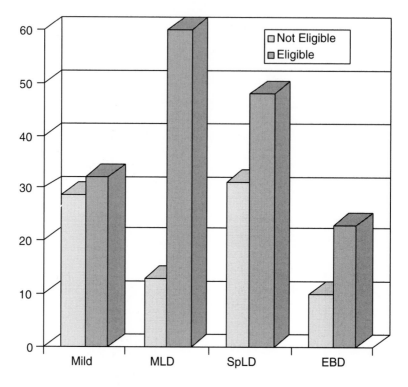

Figure 3.10   Eligibility for free school meals and SEN categorization

Figure 3.11   Free school meals eligibility by home background

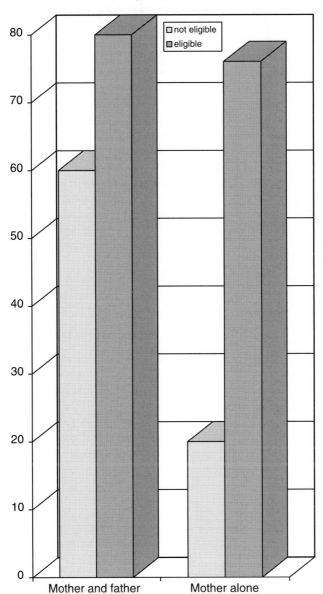

Conclusion

The pursuit of equity in education has been guided and enhanced by an analysis-focused equality of opportunity. But this often has analyses of educational practice which consider one category of inequality at a time. Similarly, groups of analysts and practitioners have developed interests and analyses which have been single-category driven. Moreover, injudicious averaging may be seen to be in play in the context of SEN resource allocation. The data presented here suggest that averaging across schools and considering categories of SEN, race, and gender in isolation are both 'injudicious'.

We would argue that social processes bias and distort the allocation of mainstream support for SEN, and therefore that the allocation of scarce and precious resources should be monitored and decision-making processes evaluated so as to improve the chances of equitable distribution. However, the pursuit of equity through equal opportunities initiatives is constrained by the extent to which the diversity of the client group is captured in the analysis. The power relations that establish and maintain categories in the discourses of analysts and practitioners create inequalities which must be challenged if *equity* is to be achieved.

In this sense we must recognize that the categories are analytical tools with which we understand the social processes we seek to monitor and ultimately change. Categories of analysis need to be selected to serve both general and local purposes. Without such tools we cannot ask whether systems are providing equality, let alone equity.

If we wish to treat all children equally fairly, then we must first try and understand how we make decisions, and then monitor the outcomes of those decisions. We know that boys and girls are not treated in the same way. We do not know whether this is fair. It may well be that we should seek to establish new forms of difference rather than impose sameness. In order to match pedagogical needs with provision, we need to be flexible in our response to diversity, rather than offering fixed solutions under the name of equality.

Notes

1   ESRC-funded study R000235059, 'Gender and Special Educational Needs Provision in Mainstream Schooling', Harry Daniels, Valerie Hey, Diana Leonard and Marjorie Smith.
2   We chose LEAs with established Equal Opportunities (EO), (gender) policies and asked LEA Advisers to indicate 'good' EO schools (i.e. 'best cases', where we thought schools would be least likely to show gender inequalities).
3   The term 'adjusted' will be used as an abbreviated form of this phrase.
4   The Additional Educational Need (AEN) budget.
5   The categories of SEN are those used by the teachers and SENCOs to describe the pupils' difficulties.
6   The categories of ethnicity used here were those adopted by the LEA.
7   There were very few Asian children living in the LEA.

References

Booth, T. (1996) 'A perspective on inclusion from England', *Cambridge Journal of Education*, 26(1), 87–100.

Carrier, J.G. (1983) 'Explaining educability: an investigation of political support for children with learning disabilities', *British Journal of Sociology of Education*, 4(2), 28.

Cooper, P., Upton, G. and Smith, C. (1991) 'Ethnic minority and gender distribution among staff and pupils in facilities for pupils with emotional and behavioural difficulties in England and Wales', *British Journal of Sociology of Education* , 12(1), 189.

Daniels, H., Hey, V., Leonard, D. and Smith, M. (1995) 'Gendered practice in special educational needs', in L. Dawtrey, J. Holland and M. Hammer (eds) *Equality and Inequality in Education Policy*. Milton Keynes: Open University Press.

Davies, L. and Burton, L. (1996) 'Effective schools and gender research'. Mimeo, University of Birmingham.

Department for Education (1994a) *The Organization of Special Educational Provision (Circular 6/94)*. London: DfE.

Department for Education (1994b) *Code of Practice on the Identification and Assessment of Special Educational Needs*. London: DfE.

Department for Education and Employment (1997) *Excellence for All Children: Meeting Special Educational Needs*. London: The Stationery Office.

Department of Education and Science (1978) *Special Educational Needs* (The Warnock Report). London: HMSO.

Department of Education and Science (1988) *Education Reform Act*. London: HMSO.

Evans, J. (1995) *Feminist Theory Today*. New York: Sage.

Haddock, L. and Malcolm, L. (1992) 'Make trouble: get results. Provision for girls in support services', *Educational Psychology in Practice*, 8(2), 45.

Haigh, J.A. and Malever, M.G. (1993–4) 'Special education referral practices by gender, ethnicity, and comparison to state and district enrolments', *CASE in Point*, 8(1), 13–24.

Lewis, A., Neill, St J. and Campbell, R.J. (1996) *The Implementation of the Code of Practice in Primary and Secondary Schools*. Coventry: University of Warwick.

Norwich, B. (1990) *Reappraising special needs education*. London: Cassell.

Office for Standards In Education (OFSTED) (1996) *The Gender Divide In Schools And How To Bridge It (Pn22/96)*. London: HMSO.

Sebba, J. and Ainscow, M. (1996) 'International developments in inclusive schooling: mapping the issues', *Cambridge Journal of Education*, 26(1), 5–18.

Solstad, K.J. (1994) 'Equity at risk: schooling and change in Norway'. PhD thesis, National Education Office, Nordland Office.

United Nations (1993) *The Standard Rules on the Equalization of Opportunities for Persons with Disabilities (adopted by the United Nations General Assembly at its 48th Session on 20 December 1993 – Resolution 48/96)*. New York: United Nations.

United Nations Educational, Scientific and Cultural Organization (UNESCO)/ Ministry of Education and Science, Spain (1994) *The Salamanca Statement and Framework for Action on Special Needs Education (adopted by the World Conference on Special Needs Education: Access and Quality, Salamanca, Spain, 7–10 June 1994)*. New York: UNESCO.

Wagner, M. (1992) 'Being female – a secondary disability? Gender differences in the transition experiences of young people with disabilities'. Paper presented at the annual meeting of the American Educational Research Association, San Francisco, April.

Weinstein, D.F. (1993–4) 'Special education referral and classification practices by gender, family status and terms used: A case study', *CASE in Point*, 8(1), 25–36.

White, J. (1991) 'The goals are the same … are they?', *British Journal of Special Education*, 18(1), 25–7.

Section 2

Pedagogic Concerns

4 Evidence-Based Practice: How Will We Know What Works?

An International Perspective

Peter Evans

Background

Including students with special educational needs (SEN) in mainstream schools remains a goal for most education systems around the world. It has been an education reform agenda item for many years, with some progress having been made in some countries and others being static.

The history of the development of education and special education systems has led, in most countries, to the creation of essentially separate entities with often very little dialogue between them. This is as true of the administrative structures as it is of the research and practice, and these are certainly some of the key macro-level obstacles to inclusion that exist all over the world.

Although the concept of SEN, as well as the term itself, has gained much ground internationally as a way of referring to students experiencing difficulties in learning, the situation on the ground in many ways has changed little since the earlier OECD publication (OECD, 1995) which brought together statistics and definitions in this field. In a recent survey (OECD, 1999) covering some 22 countries, all of them, with the exception of the UK, used disability categories to identify special needs students. The number of categories in use, from six to over twenty, varies as much as the estimates of proportions of children with SEN. In the US, for instance, 12 per cent of students are categorized as disabled and have individual education programmes (IEPs). In other countries the figure is 5 per cent or less. In the UK only 2.9 per cent have statements. These differences are more indicative of definitional differences and administrative features of the system rather than being true estimates of prevalence, a possibility implied by categorical descriptions, and they pose substantial interpretative challenges to international comparisons.

These examples are not given in order to argue the merits or demerits of any particular system, but merely to show that there are substantial differences between countries in the way special needs issues are conceptualized and discussed. In addition, the examples show the difficulties in generalizing from research from one country to another if the exact details of the sample of students being studied is unclear. In order to facilitate international comparisons and to tackle some of these issues, the OECD has been developing a new framework intended to overcome some of the comparability issues (OECD, 1998), but a fuller discussion of this approach is outside the scope of this chapter.

Most countries in the world provide special schools to educate widely varying percentages of their special needs students. Some educate under 0.5 per cent in special schools, but many have significantly more: for example, in Germany and the Netherlands approximately 4.0 and 6.0 per cent respectively of those of compulsory school age. Furthermore, few countries have achieved the level of inclusion whereby all students, however seriously disadvantaged, can be effectively supported in mainstream classrooms. Some would debate the desirability. Whatever the philosophical position held, however, the reality is that there are very few examples of inclusion at this level (updating the Warnock concept (Warnock, 1978) I shall call it 'functional inclusion'). In terms of identifying what works in achieving functional inclusion, it is therefore necessary to draw on the many examples at regional or local levels, often coming down in practice to individual districts and schools. As a consequence, the database does not allow for ready generalizations to be made, especially about the important issues of going to scale, or identifying the implications for educational systems as a whole, since local developments are so frequently special cases, often being associated with particular individuals and charismatic leadership.

Over the past few years the Centre for Educational Research and Innovation (CERI) has been continuing its work looking at inclusive education practices. Case studies have been completed and data gathered in eight countries: Australia, Canada (New Brunswick), Denmark, Germany, Iceland, Italy, the UK and the USA. Based mainly on this work (OECD, 1999a), the remainder of this chapter will discuss some basic issues and identify some general principles that seem to be associated with developing and sustaining functional inclusion.

Developing functional inclusion is a systemic issue. It cannot be achieved nationally by focusing on one or only a small number of elements of the system, since ultimately it is part of a political process in which there are different points of view and a range of different factors which need to be taken into account. Different evaluation models are in use, and these issues must be considered when responding to the question of what works in inclusive practice. Different constituencies also have to be persuaded, which include politicians, administrators and policy-makers, parents, teachers and other professionals. The discussion which follows will reflect these broad considerations. Other chapters in this book take up the specific issues in more detail.

General Context

There are many pressures on governments to move towards more inclusive education and there are many examples of changes taking place. International pressure, such as the European Union's resolution on the 'integration of children and young people affected by a handicap into mainstream education systems' (Council of the European Union, 1990) and the United Nations (UN) have led to a number of programmes and statements to promote inclusion. For example, a UNESCO conference in Salamanca, Spain (1994), proclaimed:

> the necessity and urgency of providing education for children, youth and adults with special educational needs within the regular education system ... Regular schools with this inclusive orientation ... provide an effective education to the majority of children and improve the efficiency and ultimately the cost-effectiveness of the entire education system.
>
> (UNESCO, 1994: viii–ix)

In parallel, there have been changes in the legal frameworks of many countries to move towards more inclusion. The main principle, which must be enshrined in the law and subsequent policy statements, is that all children, however disabled, have the right to attend their neighbourhood school. In the New Brunswick Province of Canada, for instance, requirements on school boards changed from being able to exclude disabled students to not being allowed to refuse the admission to school of disabled children unless they are able to convince the Ministry that it is not in the child's best interest. In Iceland, the recent law on education covers all students, including those with SEN, and deliberately avoids mentioning special education as a particular issue in order to avoid the education/special education dualism referred to above.

It must, then, be remembered that, in developing policies to support inclusion, this is only a part of a wider reform process which is taking place in all our education systems and cannot as a result be treated in isolation. Two issues are of signal importance: funding and standards. However, in discussions of inclusion these issues are not generally put at the top of the list of imperatives, where the prizes go to humanitarian and equity concerns (see the organization of the present book!). Nevertheless, they are probably the most important issues in the general context of educational reform and for this reason are discussed first.

Funding and Resourcing

In most of the countries visited, funding arrangements for students with special needs were in a state of flux. This was partly because the form of educational provision was changing towards greater inclusion, and partly because the locus of funding was changing under general policies of decentralization which are impacting on the degree of control effected by central administrations. In addition, relevant data were not readily available. This may be because, up to now, the provision of appropriate education for disabled students has been viewed as of greater significance than the costs. However, there have been increases in the numbers of students identified with SEN which have brought the issues of costs and the link with efficiency and effectiveness into sharper relief. For example, in the UK the numbers of students on statements increased from 2.1 per cent to 2.9 per cent between 1992 and 1997 (Department for Education and Employment, 1998). In the USA, the number on IEPs increased from 7 per cent to 12 per cent between 1990 and 1996 (US Department of Education, 1996).

A Comparison of Costs Entailed in Integrated and Segregated Provision

Calculating the costs of special educational provision is notoriously difficult, although it is generally assumed that the per capita cost is higher (OECD, 1995). This seems a fairly safe assumption, since teacher–student ratios are more favourable for SEN students and teachers' salaries make up a large proportion of the costs. In New Brunswick in Canada, where there was functional inclusion, the cost of disabled students, estimated at 5 per cent of the student population, was twice that of non-disabled students. In Italy's national system it was four times, for 2.4 per cent. In a specially resourced functionally inclusive school studied in Derbyshire in the UK, the cost was 2.5 times, with some 3 per cent of students on statements.

It is also generally agreed that inclusive settings are less expensive than segregated ones. The question of comparative costs was carefully followed during the course of the study with administrators and schools; based on the funding allocated to schools it emerges that, for systems as a whole, special school provision tends to be more costly than regular school provision, a common ratio being about 1:1.2. However, a closer inspection comparing per capita costs between a special school and a regular school in the UK revealed the regular inclusive school to be more costly (OECD, 1999a). This finding can only be treated tentatively and needs replication both within and among countries. What the data point to is the importance of analysing costs in the context of different educational governance policies such as decentralization. They also argue for giving greater consideration to the links between the costs and the effectiveness of different settings about which there is little, if any, available data.

Allocation of Resources

From the point of view of encouraging inclusive practices, it is important that funding arrangements help to create a level playing field, so that special school provision is not given preferential treatment for resources. In New South Wales, for instance, special school teachers are paid an additional daily sum of A$6.14, which is not available to those working with equivalent children in regular schools. In Germany, too, special school teachers are paid at the top end of the scale at an equivalent rate to grammar school teachers. In Switzerland, recent additional funding for the education of disabled students has only been available if the provision has been made in special schools.

Among the countries visited, there has been a trend in recent years towards the devolution of the management of funding, from central government to regions, from regions to districts, and in some instances to individual schools. Where the extent of devolution of funds for ordinary education differs from that for special education, this can influence the extent to which inclusive education occurs. If funds for ordinary schooling are borne from district budgets but those for special schooling are managed at regional level, as in parts of Denmark, for example, districts may be tempted to press for special schooling for their more expensive students.

In some countries, funding models are being used as a policy instrument to influence inclusive practices. In Colorado, for example, a checklist has been identified with criteria that funding formulae should meet if they are to support inclusive education. Five are identified:

- allocating a single amount for each child;
- tying special education funds to a general school funding formula;
- adding a flat percentage to allow for special needs generally;
- considering an adjustment for poverty;
- including arrangements to evaluate the formula's effectiveness across the state.

In addition, mainstream schools are given the choice of keeping the child with SEN plus the extra resources, or letting the child go to a special school and losing the resources. This has led to many schools choosing to keep their disabled pupils. As a further incentive, transport budgets for regular and special schools have been merged into a single item, thus discouraging expensive transport to special schools often outside the community base.

In Australia, in New South Wales, individual schools may apply for state integration funding for students who they think can be educated in regular classrooms. Allocation of funds is not automatic and depends on five criteria:

- the student is enrolled in a regular class;
- additional support is essential to the provision of an age-appropriate programme;
- this support meets individual needs that cannot be met through in-school resources already available;

- the support includes an individual education plan;
- the support encourages the student's maximum independence.

In the Australian state of New South Wales, the procedures developed for determining the funds to be allocated for helping students with disabilities in ordinary classes were particularly detailed. Stringent criteria were set at state level, and bids were being made by the schools on an annual basis.

For each student for whom extra help was being sought, the school principal had to complete a form. The completed form had to specify the number of hours of special help required over the coming year, present the results of tests administered, state the teaching methods to be used, set objectives for student outcomes, and list any extra special educational help already received, with respect to both this student and any other students with disabilities in the school. The completed forms were monitored at district level and then submitted for consideration by staff in the state's education department.

Standards, Accountability and Evaluation

Along with funding arrangements, accountability and evaluation methods are policy tools of growing value in shaping education systems, and they have an increasingly significant international dimension. It is of great importance that issues of inclusion are borne in mind at the time accountability schemes are devised, to avoid creating further obstacles to inclusion. For instance, in the UK, school inspection systems and the publication of league tables have become part of the process to improve school performance generally. However, at the same time they may militate against inclusion, by discouraging schools from taking on students likely to perform poorly in examinations or encouraging them to expel students who are difficult to teach or omit those with difficulties from testing programmes. Thurlow (1997) reported work in the USA, showing that some two-thirds of students with disabilities were excluded from the administration of the National Assessment of Educational Progress tests. Some countries recognize that flexibility in the examination process is important for inclusion.

Many countries operate a system of monitoring SEN provision and the professional staff involved. In one country, indicators had been developed, based on the provision of equal academic opportunities, performance quality and accountability to the community, which were used to evaluate school districts. For instance, in the Woodstock district of New Brunswick, Canada, where the educational strategies were seen to be particularly effective, in a pan-Canadian comparison the measured educational achievements of students in general were above what might have been expected on the basis of socio-economic factors, and the Director of Education concerned publicly attributed these results to inclusive education. In New South Wales in

Australia, the government had commissioned a particularly extensive independent feasibility study of inclusion. The report identified weaknesses still to be addressed but also recognized the substantial and beneficial growth over recent years in the education of SEN students in regular classes.

Organization, Staffing and Training

Educational systems that support effective functional inclusion have developed some common features, which serve to provide flexibility and responsiveness on the part of the school and its teachers. These are discussed under the headings of school organization and management, curriculum development, classroom organization, within-school support, other support, parental and community involvement, and training.

School Organization and Management – Opportunities for Whole School Development

Educating students with special needs is an issue for the whole school, not just for individual teachers. Furthermore, planning successful inclusion has to go beyond the teaching of traditional subjects and give equal close attention to the social and affective side of development. The work described in the report on the UK provides a useful example (OECD, 1999a).

In the whole school approach, headteachers and the school management clearly need to be closely involved in innovations, especially since they are accountable for how the school works, its ethos, and in motivating teachers to work for all the children on the roll. In all of the schools visited, headteachers and the management team were committed to inclusive education. In the secondary school in Derbyshire, for example, the head of the upper secondary school had had an earlier career in special education and the chairman of the Board of Governors had previously been appointed to the Board to represent the interests of children with special needs.

There was particular interest in this school in coherence of practices across the school, not only in curriculum but also in the pastoral work. For instance, they had implemented an 'assertive discipline' programme across the school, adhered to by all teachers, which specified classroom rules about acceptable behaviour, and when students transgressed there were scaled constructive punishments which often incorporated parents. This programme was also associated with rewards for good behaviour. If students felt that they had been unfairly treated there were 'appeal' procedures. The school claimed that this approach was very useful in preventing 'exclusions' from school, a particular problem in the UK, because it provided a means of dealing with poor behaviour before it crossed the threshold of unacceptability. For some countries, this is an area of great concern; during the course of the visits, many headteachers raised the question of coping with violence, which is occurring at younger and younger ages. In Australia, for instance, new special schools were being opened to deal with violent children.

In the UK school, careful attention was also given to allocating students to tutor groups so that they would be with other tolerant students and also more accepting teachers. In addition, when there are problems relating to the management of individuals, they are dealt with constructively with an individual focus. The learning support team also provided a 'safe haven' for students with special needs which was extensively used by them and other students at break times.

Curriculum Development

Curriculum development is another key area in the development of inclusion, and all countries visited had addressed this issue to a greater or lesser extent. In Australia, for example, the National Strategy for Equity in Schooling (Department of Employment, Education and Training, 1994) identified curriculum and assessment as a key area for development for students with SEN. In New South Wales, outcomes-based education (a structured approach to education, stressing the outcomes students should achieve in making progress through the curriculum) has been emphasized, and the state's board of studies has developed generic life-skills courses to complement the key learning areas of the regular curriculum and to help in the development of IEPs. The reading recovery programme (Clay, 1994) has also been adopted and is implemented in schools. In the UK and Canadian examples, SEN students follow the standard curriculum and teachers make the necessary adaptations for those with SEN. In Colorado, a federally funded curriculum development systems change project (Supporting Inclusive Learning Communities – SILC) is being used to stimulate school improvement via action research methods. Progress towards agreed goals is reviewed monthly.

In one of the high schools visited there, affective education was part of the curriculum for those with special needs and covered such areas as socio-emotional development and conflict management. Life-skills and functional independence were also stressed for those with severe learning difficulties.

In other countries, curriculum modification for SEN may also include dropping certain subjects, e.g. a foreign language, and providing more practical subjects instead. It might well include adjustments to assessment arrangements.

The use of teachers' time has also been subject to change. In Italy, primary teachers work on modules comprising two teachers per three classes or three teachers per four classes, with each teacher taking responsibility for a cluster of subjects for two to three years. This approach in collaboration with support teachers has the potential of providing a coherent approach to curriculum planning for SEN students. In addition, in lower secondary education, teachers stay with pupils for three years, and to help students with SEN, teachers may stay with students across the primary/lower secondary boundary. In many countries progress is planned and monitored via IEPs, the development of which is often collaborative and may involve school inspectors, as in Italy, or other officers from the local education authority or support services.

A central feature of curriculum development is the provision of teaching materials. In no country was this comprehensively carried out through central services or via private sector publishers, and teachers were left to develop their own supplementary materials, sometimes in isolation and sometimes in collaboration with others in the school. In the school in Derbyshire in the UK, this was a main pivot of the successful inclusion programme. There, teachers supplemented the regular curriculum with additional resource material specially prepared for each curriculum subject, which allowed for real classroom-based differentiated teaching. These materials were stocked in the special education resource room and could be used by any staff member. The ready availability of teaching resources is obviously essential for teaching and becomes ever more important during the secondary years, where the curriculum becomes more varied and the pressure more intense. There is clearly a role here for information technology, which is used extensively in some schools. Whether the currently available software really meets all of the needs is unknown, but it seems unlikely.

Curriculum differentiation is a key part of successful inclusion, but in Italy, where compulsory schooling ends at age 14, it was pointed out that this onerous process is less extensive in upper secondary school, where students have more choice and transition to work programmes is evident, and where there are counsellors to provide additional support.

Classroom Organization

Classroom teachers undertaking inclusive education usually had the assistance of at least one other adult. Classroom assistants were often assigned specifically in relation to individual children with moderate or severe disabilities, not in relation to children with special needs more generally, although they would often help the latter as well as the former. They were not necessarily assigned on a full-time basis, and the work often proved attractive to people – mothers with children of primary school age for example – whose other activities made it difficult or undesirable for them to take on full-time paid employment.

The assistants worked under the direction of the classroom teachers, whose lesson planning with respect to children with special needs was helped if necessary by the school's special education support staff. For the lessons to be effective, class teachers generally had to spend a significant amount of time on planning them, and planning adaptations to meet special needs required time additional to that required for the majority of the class. For a child with a severe learning difficulty, for example, this could take as much as a quarter of the time needed to plan for the rest of the class. In addition, time was needed to discuss the lesson with the classroom assistant.

Instances were seen in which the thoroughness of planning was such that the children had all the information and instructions they needed presented to them in written form at the start of the lesson, with adapted materials, perhaps in the form of simplified instructions with supporting illustrations, prepared for those with learning difficulties. This enabled most of the children to carry out their tasks unaided, thus freeing teacher and assistant to circulate round the class from the beginning, helping individuals as necessary.

The most frequently observed pattern in the countries visited was for the assistant to work in the classroom with a child with a disability on the same topic as that set for the class as a whole, although this was not always the case. Effective work was seen, for example, in which the assistant took a child or a small group out for a particular purpose, or went round helping various children, including some without special needs, or looked after the class as a whole while the class teacher helped children with special needs.

In some cases the child with a disability was working in the ordinary classroom on a topic unrelated to that of the class generally. While this could be effective, and might have been the only way of meeting the child's particular needs in that lesson, it did tend to keep the child isolated from the rest of the class. Even here, though, there are ways of keeping children with disabilities in touch with their classmates. In Berlin, for example, when an assistant bringing a boy with Down's syndrome back from a shopping expedition talked to the class about the boy's achievements, the children were spontaneously supportive.

In-class help for children with disabilities was at its most effective when planned within the framework of the general school curriculum, when it was targeted precisely to meet their identified special needs, when their progress towards these targets was systematically assessed, and where the results of assessment guided further planning.

Targeting was usually a statutory requirement for some of a country's children with special needs, with learning targets being referred to in formal documentation, for example, through IEPs. The targeting of education programmes varied appreciably in its specificity, as did assessment of progress.

Within-school Support

The extent to which class teachers were themselves able to provide support for children with special needs depended not only on their own expertise but also on factors such as the extent to which the organization of the school helped the teachers become familiar with the children's needs. Classes would often be smaller and teacher–student ratios adjusted. In Italy, for example, the regular teacher–student ratio of approximately 10:1 is reduced to 7.5:1

In Denmark and in Iceland, it was customary for class teachers to remain with the same children during the children's year-by-year moves up through the school. In the Danish system, a teacher given special training to help her teach a child with visual impairment was likely to be able to use the expertise gained to continue to help that child throughout the child's period in that school.

This kind of continuity can also be enhanced if the chronological ages of the children within a class span two years or more, but such arrangements were not features of the schools visited and in most instances a primary school class teacher would take a child for one year only. Classroom assistants and schools' special education specialists, on the other hand, did get to know children with disabilities over a longer period of time, often over the whole period of a child's stay in the school, and this experience was of considerable advantage to them in carrying out their duties.

In the most effective examples of inclusive education seen, class teachers and their classroom assistants had access to a network of support provided within the school by teachers with advanced qualifications and associated expertise in special education. When called upon by the class teacher, these specialist teachers might help with the setting of individual targets, with the planning of lessons and their adaptation to meet special needs, with classroom teaching, and with the assessment of children's progress. And if necessary, and by agreement with the class teacher, they might withdraw children for a time, individually or in groups, either to carry out a particular intensive programme or to help cope with a crisis.

The longer-term strategies of these specialist teachers could include preparing adapted curriculum materials designed to help successive cohorts of children with learning difficulties at particular stages of the syllabus in particular subjects. In order to facilitate this kind of curriculum development, where several specialist teachers were employed in one school, as was seen in a secondary school in the United Kingdom, for example, it was possible for their subject strengths to complement one another. Thus, one of the specialists might have expertise in language development, another in mathematics and another in science.

In these circumstances special education specialists might maintain their own subject expertise, and their credibility within the school, by spending part of their time relieving class teachers to take their classes for lessons in these subjects.

At their best, these special education specialists were fully integrated within the school as a whole, both sharing in the teaching and being members of the school's management team. Their contributions to school management could be as problem-solvers, not just with respect to special education but with respect to problems experienced generally. They might also have some expertise in aspects of school life affecting all students, for example in assessment of students' progress or in staff appraisal. Where these roles were developed fully, the posts of specialist in special education were highly regarded, much sought after, and recognized as stepping stones to school headship.

While examples of fully developed within-school support systems were seen, they were by no means pervasive, even where all or virtually all children with special needs were being educated in ordinary schools. In New Brunswick, for example, where the same inclusion policy and legislation applied across all districts and where fully developed support systems were seen to operate in the schools of one district, this was not the case in another district visited. In the latter, people designated as special education specialists often lacked special training and spent most of their time, helped sometimes by classroom assistants, teaching groups withdrawn from ordinary classes for extra help in basic subjects.

Other Support

In all countries visited, schools received substantial further support for their work with students with SEN, and this is plainly a key area for successful inclusion and education of these students. The countries identified a large number of professionals who serve in other roles, comprising, in general terms: peripatetic teachers with various forms of specialism, SEN co-ordinators, teacher assistants/aides, school counsellors, educational psychologists, clinical psychologists, youth service psychologists, psychotherapists, social workers, physiotherapists, speech therapists, occupational therapists, doctors and nurses. In addition, it must not be forgotten that parents and communities and voluntary bodies also provide extra support; this can include 'civic servants', for instance those working in communities in place of national service in the armed forces. Transportation is often also provided, and finally there are local education authority advisers and officers who also work with schools specifically in the special needs field. These services provide front-line support for students and teachers and are also closely involved in the formal assessment arrangements that all countries undertake in order to allot additional resources to, and make special arrangements for, students with SEN.

The organization of these services varies substantially between and within countries, especially with the growing decentralization of provision. What is important is getting the skills and support to the schools according to need. Thus, an appropriate balance has to be struck between the skills available within the school staff, the degree of disabilities in the children in the schools, and the availability of the support service personnel, who often find themselves in high demand. In this vein, it is worth noting that speech therapists were frequently far too thin on the ground and hence highly sought after, with those who were available often unable to meet the demand.

In using these services to develop effective inclusive provision it is important to consider how they work with the school. One possibility is that they work with the students themselves in essentially a clinical model, i.e. on a one-to-one basis isolated from the school as a whole. Another is that they support schools and staff in developing their own effective approaches to teaching the disabled students in the school, as in New Brunswick. This latter approach is clearly preferred, and the schools visited were working in this way, usually having identified a teacher or teachers to take responsibility for co-ordinating special needs support in the school. Nevertheless, there were still big differences between the schools visited in the approach taken by support services, particularly in the degree to which the support services explicitly saw themselves as encouraging and supporting schools to solve their own problems. This can be dramatically illustrated by referring to the three districts visited in Iceland. In the first district, the ratio of SEN students to support staff was 47:1, in the second 520:1 and in the third 1320:1. In the last two districts there had been substantial investment in within-school support, thus changing the form of the external support. In Germany and Canada (New Brunswick), we were told that relying on external professionals to sort out problems can often involve inordinate delays and inconsequential advice. If a school can handle the sparks, the fire brigade is not required!

The role and function of support services has to be a key feature of successful inclusive practice. Certainly, the model developed in New Brunswick, especially in Woodstock, which stresses support and training of all staff, is well regarded by them and by parents and students; furthermore they also support *all* students, throughout their whole school lives, however severely disabled they may be. A similar model was a feature of the successful integration practices in Berlin. Approaches that strengthened the ability of the staff to accept and work constructively with SEN pupils were a feature of all of the countries visited, and the role that teachers can play has already been discussed more fully in the section on curriculum development. The training of non-teaching professionals to work with disabled students in the school setting is another central issue to successful inclusion and remains an unexplored area.

Parental and Community Involvement

Parents can be involved in schooling at several levels. In some of the countries visited – e.g. Canada (New Brunswick) – they are strongly represented in the school governance process, where they can even be in the majority on committees and directly influence school policy-making. In others there is relatively little involvement at this level.

In terms of more direct involvement with their children vis-à-vis schooling, in all of the countries visited it was clear that parents are able to be a very strong part of the education of children with special needs: for example by listening to them read. In fact, in many they have spearheaded the inclusion movement and have lobbied for reform. In all of the countries visited, parents are closely involved in the decision-making concerned with assessment arrangements. In Denmark, for instance, except in very exceptional circumstances, they can virtually prevent certification.

There is more variation in the degree to which parents seem to be welcomed as part of the education process. In some countries there appears to be very full involvement. For instance, in Canada they can take part in training sessions with teachers in problem-solving approaches and can be involved in schools. It is essential to make specific arrangements to liaise between schools and parents, and the discussions that take place should be problem-centred and should emphasize practical solutions.

Community involvement seems likewise very variable. In Colorado, accountability committees ensure community involvement in the development and evaluation of school improvement, with the results being fed back directly to the community. An on-line database forms part of the work of PEAK (Parent Education and Assistance for Kids), the local branch of which also publishes Colorado-based resources for parents and educators wanting to promote inclusion.

Other members of the community can also become involved in schools. In Colorado again, Americorps volunteers work in the classroom with children at risk and child-find co-ordinators also ensure that students with disabilities get the services to which they are entitled, by working via community awareness approaches and training sessions. In Italy, in Rome, it was reported that both professionals and parents and other members of the community work with churches and other voluntary agencies in local provision.

In Colorado, education department, university and parent body representatives had collaborated to implement a project providing in-service training for school leadership teams in developing strategies for inclusive education. Their stated emphasis, similarly broad in its scope, was on catering for ethnic, cultural and intellectual diversity.

Training

The preparation of teachers and other professionals to work in the multidisciplinary environment of functionally inclusive schools is of paramount importance. The crucial role of support staff in providing on-going training for teachers and others has already been noted. By contrast, international reviews of teacher training programmes and for the training of other professionals which were carried out as a part of this study provided a disappointing picture. Suffice it to say that, for very many countries, this is an area where substantial reforms are desperately needed. The work is reported more fully in OECD (1999a).

Conclusions

If the conditions which have been described above are met in the appropriate policy context, then there is no reason to believe that functional inclusion cannot be achieved for all countries, even though it will demand changes at a large number of levels of the system. Certainly, bringing together the special education and the education factions and considering policy implications for all children would be a very useful first step, as would a thorough review of the training teachers and other professionals receive and the way they work with the schools. Evidence is accumulating for the benefits of inclusive education for disabled and non-disabled students alike across academic and non-academic domains (e.g. OECD, 1993; McGregor and Vogelsberg, 1998). In addition, there is also evidence that inclusive provision benefits the academic level of non-disabled students (Manset and Semmel, 1997), a finding consonant with the experience described from Woodstock in Canada. More work is needed in this area, linked into the funding of inclusive education. Although formal analyses have not been carried out, the evidence which exists suggests that functionally inclusive education would improve standards for all students, with some savings on costs.

References

Clay, M. (1994) *Reading Recovery: A Guidebook for Teachers*. Auckland, New Zealand: Heinemann.

Council of the European Union (1990) *The Integration of Children and Young People Affected by a Handicap into Mainstream Education Systems*, Resolution 90/C162/02 of the Council and Ministers of Education. Brussels: European Union.

Department for Education and Employment (1998) *Special Educational Needs in England*. Norwich, UK: The Stationery Office.

Department of Employment, Education and Training (1994) *National Equity Programs for Schools (NEPS)*. Canberra: Australian Government Publishing Service.

McGregor, G. and Vogelsberg, R.T. (1998) 'Inclusive schooling practices: pedagogical and research foundations'. Mimeo, University of Montana.

Manset, G. and Semmel, M.I. (1997) 'Are inclusive programs for students with mild disabilities effective? A comparative review of model programs', *Journal of Special Education*, 31(2), 155–80.

OECD (1993) *European Journal of Special Needs Education*, 8, special issue on integration.

OECD (1995) *Integrating Students with Special Needs into Mainstream Schools*. Paris: OECD.

OECD (1998) *Education at a Glance (OECD indicators)*. Paris: OECD.

OECD (1999) *Special Education Statistics and Indicators*. Paris: OECD.

OECD (1999a) *Sustaining Inclusive Education: Educating Students with Disabilities in Mainstream Schools*. Paris: OECD.

Thurlow, M. L. (1997) 'Standards and assessment in the United States including students with disabilities in public accountability systems', in D. Labon and P. Evans (eds) *Implementing Inclusive Education*, Paris: OECD.

UNESCO (1994) *The Salamanca Statement and Framework for Action on Special Needs Education*. Paris: UNESCO.

US Department of Education (1996) *Eighteenth Annual Report to Congress on the Implementation of the Individuals with Disabilities Education Act*. Washington: US Department of Education.

Warnock, M. (1978) *Special educational needs – The Warnock Report*. London: HMSO.

5 Questioning, Understanding and Supporting the Inclusive School

Alan Dyson

The Inclusive School

In recent years, the development of inclusive education has come to constitute what Pijl et al. (1997) characterize as 'a global agenda'. Not only do we see schools and (in the English context) local education authorities (LEAs) developing inclusive provision, we also see the emergence of a wide range of inclusion lobby groups, the formulation of international declarations in favour of inclusion, and the adoption of more or less inclusive policies by a range of national governments. A central plank of the inclusion platform is the notion of the 'inclusive school'. The Salamanca 'Framework for Action' (UNESCO, 1994) defines the inclusive school in the following way:

> The fundamental principle of the inclusive school is that all children should learn together, wherever possible, regardless of any difficulties or differences they may have. Inclusive schools must recognize and respond to the diverse needs of their students, accommodating both different styles and rates of learning and ensuring quality education to all through appropriate curricula, organizational arrangements, teaching strategies, resource use and partnerships with their communities. There should be a continuum of support and services to match the continuum of special needs encountered in every school.
>
> (UNESCO, 1994: 61, para. 7)

Definitions of this sort have become so common in the inclusive education literature that they tend to be somewhat taken for granted. However, they raise two issues which are worthy of comment. The first is that, since the majority of education systems in the world are based on more or less exclusive segregationist principles, the implementation of inclusion constitutes a major change for most schools and most teachers. UNESCO's matter-of-fact statements – about responding to diverse needs, accommodating different styles and rates of learning, developing appropriate curricula and so on – have to be realized by schools which have commonly been established to accomplish the quite different tasks of educating a finite range of students within a predetermined, and often centrally prescribed, curriculum. The scale of the transformation that is required is significant.

Second, the inclusion movement, through the notion of the 'inclusive school', has defined the 'unit of participation' for students as the mainstream school – or, indeed, the mainstream classroom – in a way that has previously not been the case. Many education systems, particularly in the 'developed' world, have been 'inclusive' for many years in the sense that *all* (or very nearly all) children have been entitled to state education. However, the unit of participation has tended to be a local network of schools (in England, the LEA's schools), with segregated special schools constituting a means of facilitating participation in this sense (Gerber, 1995). From the point of view of policy-makers, this has provided a stress-free means of resolving the dilemma of how to provide a common education to children who have manifestly different educational characteristics and needs (Clark et al., 1997). However, the notion of the inclusive school shifts the resolution of this dilemma to the level of the school rather than the system. It is the mainstream school – and, more particularly, the mainstream teacher – who must now square the circle of offering a common education to diverse learners.

The implication of this analysis is that schools which are seeking or are required to become inclusive are likely to find the process *difficult*, because of the extent of the changes required of them, and *problematic* because of the dilemmas it requires them to resolve. In this chapter, therefore, I wish to explore the sorts of external support which schools need to help them through this process. In particular, I wish to suggest that the support needed, like the process itself, is multi-faceted. In order to overcome the difficulties of implementing inclusion, schools need what I shall call *enabling* and *catalytic* support – forms of support which are well-documented in the literature. In order to deal with the problematic nature of inclusion, however, schools need a different and less well-understood form of support, which I call *critical* support.

The Difficulties of Inclusion

A number of commentators have attempted to identify and articulate the features that enable a school to overcome the difficulties associated with becoming inclusive. A range of features has been offered, but they can be usefully seen as falling into three distinct, though interacting, areas:

1 *Technology* A common theme in the literature is what we might call the 'technology' of inclusion. This simply means that inclusive schools need to develop a range of systems, structures and practices which, in practical terms, enable teachers to educate a diverse range of learners in the same classroom. Much of the effort in developing such a technology has focused on pedagogical and curricular adaptation (see, for instance,

Lipsky and Gartner, 1997; Stainback and Stainback, 1992; Udvari-Solner, 1995; Udvari-Solner and Thousand, 1995; Villa and Thousand, 1995). However, other aspects of this technology include systems for making adult support available, accessing specialist teaching skills in the ordinary classroom, promoting students' social development and acceptance, and so on (see, for instance, Sebba and Sachdev, 1997).

2   *Problem-solving*   A number of commentators regard technique in itself as being inadequate, partly because the diversity of learner characteristics tends to elude any predetermined technology and partly because what we know about teacher learning suggests that a simple 'transfer' of techniques into schools is unlikely to be successful. Instead, therefore, these commentators have argued that the key to inclusiveness lies in the capacity of teachers within the school to solve for themselves the pedagogical problems that are presented by diversity (see, for instance, Ainscow, 1994, 1997; Skrtic, 1991a, 1991b, 1991c). This in turn has implications for the organization of inclusive schools. Teachers are likely to be more effective as problem-solvers if they work in problem-solving teams where they can pool ideas and expertise. The inclusive school, therefore, has to be organized around such teams rather than around the traditional model of the individual teacher isolated in her/his classroom.

3   *Political commitment*   For other commentators, the key barriers to inclusion are the vested interests ranged against it at every level of the education system. Neither technology nor problem-solving will be enough, therefore, unless they are accompanied by a genuine commitment within schools to inclusive principles (see, for instance, Ballard, 1995; Fulcher, 1993; Vlachou and Barton, 1994; Vlachou, 1997; Ware, 1995). For these commentators, the realization of inclusion is essentially a political struggle in which inclusion advocates fight against both the explicit opposition of their colleagues and the undermining effects of exclusive attitudes, practices and structures in the education system as a whole.

Although these three features are emphasized to different degrees by different commentators, it is not difficult to see how they might complement and enhance one another. Inclusive schools need a commitment to inclusion on the part of at least a critical mass of their staff; they need to acquire a broad repertoire of techniques for educating a wide range of students; and they need to develop a problem-solving capacity which will enable them both to apply their acquired techniques to the unique characteristics of individual students and to develop new techniques to respond to students who fall outside even the extended range of student characteristics to which they are accustomed to respond.

Enabling and Catalytic Support

Once these characteristics of inclusive schools are understood, it becomes relatively clear what sort of external support they might need. I wish to suggest that, essentially, this support is of two kinds. The first is *enabling* support – that is, support which creates an environment in which the inclusive school can flourish. For instance, the extent to which local and national policy is *unequivocally* committed to inclusion has a major impact on the capacity of individual schools to become inclusive (Dyson and Millward, 1997; Fulcher, 1989; Fulcher, 1993; Lipsky and Gartner, 1997; Porter, 1997; Slee, 1995; Slee, 1996; Villa et al., 1992). More specifically, the way in which resources – in terms of funds, personnel and expertise – are distributed throughout the education system can offer incentives and disincentives for schools to become inclusive (Lee, 1996; Lunt and Evans, 1993; Parrish, 1997; Pijl and Dyson, 1998; Porter, 1997). If schools derive a financial advantage from segregating students, or if that is the only way in which students can access the additional resources they need, then there will be powerful incentives for the retention of segregated special education. On the other hand, if additional resources are readily available in regular schools and if such schools have some flexibility in the way they deploy those resources, then there is a greater likelihood not only that regular schools will retain their more problematic students, but also that they will develop creative approaches to making provision for them.

The second form of support we might usefully describe as *catalytic*. Such support takes the forms of interventions in schools aimed at changing them so that they become more inclusive. The precise nature of this support is likely to vary according to which of the three broad aspects of inclusive schools the change-agents consider most important. For instance, while Ainscow (1994) describes an international project aimed at intervening in schools in order to establish problem-solving cultures, and Udvari-Solner (1995; Udvari-Solner and Thousand, 1995) describes projects aimed at developing and teaching specific techniques to teachers, Jordan and Goodey (1996) describe an attempt to energize schools through the powerful advocacy of a human rights perspective. Given what we said earlier about the interdependence of the main features of inclusive schools, it seems likely that all three forms of catalytic support will be necessary at some point.

The Problems of Inclusive Schools

It is clear that our analysis so far makes it possible to identify both a finite set of features which inclusive schools need to develop and a specific range of support which such schools will need in order for this development to take place. Indeed, in the past, my colleague Alan Millward and I have attempted to formalize these requirements in a form which would be useful to both policy-makers and practitioners in an education system which was seeking to become more inclusive (Dyson and Millward, 1997). While I continue to be happy to stand by the usefulness of such prescriptions, recent investigations in which I have been involved leave me with an underlying concern that they might underestimate the challenges of the inclusion project. In particular, they suggest that, alongside the *difficulties* which would-be inclusive schools face and which they can, with appropriate support, overcome, such schools also confront a series of complex *problems*, the solutions to which are far less apparent.

Over the past three years, I have been involved with colleagues in three studies of comprehensive schools in England which were, in terms of their avowed policies and some (at least) of their actual practices, seeking to become more inclusive. The first study concerned 'Richard Lovell School' – a school on the fringes of the inner area of a large industrial city (Booth et al., 1997, 1998). Richard Lovell not only had to respond to the significant needs of a range of students, many of whom were drawn from the inner-city area, but also included students with sensory and intellectual impairments who would more usually, in England, be educated in segregated special settings.

The second study focused on four comprehensive schools – 'Moorgate', 'Lakeside', 'St Joseph's' and 'Seaview' – which were selected because they had developed a set of 'innovatory' (Clark et al., 1995b) approaches to educating students with special educational needs (Clark et al., 1999a, 1999b).[1] Each of the schools displayed a commitment to including students who might otherwise have been placed in segregated special settings, and Lakeside in particular included students with significant intellectual impairments. Moreover, the 'innovatory' approaches which these schools had developed were aimed at encouraging the full participation of *all* students – including those with special educational needs – in regular classrooms and the mainstream curriculum.

The third study likewise focused on a comprehensive school – 'Downland' School – which had been identified as 'innovatory' to the extent that it had rejected both the language and the structures of special needs education through which almost all schools respond to students who experience difficulties in learning (Clark et al., 1995a). Instead, this school sought to develop an entirely new approach in which all students were regarded as characterized by 'individual differences' which called on the teachers to develop infinitely flexible pedagogical techniques to respond to those differences.

In many ways, these schools shared the features of inclusive schools which we identified above. However, their attempts to become inclusive also shared a series of problematic features:

1   *The resilience of special education*   In each of the case-study schools, there was a conscious attempt either to dismantle separate special needs provision entirely, or to restructure it in such a way as to break down the

barriers between it and mainstream provision. However, in each case, it was possible to identify ways in which rather traditional forms of special needs provision continued to reassert themselves. To take a specific example: in St Joseph's School, thinking skills approaches were advocated as an means of releasing the learning potential of all students and offering an alternative to traditional forms of provision for students with special educational needs. However, it was striking that students with special educational needs actually followed a programme of thinking skills which was quite different from that followed by their peers, and did so in segregated groups. Moreover, instead of replacing traditional interventions, this thinking skills programme sat alongside a programme of reading instruction in withdrawal groups that would not have been out of place in a comprehensive school twenty years ago.

Elsewhere, we were able to see a proliferation of segregated groups, setting by 'ability', special education teachers, alternative curricula, and so on. Even Downland School, which was the most vehemently opposed to traditional special education structures, succumbed to the appointment of a Special Educational Needs Co-ordinator when the government introduced its somewhat traditionally oriented Code of Practice (DfE, 1994) and in the face of pressure from some parents and staff who were disturbed by the school's apparently radical approach.

2   *The inadequacy of the technology of inclusion*   Each of the schools established a 'technology' of inclusion – a set of structures and practices aimed at making it possible for students with special educational needs to be included in regular classrooms. Typically, this technology comprised in-class support from teachers or Learning Support Assistants (LSAs), a programme of 'differentiation' through which the common curriculum was adapted or delivered in such a way as to be accessible to students with difficulties, and a proactive SENCO (or equivalent) managing the school's response to diversity and seeking to develop the skills of the staff in contributing to that response.

In each of the schools, the implementation of this technology was characterized by patchiness and ambiguity. The patchiness stemmed both from the variable degree to which individual teachers and their subject departments adapted their teaching and from the strictly limited level of in-class support available in the schools. Typically, students with special needs would move lesson by lesson from classrooms in which they had access to support and were able to participate in the common curriculum to classrooms where there was no support and/or the teacher operated in a traditional, didactic manner which made few concessions to the diversity of the student group.

The ambiguity of the technology stemmed from its dual role as a means of promoting inclusion and as a means of reinforcing difference. On the one hand, differentiation and support were means of enabling students to access the common curriculum in regular classrooms; on the other hand, they were means of offering students with special needs a somewhat restricted and degraded version of the curriculum which was offered to their peers, in order that some appearance of inclusion could be maintained without any radical restructuring of teaching and learning activities. In Richard Lovell School, for instance, we even had an example of an LSA attending a lesson despite the fact that the student she was supporting was absent. Nonetheless, she followed the lesson carefully and did all the work set by the teacher in the student's book; he effectively was 'included' in the lesson without even being present.

3   *The problem of behaviour*   In each of these schools, one of the sternest tests faced by the policy of inclusion was in responding to the problematic behaviour of some students. Many teachers in each of the schools reported concern about what they took to be a rising tide of misbehaviour – a tide which could not be contained by the technologies of inclusion described above. Some went so far as to question openly whether such students could and should be included in regular schools. Increasingly, the schools felt themselves compelled to set up 'behaviour management' systems which appeared to fly in the face of their avowed commitment to inclusion – separate teaching groups for 'disruptive' students, 'time-out' rooms where students could be removed from regular classrooms, 'behaviour specialists' who would intervene with 'difficult' students, and classroom management systems which were punitive in their orientation and involved excluding students from the classroom as part of the punishment regime.

Again, there is a certain ambiguity in these developments, which on the one hand maintained students in the school but on the other hand singled them out and excluded them from common learning experiences in regular classrooms. This ambiguity was most keenly evident in Lakeside and Downland, where a powerful rhetoric at management level of inclusion was accompanied by rather high rates of disciplinary exclusion from the school. The account offered by the headteachers of these schools was to the effect that excluding some students enabled the school to function as an inclusive community for its remaining students.

4   *The impact of the policy environment*   The difficulties faced by schools in managing behaviour, and their need, in certain cases, to remove troublesome students, cannot entirely be disentangled from the policy environment in which the schools found themselves. It has been well documented that the sweeping education reforms in England introduced in the 1988 Education Act and after made it increasingly difficult for regular schools to pursue liberal policies in respect of special needs education (Bines, 1995; Clark et al., 1997; Gold et al., 1993; Riddell and Brown, 1994; Vincent et al., 1994). The introduction of an education market-place in

91

which parents are encouraged to choose their child's school largely on the basis of the school's 'academic excellence' has introduced powerful incentives for schools to emphasize achievement – and hence high-achievers – at the expense of students with special educational needs.

The impacts of these developments were clearly evident in the case-study schools. Getting a 'grip' on behaviour – even to the extent of excluding students, for instance – is likely to enhance the perception of the school as one where hard work and academic endeavour are valued. So too is the practice of grouping students by ability, which was increasing in these schools. All the schools – especially Lakeside, Moorgate and Richard Lovell – were in direct competition for new students with other schools in their localities, and it was not uncommon for senior managers to wonder out loud whether their good reputations for special needs education did not disadvantage them in the market-place. Indeed, Moorgate was beginning to consider actively restricting the numbers of students with special needs which it accepted, for precisely this reason. In some schools, moreover, additional resources, which might traditionally have gone to the most vulnerable students, were being redirected to students on the borderline of examination success, since it was those successes which would appear in the local media and mark the school out as a 'good' one.

5 *The endemic nature of resistance*   Resistance to the implementation of inclusive education is not something that is entirely unanticipated. If the creation of an inclusive school requires political commitment, then it is not surprising that where such commitment is absent or where there are other political commitments in operation, conflict will ensue. In some of our case-study schools, the immediate causes of such conflict were not difficult to find: idealistic and pro-inclusionist headteachers had taken over schools where very different values prevailed among the staff, and their attempts to impose their own values were, predictably, resisted.

What was striking, however, was the way in which resistance was endemic even in those schools where there had been a careful and, in some cases, lengthy process of consensus-building. Moorgate, for instance, had been characterized by a liberal approach to education in general and to student diversity in particular for at least two decades. The staff as a whole were only too willing to tell us that this was a school committed to the 'comprehensive ideal' and to building a welcoming community for all students. Nonetheless, they were also able to direct us towards, or identify themselves as, resisters who were sceptical about the current policies being pursued by the school. Similarly, at Downland, where there was a very powerful pro-inclusion rhetoric from the majority of the staff, we found at least one dissident subject department and a number of other individuals and groups who were scathing about the 'official' policy of the school.

6   *The indeterminacy of ideals*   This conflict between the 'official' policy of these schools and the resistance to those policies which we found points to another salient characteristic of the schools. In all cases, the policy of the school was supported by an 'official rhetoric' which was espoused by senior managers and was broadly pro-inclusionist. Commonly, this rhetoric hinged on a broad characterization of the ideal to which the school was committed – the 'comprehensive ideal', or a 'community school', or 'unleashing the potential' of students, or the infinite 'capacity to learn' of all students. This, in itself, was not surprising. What was surprising, however, was that even dissidents among the staff sometimes espoused this same rhetoric while resisting the specific policies and practices designed to realize it – and did this without any sense of contradiction between the two.

Indeed, it was striking that the ideals that were espoused in the schools appeared to be compatible with a wide range of apparently contradictory policies and practices. Hence, for instance, the 'community school' included students with severe learning difficulties while being willing to exclude students whose behaviour disrupted the school; the school which saw all students as having infinite capacity to learn nonetheless operated a system of strict 'ability' grouping and, in important ways, offered different curricula to different groups; a school that prided itself on being inclusive and accepting in its attitudes nonetheless created a multiplicity of special groups, bases and courses which effectively segregated students from each other.

In none of these cases was there reason to suspect simple bad faith. Headteachers and their staff seemed to be genuinely committed to their ideals. However, those ideals were so generalized that they were compatible with almost any practice. As a result, they seemed to offer only the most minimal of guidance to action within the school.

The Problematic Nature of Inclusion

To a certain extent, difficulties such as these in the realization of inclusion are entirely predictable from the characteristics of inclusive schools which we outlined earlier in this chapter. If inclusion requires the significant changes we suggested, then we must expect the difficulties and complexities of all educational change processes (Fullan with Stiegelbauer, 1991). By the same token, of course, we might also expect that the sorts of enabling and catalytic support we outlined above would be adequate to overcoming these difficulties.

However, there is an alternative position which can be argued. Although the problems of inclusive schools can be treated as symptoms of a change process which will ultimately be successful, they can also be treated as indicative of much more deep-seated ambiguities in the inclusion project itself. Those ambiguities stem from the basic dilemma of mass education systems which I outlined at the start of this chapter: on the one hand, such systems aim to give all learners access to broadly *common* educational experiences within a broadly *common* organizational framework; on the other hand, they attempt to give all learners somewhat *different* experiences through more or less *different* structures in order to meet their individual needs, interests and characteristics (Clark et al., 1997, 1999a, 1999b).

This 'commonality–difference dilemma' remains submerged where learners can be assumed to have much in common with one another and/or where the organization of schooling permits considerable flexibility. However, it becomes acute where learners are markedly different from each other in characteristics that bear directly upon learning and/or where the framework of schooling permits little flexibility. The 'inclusive school', where a wide range of learners is to be educated together, is, therefore, a site where this dilemma inevitably surfaces. Furthermore, the more that school takes a 'hard' position on inclusion (Low, 1997), insisting, for instance, that all learners be educated in the mainstream classroom, following a common curriculum and participating in shared learning experiences, the less flexibility there is to accommodate difference and the more acute the dilemma becomes. Finally, if, as is inevitably the case, the inclusive school operates in the context of an education system which imposes significant constraints on the school and requires it to obey a series of imperatives in addition to inclusion, the dilemma may verge on the unmanageable (Booth et al., 1997, 1998; Rouse and Florian, 1997).

On this analysis, the problems outlined above are not soluble through a 'management of change' process, however sophisticated that process may be. Indeed, at bottom they are not *soluble* at all: the acuteness of the dilemma can be lessened, but the dilemma itself cannot be eradicated; schools and teachers can be helped to teach diverse groups and manage difficult behaviour more effectively, but the tensions created by diversity and disruption cannot be entirely resolved; national policy can become more supportive of inclusion, but it cannot have inclusion as its *only* goal. The issue for schools, therefore, is not so much how they *solve* the problems associated with inclusion, but how they *resolve* the dilemmas created by responding to diversity within the framework of a common educational system.

Critical Support for Schools

This, in turn, has major implications for the nature of the 'support' which inclusive schools are held to need. The sorts of 'enabling' and 'catalytic' support we described earlier in this chapter are entirely appropriate for supporting change. However, they assume that, however complex the change process, the direction of change itself is unproblematic and its outcome is something that can unequivocally be recognized as 'improvement'. Put another way, there is no question about where schools have to end up as a consequence of the change process – they have to become 'inclusive'; the only issue is how to get them to that end-point efficiently and effectively.

The dilemmatic perspective, however, makes the end-point itself problematic. Since there are no *solutions* of dilemmas, any proposed *resolution* simply reorders the basic elements of the dilemma in a different way. There is, therefore, no unequivocal 'improvement' since the fundamental conditions out of which the dilemma arose in the first place have been rearranged rather than changed. The question which then arises is what kind of support, promoting what kind of change, is appropriate when the end-point of that change is surrounded by so much ambiguity?

These issues frequently surface in the inclusion arena around what we might call the participation versus appropriateness debate. A bone of contention between inclusion advocates and inclusion sceptics is whether the participation of learners with special educational needs in mainstream classrooms and curricula can only be 'bought' at the cost of the appropriateness of provision. In Zigmond and Baker's (1995, 1996) terms, can good 'general' education for these learners only be achieved by sacrificing those elements of 'special' education which are specifically targeted at their distinctive characteristics? On the standard inclusionist analysis, the reality of this set of alternatives tends to be denied. Either participation in general education is so overwhelmingly superior to 'special' education that there is simply no contest or, more likely, teachers can be supported in developing techniques which enable them to deliver both forms of provision simultaneously (McLaughlin, 1995; Udvari-Solner and Thousand, 1995).

On a dilemmatic analysis, however, not only is the reality of dilemma granted, but it is seen to highlight questions of underlying values which are not easily resolved. There may indeed be contradictions between important educational principles such as participation and appropriateness – contradictions, moreover, which cannot simply be discounted because of the overwhelming superiority of one principle over another and cannot be caused to vanish by improved teaching techniques. If this is the case, then at some point *choices* have to be made between those principles. And such choices are inevitably both *ethical*, in that they require some resolution to be arrived at between competing values (Lindsay, 1997; Lindsay and Thompson, 1997), and *political* in that such choices are structured by and contribute to the structuring of the political context within which they have to be made (Barton, 1995, 1997).

This brings us back to the issue of support. It is evident that 'enabling' support is not concerned with choices but rather with implementing choices that have already been made. Catalytic support, on the other hand, is most definitely concerned with choices, but starts from the assumption that the choice is between one unequivocally better (i.e. inclusionist) alternative and one unequivocally poorer (i.e. segregationist) one. Its principal agenda, therefore, is to do with getting better choices made by energizing and (in a particular sense) politicizing teachers. What is needed, therefore, is a third form of support, which I suggest might be called *critical* support. This is very much concerned with getting choices made; however, it starts from the assumption that the choices are between real alternatives, posing real dilemmas and requiring real trade-offs between equally important principles.

I call this support 'critical' because its principal characteristic is that it is essentially concerned with deconstructing any proposed course of action in terms both of its political and ethical assumptions and of the alternatives which have to be rejected if that course is adopted. To that extent, I see critical support as fostering a process akin to that sustained by Skrtic's (1995) 'critical pragmatism' whereby forms of educational provision are constantly constructed and deconstructed through critical debate. However, whereas Skrtic seems to see such a process as one of continual progress towards a democratic ideal, I am, for the reasons set out above, somewhat less convinced of the linear and progressive nature of change. 'Critical support', therefore, is not simply about moving from the unequivocally worse to the undeniably better, so much as about interrogating fundamental assumptions as to what counts as 'better' at a given time and place.

Providing Support to Schools

In the bulk of this chapter, I have concentrated on outlining the broad types of support which would-be inclusive schools may need. However, this inevitably begs the question of how such support is to be provided. This question is particularly *à propos* at the current time in England, where the incoming New Labour government has initiated a series of education reforms which effectively weaken the autonomy of LEAs and increase the direct control over schools and other parts of the education system exercised by central government. Whatever the merits of such reforms, they have two effects which are relevant to the issue of support for inclusion.

First, they drive schools hard in the direction of the education agenda as determined by central government. Currently, that agenda has inclusion as one of its sub-themes (DfEE, 1997), but is heavily dominated by a so-called 'crusade for standards' which is effectively about raising attainments as measured by national tests and examinations. Second, they direct elements of the education system which have traditionally offered external support to schools – notably LEAs and the professional development and research roles of higher education – towards supporting that same agenda.

The consequences of this for the provision of enabling and catalytic support are, it seems to me, ambiguous. Schools are offered considerable support in complying with the government's agenda but very little support for anything which deviates therefrom. It remains to be seen, therefore, whether the government's commitment to inclusion is real enough for significant support to be offered to schools and, perhaps more important, whether it can be reconciled with a much stronger commitment to 'standards', defined in such a narrow way.

Perhaps more worrying, it is difficult to see in the current situation how critical support is to be provided. It is of the essence of critical support to help schools and teachers *problematize* agendas, whether their own, the government's or anyone else's. Critical support is only possible in an education system characterized by openness to doubt and uncertainty, and, moreover, by openness to debate. It does not, therefore, sit easily with the hard driving of fixed and limited agendas. In the long run, the real concern is that the mixture of doctrinaire government policy on the one hand, competing with an advocacy of inclusion which can sometimes be equally doctrinaire on the other, will leave schools bereft of any sort of open debate. The prospects for the realization of inclusion under such circumstances look bleak; the prospects for ultimately finding our way beyond inclusion look even bleaker.

Notes

1   This study was supported by the Economic and Social Research Council, project number R000234770, 'Policy, practice and understandings in emerging approaches to special needs'.

References

Ainscow, M. (1994) *Special Needs in the Classroom: A Teacher Education Guide*. London: Jessica Kingsley/UNESCO.

Ainscow, M. (1997) 'Towards inclusive schooling', *British Journal of Special Education*, 24(1), 3–6.

Ainscow, M., Hopkins, D., Southworth, G. and West, M. (1994) *Creating the Conditions for School Improvement*. London: David Fulton.

Ballard, K. (1995) 'Inclusion, paradigms, power and participation', in C. Clark, A. Dyson and A. Millward (eds) *Towards Inclusive Schools?*. London: David Fulton.

Barton, L. (1995) 'The politics of education for all', *Support for Learning*, 10(4), 156–60.

Barton, L. (1997) 'Inclusive education: romantic, subversive or realistic?', *International Journal of Inclusive Education*, 1(3), 231–42.

Bines, H. (1995) 'Special educational needs in the market place', *Journal of Education Policy*, 10(2), 157–72.

Booth, T., Ainscow, M. and Dyson, A. (1997) 'Understanding inclusion and exclusion in the English competitive education system', *International Journal of Inclusive Education*, 1(4), 337–54.

Booth, T., Ainscow, M. and Dyson, A. (1998) 'England: inclusion and exclusion in a competitive system', in T. Booth and M. Ainscow (eds) *From Them to Us: An international study of inclusion in England*. London: Routledge.

Clark, C., Dyson, A., Millward, A. and Robson, S. (1999a) 'Inclusive education and schools as organizations', *International Journal of Inclusive Education*, 3(1), 37–51.

Clark, C., Dyson, A., Millward, A. and Robson, S. (1999b) 'Theories of inclusion, theories of schools: deconstructing and reconstructing the "inclusive school"', *British Educational Research Journal*, 25(2), 157–77.

Clark, C., Dyson, A., Millward, A. and Skidmore, D. (1995a) 'Dialectical analysis, special needs and schools as organizations', in: C. Clark, A. Dyson and A. Millward (eds) *Towards Inclusive Schools?*. London: David Fulton.

Clark, C., Dyson, A., Millward, A. and Skidmore, D. (1995b) *Innovatory Practice in Mainstream Schools for Special Educational Needs*. London: HMSO.

Clark, C., Dyson, A., Millward, A. and Skidmore, D. (1997) *New Directions in Special Needs: Innovations in Mainstream Schools*. London: Cassell.

Department for Education (1994) *Code of Practice on the Identification and Assessment of Special Educational Needs*. London: DfE.

Department for Education and Employment (1997) *Excellence for All Children: Meeting Special Educational Needs*. London: The Stationery Office.

Dyson, A. and Millward, A. (1997) 'The reform of special education or the transformation of mainstream schools?', in S.J. Pijl, C.J.W. Meijer and S. Hegarty (eds) *Inclusive Education: A Global Agenda*. London: Routledge.

Fulcher, G. (1989) *Disabling Policies? A Comparative Approach to Education Policy and Disability*. Lewes: Falmer Press.

Fulcher, G. (1993) 'Schools and contests: a reframing of the effective schools debate?', in: R. Slee (ed.) *Is There a Desk With My Name On It? The Politics of Integration*. London: Falmer Press.

Fullan, M. with Stiegelbauer, S. (1991) *The New Meaning of Educational Change*. London: Cassell (second edition).

Gerber, M. M. (1995) 'Inclusion at the high-water mark? Some thoughts on Zigmond and Baker's case studies of inclusive educational programs', *Journal of Special Education*, 29(2), 181–91.

Gold, A., Bowe, R. and Ball, S. (1993) 'Special educational needs in new context: micropolitics, money and "education for all"', in R. Slee (ed.) *Is There a Desk With My Name On It? The Politics of Integration*. London: Falmer Press.

Jordan, L. and Goodey, C. (1996) *Human Rights and School Change*. Bristol: CSIE.

Lee, T. (1996) *The Search for Equity: The Funding of Additional Educational Needs under LMS*. Aldershot: Avebury.

Lindsay, G. (1997) 'Values, rights and dilemmas', *British Journal of Special Education*, 24(2), 55–9.

Lindsay, G. and Thompson, D. (eds) (1997) *Values into Practice in Special Education*. London: David Fulton.

Lipsky, D. K. and Gartner, A. (1997) *Inclusion and School Reform: Transforming America's Classrooms*. Baltimore: Paul H. Brookes.

Low, C. (1997) 'Is inclusivism possible?', *European Journal of Special Needs Education*, 12(1), 71–9.

Lunt, I. and Evans, J. (1993) 'Allocating resources for special educational needs provision'. Paper presented to *Policy Options for Special Needs*, Institute of Education, London, 9 November 1993.

McLaughlin, M. (1995) 'Defining special education: a response to Zigmond and Baker', *Journal of Special Education*, 29(2), 200–207.

Parrish, T.B. (1997) 'Fiscal issues relating to special education', in D.K. Lipsky and A. Gartner (eds) *Inclusion and School Reform: Transforming America's Classrooms*. Baltimore: Paul H. Brookes.

Pijl, S.J. and Dyson, A. (1998) 'Pupil-bound budgets in special education: a three-country study', *Comparative Education*, 34(3), 261–79.

Pijl, S.J., Meijer, C.J.W. and Hegarty, S. (eds) (1997) *Inclusive Education: A Global Agenda*. London: Routledge.

Porter, G. (1997) 'Critical elements for inclusive schools', in S.J. Pijl, C.J.W. Meijer and S. Hegarty (eds) *Inclusive Education: A Global Agenda*. London: Routledge.

Riddell, S. and Brown, S. (eds) (1994) *Special Educational Needs Policy in the 1990s: Warnock in the Market Place*. London: Routledge.

Rouse, M. and Florian, L. (1997) 'Inclusive education in the market-place', *International Journal of Inclusive Education*, 1(4), 323–36.

Sebba, J. and Sachdev, D. (1997) *What Works in Inclusive Education*. Ilford: Barnardos.

Skrtic, T.M. (1991a) *Behind Special Education: A Critical Analysis of Professional Culture and School Organization*. Denver: Love.

Skrtic, T.M. (1991b) 'The special education paradox: equity as the way to excellence', *Harvard Educational Review*, 61(2), 148–206.

Skrtic, T.M. (1991c) 'Students with special educational needs: artifacts of the traditional curriculum', in M. Ainscow (ed.) *Effective Schools for All*. London: David Fulton.

Skrtic, T.M. (ed.) (1995) *Disability and Democracy: Reconstructing (Special) Education for Postmodernity*. New York: Teachers College Press.

Slee, R. (1995) 'Inclusive education: from policy to school implementation', in C. Clark, A. Dyson and A. Millward (eds) *Towards Inclusive Schools?*. London: David Fulton.

Slee, R. (1996) 'Inclusive education in Australia? Not yet!', *Cambridge Journal of Education*, 26(1), 19–32.

Stainback, S. and Stainback, W. (eds) (1992) *Curriculum Considerations in Inclusive Classrooms: Facilitating Learning for All Students*. Baltimore: Paul H. Brookes.

Udvari-Solner, A. (1995) 'A process for adapting curriculum in inclusive classrooms', in: R.A. Villa and J.S. Thousand (eds) *Creating an Inclusive School*. Alexandria, Va.: ASCD.

Udvari-Solner, A. and Thousand, J. (1995) 'Effective organizational, instructional and curricular practices in inclusive schools and classrooms', in: C. Clark, A. Dyson and A. Millward (eds) *Towards Inclusive Schools?*. London: David Fulton.

UNESCO (1994) *Final Report: World Conference on Special Needs Education: Access and Quality*. Paris: UNESCO.

Villa, R. and Thousand, J.S. (eds) (1995) *Creating an Inclusive School*. Alexandria, Va.: Association for Supervision and Curriculum Development.

Villa, R.A., Thousand, J.S., Stainback, W. and Stainback, S. (eds) (1992) *Restructuring for Caring and Effective Education: An Administrative Guide to Creating Heterogeneous Schools*. Baltimore: Paul H. Brookes.

Vincent, C., Evans, J., Lunt, I., Steedman, J. and Wedell, K. (1994) 'The market forces? The effect of local management of schools in special educational needs provisions', *British Educational Research Journal*, 20(3), 261–78.

Vlachou, A.D. (1997) *Struggles for Inclusive Education: An Ethnographic Study*. Buckingham: Open University Press.

Vlachou, A.D. and Barton, L. (1994) 'Inclusive education: teachers and the changing culture of schooling', *British Journal of Special Education*, 21(3), 105–7.

Ware, L. (1995) 'The aftermath of the articulate debate: the invention of inclusive education', in: C. Clark, A. Dyson and A. Millward (eds) *Towards Inclusive Schools?*. London: David Fulton.

Zigmond, N. and Baker, J. M. (1995) 'Concluding comments: current and future practices in inclusive schooling', *Journal of Special Education*, 29(2), 234–50.

Zigmond, N. and Baker, J. M. (1996) 'Full inclusion for students with learning disabilities: too much of a good thing?', *Theory into Practice*, 35(1), 26–34.

6 Reaching Out to All Learners

Some Opportunities and Challenges

Mel Ainscow

Two phrases seem to stand out from the government's education agenda, 'raising standards' and 'social inclusion'. For those who are committed to the development of state schooling this emphasis presents few problems. All our work has been driven by a desire to provide high-quality learning opportunities for all children and young people. So, it seems, our moment has come. Now we have to take the opportunities that all of this seems to provide.

Having said that, it is also important to be realistic. There are those within our country who, for a variety of reasons, may not be so enthusiastic to see the deep changes in the education system that will be necessary in order to provide 'excellence for all children' (DfEE, 1997). Some see the existence of a system that ensures prizes for some at the expense of others as being to their advantage. Then, at a more practical level, there are other barriers that are likely to be in the way of progress. Two immediately come to mind.

First of all, there is the major problem of how to redesign a system of education that still bears many of the features of the purpose for which it was originally formulated, that of educating those who will take on elite roles in society. The implication, therefore, is that substantial changes are needed. This leads to a second problem. Put simply it is this: how do we raise the morale and confidence of the one group that is most critical to these profound reforms, the teachers? Having had some ten years of being undermined and ridiculed, it would be hardly surprising if they did not find the idea of yet further proposals for change unpalatable. Certainly those who are arguing for yet further reforms need to remember that ultimately education policies are what happens behind the classroom door. In this sense teachers are policy-makers. How they choose to interpret external demands as they interact with their classes is, in effect, the policy that matters.

So if movement is to occur, it needs to be handled in ways that ensure the support of a committed and confident teaching force. Consequently, attention has to be given to ways in which this can be fostered. With this in mind this chapter draws on work I have been involved in with colleagues in this country and overseas in order to explore ways in which schools and classrooms can be developed in response to pupil diversity. My central question is: how do we create educational contexts that 'reach out to all learners'?

Responding to Today's Pupils

In the years since the right to educational opportunity was extended to all members of the community, it has become increasingly apparent that traditional forms of schooling are no longer adequate for the task. Today's pupils live in a world of remarkable interest and excitement. Many have opportunities to travel, while even those who do not are accustomed to a rich diet of stimulation through television, films and computers. In this sense they present challenges not faced by earlier generations of teachers. The pupils of today are, therefore, demanding and discriminating; they also, of course, bring to the classroom experiences and ideas that can provide important foundations upon which lessons can be planned.

Faced with this increased diversity, including the presence of pupils whose cultural experience or even language may be different from their own and others who may experience barriers to their learning within conventional arrangements, teachers have had to think about how they should respond. Broadly speaking, there seem to be three options:

- continue to maintain the status quo in the belief that those members of the class who do not respond have some 'problem' that prevents their participation;
- make compromises by reducing expectations in the belief that some pupils will simply never be able to achieve traditional standards;
- seek to develop new teaching responses that can stimulate and support the participation of all class members.

The problem with the first option, maintaining the status quo, is that it is likely to lead to conflict with some pupils, and possibly their parents. It may also damage the working atmosphere for everybody, thus making life more stressful for the teacher. The second option, making compromises, involves a reduction in standards, not least for some pupils who may already be vulnerable in our increasingly competitive society. The third option, demanding though it is, has the potential to bring about improvements that can enhance the learning of all pupils while at the same time reaching out to those who otherwise have been marginalized.

So what kinds of practices might help teachers to adopt this third option, that of seeking to 'reach out' to all members of the class? In addressing these questions I will to a large extent draw on research carried out with schools in our project 'Improving the Quality of Education for All' (IQEA). The project involved a team of university academics working in partnership with schools to explore ways in which the learning of all members of these communities, including students, parents and staff, can be enhanced (see Ainscow, 1999; Ainscow et al., 1994; Hopkins et al., 1994, for more detailed accounts of the project).

The experience of working with these and other schools leads me to suggest certain ingredients that seem to assist in developing schools and classrooms that can be more effective for all pupils. It is important here to note my use of the word 'ingredients' in order to make it clear that what I am outlining is not a recipe! Unfortunately, the fields of school effectiveness and school improvement have been prone to the formulation of lists of characteristics that appear to offer deceptively simple technical solutions to what are in essence complex social issues. Our own work illustrates the fact that schools are idiosyncratic communities, each with their own biographies, circumstances and profiles. Within these communities, many competing views are held, particularly when it comes down to the fundamental beliefs that guide teachers' interactions with their classes. This being the case, each school has to develop its own way forward, and while outsiders can and must be involved there is strong evidence to suggest that improvement has to be driven from the inside (Barth, 1990; Fullan, 1991; Hopkins et al., 1994).

In what follows I outline some 'ingredients' that provide possibilities for those who are interested in the development of schools that can be more effective in reaching out to all learners. My suggestions challenge those currently leading the national strategy to raise standards to consider how far their work really does take account of the learning of *all* pupils. They also challenge those involved in the field of special education to reconsider their ways of working.

Starting with Existing Knowledge

Recently, as part of a study I am carrying out with my colleagues Tony Booth and Alan Dyson, I watched a year 7 geography class in an urban comprehensive school (Booth et al., 1998). The students were seated in rows, two at a table, each with a textbook in front of them. The teacher began the lesson by explaining, 'This is the first of a series of lessons about the USA.' He went on to say that before they opened their books he wanted to know what the class already knew about this subject. Immediately lots of hands went up and within minutes the blackboard was full of information. Despite the fact that none of these young people from a poor city estate had ever been out of the country, their regular viewing of films and television programmes meant that their knowledge of the American way of life was extensive. Sitting on the front row was James, a student who has Down's syndrome. Next to him was a classroom assistant who is there to support this student's participation. James raised his hand and, when called on by the teacher, said, 'They have yellow taxis.'

So here, the teacher was using a familiar tactic to 'warm up' his class: that of using questioning to draw on existing knowledge, prior to introducing new material. It is an approach that many teachers use. Certainly it is not 'special education' but, nevertheless, it proved to be a means of facilitating the participation of members of the class, including one who is seen as needing a permanent adult helper.

This story points to what I see as the most important starting point for learning: that is, the knowledge and understandings that already exist in any context. Interestingly this seems to apply to the learning of both pupils and teachers. So, as in this example, we find that teachers who appear to be effective in providing experiences that facilitate the participation of all members of the class – while they each have their own style of working – do pay attention to certain key aspects of classroom life. First of all, they seem to recognize that the initial stages of any lesson or activity are particularly important if pupils are to be helped to understand the purpose and meaning of what is to occur. Specifically they aim to help their pupils to recall previous experiences and knowledge to which new learning can be connected. As one teacher put it, 'I have to warm the class up – I need hot learners, not cold learners.'

Noticeable too is the way that some teachers use available resources in order to stimulate and support participation. Most significantly, they seem to be aware that the two most important resources for learning are themselves and their pupils. The idea of using the potential of pupils as a resource to one another seems to be a particularly powerful strategy, but regrettably in some classrooms it is one that is largely overlooked. A striking feature of lessons that encourage participation is the way in which pupils are often asked to think aloud, sometimes with the class as a whole, as a result of the teacher's sensitive questioning, or with their classmates in well-managed small group situations. All of these provide opportunities for pupils to clarify their own ideas as they 'think aloud', while at the same time enabling members of the class to stimulate and support one another's learning.

Current thinking in cognitive psychology emphasizes the idea that learning is a personal process of meaning-making, with each participant in an event 'constructing' their own version of that shared experience (Udvari-Solner, 1996). The implication is that even in what might be seen as a rather traditional lesson, with little apparent concession being made by the teacher to the individual differences of members of the class, each pupil experiences and defines the meaning of what occurs in their own way. Interpreting the experience in terms of their own mental frames, individuals construct forms of knowledge which may or may not relate to the purposes and understandings of the teacher.

Recognizing this personal process of meaning-making leads the teacher to have to include in their lesson plans opportunities for self-reflection, in order that pupils can be encouraged to engage with and make a personal record of their own developing understandings.

However, the story of the geography class also points to the importance of teachers' existing thinking and practice as a starting point for development. Indeed, in my experience the expertise that is necessary in order to facilitate the participation and learning of all the pupils within a school is often already there. Often, it seems, teachers within a school know more than they use! Thus the improvement strategy is less to do with importing new expertise and much more about creating the organizational conditions within which existing skills and knowledge can be used more effectively.

Planning with All Members of the Class in Mind

It has taken me a long time to appreciate that existing practice represents the best starting point for development activities, not least because of my previous experience and training in the field of special education. Specifically, it took me many years to recognize the ways in which earlier attempts to develop integrated arrangements for pupils said to have special needs had often, unintentionally, undermined our efforts. As we tried to integrate such pupils into mainstream schools, we adopted practices derived from earlier experience in special provision. What we learned was that many of these approaches were simply not feasible in primary and secondary schools. Here I am thinking, in particular, of the individualized responses, based on careful assessments and systematic programmes of interventions, that have been the dominant orientation within the special needs world. For many years this was very much the orientation that shaped my own work (e.g. Ainscow and Tweddle, 1979, 1984). Gradually, however, experience has taught me that such approaches do not fit with the ways in which mainstream teachers plan and go about their work. For all sorts of sensible and understandable reasons, the planning frame of such teachers has to be that of the whole class. Apart from any other considerations, the sheer numbers of children in the class and the intensity of the teacher's day makes this inevitable.

Consequently, when integration efforts are dependent upon the importing of practices from special education they seem almost certain to lead to difficulties. Indeed, they are likely to lead to yet new forms of segregation, albeit within the mainstream settings (Fulcher, 1989), through the use of what Slee (1996) calls 'dividing practices'. For example, we have seen the proliferation of largely untrained classroom assistants who work with some of the most vulnerable children and their individual programmes. When such support is withdrawn, teachers feel that they can no longer cope. And, of course, the formal requirement for individualized education plans laid down by the Code of Practice has encouraged colleagues in some schools to feel that many more children will require such responses, thus creating the massive budget problems currently faced by some local authorities.

The gradual recognition that schools for all will not be achieved by transplanting special education thinking and practice into mainstream contexts has opened my mind to many new possibilities that I had previously failed to recognize. Many of these relate to the need to move from the individualized planning frame, referred to above, to a perspective that emphasizes a concern for and an engagement with the whole class. Thus, as one teacher explained, what is needed are strategies that *personalize* learning rather than individualize the lesson. An understanding of what these might involve can be gained from the study of practice, particularly the practice of class teachers in primary schools and subject teachers in secondary schools. As my awareness of the value of such studies has developed, so my interest in observing and trying to understand practice has grown. Put simply, I am arguing that a scrutiny of the practice of what we sometimes call 'ordinary teachers' provides the best starting point for understanding how classrooms can be made more inclusive.

Our own observations of planning processes used by teachers who seem to be effective in responding to diversity suggests certain patterns that might be borne in mind (Ainscow, 1995a; Hopkins et al., 1997). Usually, experienced teachers have developed a range of lesson formats that become their repertoire and from which they create arrangements that they judge to be appropriate to a particular purpose. Here they seem to take account of a range of interconnected factors, such as the subject to be taught, the age and experience of the class, the environmental conditions of the classroom, the available resources and their own mood, in order to adapt one of their usual lesson outlines. Such planning tends to be rather idiosyncratic and, indeed, often seems to be conducted at a largely intuitive level. In this sense it is unlike the rather rational procedure introduced to student teachers in that it consists, to a large degree, of an on-going process of designing and redesigning established patterns.

Much of this planning, therefore, goes on incidentally in the background as teachers go about their day-to-day business. While some of it may occur over the weekend or in the evening, it also continues on the way to school in the morning and on into the building as the teacher gathers things together for the lesson. Indeed, it sometimes strikes us that final adjustments are still being made as the teacher enters the classroom and judges the mood of the class.

All of this may sound rather informal, even hit-and-miss, but our observations indicate that for many experienced teachers it involves an intellectually demanding process of self-dialogue about how best to stimulate the learning of the class. Attempts to encourage and support further improvements in practice in this area must, therefore, take account of the nature of this complex approach to planning.

There is a rather obvious limitation to this approach to classroom planning that arises from the largely private way in which it is conducted. This is that the teacher is confined to the range of possibilities that is suggested from earlier experiences. This is why within our IQEA project schools are encouraged to develop organizational conditions that lead to discussions of teaching and sharing of experiences about how lessons might be planned (see Ainscow et al., 1994, in particular Chapter 7).

It is also essential to recognize that planning does not conclude when the lesson commences. Indeed, often the most significant decisions are those that are made as the lesson proceeds, through what I have characterized as a process of improvisation that is somewhat analogous to the practice of jazz musicians (Ainscow, 1995a, 1996). In this respect one researcher compares the work of teachers to that of artisans (Huberman, 1993). An example will illustrate the point he makes. Faced with a leak in a sink, an experienced plumber sets about the task in the certain knowledge that he (or she) has the wherewithal to solve the problem. Since he has fixed many similar leaks before he is confident that one of his usual responses will do the trick. Occasionally, however, he experiences a surprise – his usual repertoire proves to be inadequate. What does he do? Does he go on a course? Call for help? Read a manual? More likely he will 'tinker' with the problem pipes until he is able to invent a solution. In this way he adds a new way of working to his repertoire, which, of course, he can then take with him to the next leaking sink.

The suggestion is that this is something like the way in which teachers develop their practices. Arguably the key difference is that teaching is far less predictable than plumbing, so much so that during each lesson there are many 'surprises' to be dealt with and, therefore, far more possibilities for 'tinkering'. For example, there is the pupil who suddenly wants to tell the teacher about something interesting that happened the previous night; another who asks a question about the subject of the lesson that the teacher has never thought of; and, inevitably, those who lose interest or misbehave in some way. All of these unexpected events require an instant decision. Just like the plumber, the teacher has no opportunity to take advice. In this way new responses are trialled and, where they are found to be of value, added to the teacher's range of usual approaches. Through this form of 'planning in action', teachers learn how to create classroom arrangements that can be more effective in responding to individuals within their classes (Ainscow, 1996).

Seeing Differences as Opportunities for Learning

Recently I watched a wonderfully gifted teacher conduct a French lesson with a year 7 class. It struck me that her style took the form of a 'performance' in which she used a range of what I saw as dramatic techniques to create high levels of engagement among the pupils. During the final moments of the lesson I became aware of Geoffrey, who was sitting just behind me. It was obvious that he was unclear about what he should be doing. A girl sitting next to me whispered, 'He's a bit slow.' After the lesson, the teacher explained that Geoffrey often has difficulty in following instructions. 'He's my failure,' she explained.

It seemed to me that this comment summed up her approach to her work. Clearly she felt that it was her responsibility to help all members of the class to learn and that if individuals experienced difficulties it was her 'failure'. I contrast this with the apparent ready willingness of some teachers to presume that difficulties that occur in their classes are a direct result of the limitations of the pupils.

Once again, here, some of the traditions of the special needs field may have encouraged this type of response. Specifically, the tradition has been to see learning difficulties as primarily a technical problem (Ainscow, 1998b; Heshusius, 1989; Iano, 1986). This leads to a concern with finding the 'right' teaching methods or materials for pupils who do not respond to existing arrangements. Implicit in this formulation is a view that schools are rational organizations offering an appropriate range of opportunities; that those pupils who experience difficulties do so because of their limitations or disadvantages; and that *they*, therefore, are in need of some form of special intervention (Skrtic, 1991). It is my argument that, through such assumptions, leading to a search for effective responses to those children perceived as being special, vast opportunities for developments in practice are overlooked.

I accept, of course, that it is important to identify useful and promising strategies. However, I believe that it is erroneous to assume that the systematic replication of particular methods will necessarily generate successful learning, especially when we are considering populations that historically have been marginalized or even excluded from schools. This overemphasis on a search for 'quick-fix' methods often serves to obscure attention from more significant questions, such as: what are the barriers experienced by learners and how might they be overcome?

Consequently, it is necessary to shift from a narrow and mechanistic view of teaching to one that is broader in scope and takes into account wider contextual factors (Skrtic, 1991). In particular, it is important to resist the temptation of what Bartolome (1994) refers to as the 'methods fetish' in order to create learning environments that are informed by both action and reflection. In this way, by freeing themselves from the uncritical adoption of so-called effective strategies, teachers can begin the reflective process which will allow them to recreate and reinvent teaching methods and materials, taking into account contextual realities that can either limit or expand possibilities for improvements in learning.

Teachers have to remember that schools, like other social institutions, are influenced by perceptions of socioeconomic status, race, language and gender. Consequently it is important to question how such perceptions influence classroom interactions. In this way the current emphasis on methods must be broadened to reveal deeply entrenched deficit views of 'difference'. Specifically, we have to be vigilant in scrutinizing how deficit assumptions may be influencing perceptions of certain pupils.

Teaching methods are neither devised nor implemented in a vacuum. Design, selection and use of particular teaching approaches and strategies arise from perceptions about learning and learners. In this respect even the most pedagogically advanced methods are likely to be ineffective in the hands of those who implicitly or explicitly subscribe to a belief system that regards some pupils, at best, as disadvantaged and in need of fixing or, worse, as deficient and, therefore, beyond fixing.

In recent years, of course, the so-called deficit model has been subject to massive criticism (e.g. Ainscow, 1991; Dyson, 1990; Fulcher, 1989; Oliver, 1988). This has helped to encourage a shift of thinking that moves explanations of educational failure away from a concentration on the characteristics of individual children and their families towards a consideration of the process of schooling. However, despite lots of good intentions, deficit thinking is still deeply ingrained and too often leads many to believe that some pupils have to be dealt with in a separate way. In a sense, it suggests that some pupils are 'them' rather than being part of 'us' (Booth and Ainscow, 1998). This further encourages the marginalization of these pupils, while at the same time distracting attention away from the possibility that they can help to stimulate the development of practices that might well benefit all pupils. In other words, I am arguing that the responses of those who do not respond to existing arrangements represent the 'hidden voices' who, under certain conditions, can encourage the tinkering that is essential to the improvement of practice. Thus, differences can be seen as opportunities for learning rather than as problems to be fixed.

Scrutinizing Processes that Lead to Exclusion

The approach I am adopting to inclusion involves a process of 'increasing the participation of pupils in, and reducing their exclusion from school curricula, cultures and communities' (Booth and Ainscow, 1998). In this way the notions of inclusion and exclusion are linked together, since the process of increasing participation of pupils entails the reduction of pressures to exclude. This link also encourages us to look at the various constellations of pressures acting on different groups of pupils and acting on the same pupils from different sources. It draws our attention to the 'comedy' played out in some schools as pupils previously sent off to special schools are welcomed in through the front door while others are ushered out at the back. Meanwhile, other schools seem to have revolving doors which allow pupils to enter with one label, such as 'learning difficulty', only to be relabelled and then excluded with another, such as 'emotional and behavioural difficulty'.

Often the processes that lead to some pupils feeling excluded are subtle ones that occur within the classroom. So, as I watched lessons in one school recently, I noted how 'throwaway' remarks by teachers appeared to suggest that a low level of participation was anticipated. For example, a teacher appeared to have targeted one boy as somebody who was unlikely to make much of a contribution: 'Grant – homework. I assume you didn't do it – you never do, despite letters home to your mum.' Similarly, an English teacher on calling the class register remarked, 'Amazingly, we have Shula here.' It can be argued that such interactions help to reduce expectations and, in so doing, discourage participation and learning.

A current area of practice that seems to lead to a feeling of exclusion concerns the role of classroom assistants. Recently with colleagues I looked closely at the impact of their work on pupil participation in one secondary school (Booth et al., 1998). In art, for example, two pupils with 'statements' completed the tasks of the lesson even though they were both absent! In fact, the classroom assistant did the work for them. Meanwhile, there was another group of pupils in the same lesson who had no support and spent most of the lesson talking. Presumably the assistant had been told to concentrate her efforts solely on the targeted pupils.

In general, our impression was that while those pupils seen as having special needs were following broadly the same activities as their classmates, the constant presence of a 'helper' meant that often the challenges posed by these activities were significantly reduced. For example, the assistant might hold the paper for a pupil with a physical disability, write the words for a pupil experiencing learning difficulties, and so on. In these ways it seemed likely that at some point the continual availability of adult support would cease to ensure participation in the lesson, while at the same time effectively trivializing the activity. To take a specific example, Carol, a student with Down's syndrome, was observed in a series of lessons. Given the level of support she received, 'she' always completed the set tasks, although it seemed apparent that some of these held little meaning for her. Having said that, in many ways she presented as a full participant in the classroom.

The constant presence of an assistant may well, of course, be socially reassuring for a student, and we saw examples of how this can facilitate interactions between students. On the other hand, however, we saw many instances where the assistants' actions acted as a barrier between particular students and their classmates. This was particularly the case where assistants elected to group students with special needs together. This tended to encourage these students to talk to and seek help from the assistant rather than their classmates or, indeed, the teacher. As a result, it was evident in some classes that the teacher spent little time interacting with students seen as having special needs and would more often address their remarks to the assistant. Thus the presence of an assistant acting as an intermediary in communication and as a supporter in carrying out the required tasks means that the teacher may, in effect, carry less responsibility for some members of the class than might otherwise be the case. Furthermore, this means that the lesson can continue in the usual way, with the teacher knowing that the implications for these students will be dealt with by the assistant. This being the case, it can be argued that the existence of support may eliminate the possibility that the demands of these individuals could stimulate a consideration of how practice might be changed in an attempt to facilitate their participation.

For these reasons, therefore, I am suggesting that yet another starting point for the development of more inclusive practices within a school has to be with a close scrutiny of how existing arrangements may be acting as barriers to learning. With this in mind, the Centre for Educational Needs at the University of Manchester is carrying out a project with the Centre for Studies on Inclusive Education, the aim of which is to develop, evaluate and disseminate an index that can be used to review and improve current practice with respect to inclusion and exclusion in schools (Ainscow, 1998b). The 'Index of Inclusive Schooling' sets out to build on existing good practice within a school in order to encourage ways of working that will facilitate the learning of all pupils; minimize the need for exclusions; and support a school's efforts to widen its capacity for responding to diversity.

The Index project builds on earlier work carried out by teams of researchers in Australia and North America (i.e. Centre et al., 1991; Eichinger et al., 1996). However, since these studies began, thinking in the field has moved on. In particular, there has been a move away from the notion of integration towards inclusion. While the two terms have tended to be used interchangeably, increasingly they are being used to establish a degree of clarity as to how the task should be formulated (Ainscow, 1998a). Specifically, the word 'integration' has been used to describe processes by which individual children are supported in order that they can participate in the existing (and largely unchanged) programme of the school, whereas 'inclusion' suggests a willingness to restructure the school's programme in response to the diversity of pupils who attend. In the light of this distinction, some writers (e.g. Ballard, 1995) have stressed the need to see inclusion as a process by which a school continues to explore new ways of developing responses that value diversity. In this way, it is suggested, a school with an inclusive orientation defines 'differentness' as an ordinary part of human experience.

This emphasis on inclusion as a process has to be linked to the need to scrutinize the ways in which schools exclude pupils. As we have seen, there is evidence that even schools that are seen as being apparently successful in including pupils with particular disabilities may, at the same time, be developing organizational or curriculum responses that have the effect of excluding or marginalizing other groups.

So far, an 'expert group' of teachers, parents, representatives of disability groups with wide experience of attempts to develop more inclusive ways of working, and researchers from three universities (Cambridge, Manchester and the Open University) have produced a pilot Index. It has been designed in a form that is intended to be powerful in analysing existing practices, while at the same time being relatively easy to fit into the busy schedules of schools. Currently it is being trialled in four local authorities.

The Index is based upon a theoretical framework that draws on evidence from two main bodies of knowledge. First of all, it uses existing research evidence regarding processes that are known to facilitate the participation of students who might previously have been excluded or marginalized (e.g. Ainscow, 1995a, 1996; Booth and Ainscow, 1998; Wang and Reynolds, 1996). Second, it draws on recent evidence regarding effective processes of school improvement (e.g. Elmore et al., 1996; Hopkins et al., 1994; Louis and Miles, 1990; MacBeith et al., 1996). Using these knowledge bases, the Index aims to encourage all members of a school community to collaborate in collecting evidence, particularly from pupils, in order to review and develop areas of policy and practice.

Using Available Resources to Support Learning

A feature of lessons that seem to be effective in encouraging pupil participation is the way available resources, particularly human resources, are used to support learning. An example illustrates what I have in mind. A history teacher recently described to me how he had been using highly structured group learning methods in order to improve achievement in his lessons. He explained how he had planned one particular lesson around the idea of the 'jigsaw classroom' (Ainscow, 1994; Johnson and Johnson, 1994). Briefly, this involves the use of small 'expert groups' that each study separate texts. Then new groups are formed, consisting of at least one member of each of the expert groups, and they pool their material.

When he arrived at the classroom, the teacher was surprised to find that the classroom assistant who was usually there to help communication with a deaf boy in the class was absent. Despite this he pressed ahead with his carefully planned lesson. His evaluation was that not only had the lesson been successful in facilitating the learning of the class, but it had also been the first occasion on which the deaf pupil had really seemed to be fully involved. Apparently the carefully planned social processes of the lesson plan had opened up opportunities for the other pupils to overcome communication barriers that had previously left this individual rather marginalized during lessons.

This example illustrates the potential of certain approaches to create classroom conditions that can maximize participation while at the same time achieving high standards of learning for all pupils. Indeed, there is strong evidence to suggest that where teachers are skilful at planning and managing the use of co-operative group learning activities as part of their repertoire, this can have a positive impact upon achievement. The evidence suggests that the use of such practices can lead to improved outcomes in terms of academic, social and psychological development (Johnson and Johnson, 1994). Furthermore, they have also been found to be an effective means of supporting the participation of 'exceptional pupils', e.g. those who are new to a class; children from different cultural backgrounds; and those with disabilities. However, it is important to stress again the need for skill in orchestrating this type of classroom practice. Poorly managed group approaches usually involve considerable waste of time and, indeed, present many opportunities for increased disruption.

Effective group work can take a variety of forms, but the central feature is that the completion of the task necessitates the active participation of all individuals within a working group and that one member of the group cannot succeed without the success of the others. It is essential, therefore, that group members perceive the importance of working together and interacting in helpful ways. This can be accomplished by incorporating the following elements into small group experiences:

- Positive interdependence – where all members of a group feel connected to each other in the accomplishment of a common goal, such that all individuals have to succeed for the group to succeed.
- Individual accountability – which involves holding every member of a group responsible to demonstrate their contributions and learning.
- Face-to-face interaction – where members are in close proximity to each other and have dialogue that promotes continued progress.
- Social skills – involving the use of interaction skills that enable groups to function effectively (e.g. taking turns, encouraging, listening, giving help, clarifying, checking understanding, probing).
- Processing – where group members assess their collaborative efforts and target improvements.

It is important to recognize, therefore, that asking pupils to work collaboratively involves presenting them with new challenges. Consequently, this aspect of the curriculum has to be as carefully planned and monitored as any other.

Developing a Language of Practice

A couple of years ago I had a meeting with the deputy headteacher of one of the schools in the IQEA project. We were discussing the remarkable improvements that had occurred in the overall working atmosphere of the school following the appointment of a new head two years earlier. As we talked he explained how, despite these undoubted improvements, the style of teaching used around the school remained largely the same. He explained how, over recent years, the school had gone through a period of considerable difficulty, including a rather painful OFSTED inspection, as a result of which a kind of house style had developed. Basically, this meant that some of the best teachers in the school had, in his words, 'stopped playing their best shots'. Consequently the forms of teaching used now involved teachers in not taking any risks. Clearly, such an emphasis is unlikely to foster the use of responses that reach out to all learners.

Much of our early work in schools like this within the IQEA project involved attempts to introduce particular policies and, in so doing, to strengthen the schools' capacity to handle change. Gradually we recognized, however, that even where such initiatives were successful they did not necessarily lead to changes in classroom practice. Other similar studies point to similar conclusions (e.g. Elmore et al., 1996). The evidence suggests that developments of practice, particularly among more experienced teachers, are unlikely to occur without some exposure to what teaching actually looks like when it is being done differently and exposure to someone who can help teachers understand the difference between what they are doing and what they aspire to do (Elmore et al., 1996; Joyce and Showers, 1988, Hopkins et al., 1994). It also seems that this sort of problem has to be solved at the individual level before it can be solved at the organizational level. Indeed, there is evidence that increasing collegiality without some more specific attention to change at the individual level can simply result in teachers coming together to reinforce existing practices rather than confronting the difficulties they face in different ways (Lipman, 1997).

Given these arguments, it is important to look closely at schools where improvement efforts have led to changes in practice in order to see what lessons might be learned from their experiences. In stating that, however, I stress that I am not suggesting that our engagement with such a school will help to devise blueprints that can point the way forward for all schools. What I have learned as a result of many years of working in schools, trying to support a variety of innovations, is that they are complex and idiosyncratic places. What seems to help development in one school may have no impact – or even a negative effect – in another. So, while we can, I believe, learn through vicarious experience, this learning has to be respected for its own qualities. Essentially, it is a form of learning that can sometimes provide a stimulus to reflection on existing experience and current understandings, rather than a means of providing prescriptions that can be transposed to other environments.

Recently I spent some time looking closely at one urban primary school where practices had been developed that have facilitated the participation of pupils with a range of disabilities and from a large variety of minority ethnic cultures (Ainscow, 1996). As a result of my observations and discussions in the school I noted, in particular, the ways in which things were structured in order to facilitate teamwork. Indeed, enormous amounts of time were given over to this process. Staff met many times during the school week for planning and in-service activities. Their formal planning processes seemed to have two main elements. First of all, there was the planning of the overall learning environment. This involved taking the programmes of study outlined in the National Curriculum and turning these into appropriate activities, materials and classroom arrangements. The second element was concerned with planning for individuals. This required the creation of individual curriculum plans for each child, based upon the best available knowledge among the staff team working with the child. Interestingly, this seemed to incorporate the notion of individual planning discussed earlier, but in a way that related to the needs of all children. In a sense their approach implies that all children are regarded as being special!

This formal planning, carried out in a collaborative way, provided a basis for yet a third form of planning. Influenced by the ideas of Schon (1987), I characterized this as 'planning in action'. It is the decision-making of individual teachers in this particular school throughout the school day in the light of their reading of the observations they are making. It has to take account of the decisions that individual children make as they engage with the opportunities that are provided. It is, I believe, guided by the knowledge, principles and sensitivities that members of staff develop as they take part in the more formal planning procedures that I have described. However, all of this takes place in what can best be described as a 'hothouse' atmosphere within which all staff are subject to the continual scrutiny of their colleagues (Hargreaves, 1995). In this context, planning in action becomes a demanding requirement on those who work in the school. Fortunately, the evidence indicates that these pressures are, to a degree, alleviated by the heavy emphasis placed on teamwork and collaboration which, in effect, provides on-going support and encouragement for individual members of staff. As one teacher noted, 'Having to justify yourself to your colleagues helps you to think about what you do in the classroom.'

At the heart of the processes in schools like this where changes in practice do occur is the development of a common language with which colleagues can talk to one another – and indeed to themselves – about detailed aspects of their practice. It seems that without such a language teachers find it very difficult to experiment with new possibilities. Frequently when I report to teachers what I have seen during their lessons they express surprise. It seems that much of what they do during the intensive encounters that occur is carried out at an automatic, intuitive level. Furthermore, there is little time to stop and think. This is why having the opportunity to see colleagues at work is so crucial to the success of attempts to develop practice. It is through shared experiences that colleagues can help one another to articulate what they currently do and define what they might like to do. It is also the means whereby taken-for-granted assumptions about particular groups of pupils can be subjected to mutual critique.

In many fields and professions opportunities for such sharing of expertise through observation and discussion happen quite incidentally on a regular basis. So, for example, young doctors shadow experienced practitioners during their training; architects often work in open-plan studios where problems can be aired; and professional musicians and sportspeople have regular opportunities to observe one another in ways that encourage peer coaching and detailed discussion of technique. A significant aspect of the forms of school organization that we have inherited from our predecessors is that many teachers rarely, if ever, have the opportunity to consider in detail how their colleagues deal with the day-to-day challenges of classroom life. It is this tradition of professional isolation, perhaps more than anything else, that prevents the risk-taking that seems to be essential to the creation of more inclusive forms of pedagogy.

Creating Conditions that Support Risk-taking

As can be seen, my interest in studying practice takes me beyond just a consideration of the work of individual teachers. Much of my research over the last few years convinces me of the importance of the school context in creating a climate within which inclusive practices can be fostered. The nature of such positive contexts can take many forms and, as I have already stressed, generalizations are very difficult. Nevertheless, the monitoring of developments in particular schools over time suggests certain patterns that are at least worthy of consideration. These suggest a series of organizational conditions that seem to facilitate the risk-taking associated with movements towards more inclusive practices. More specifically, they indicate that such movement is not about making marginal adjustments to existing arrangements, but rather asking fundamental questions about the way the organization is currently structured, focusing on aspects such as patterns of leadership, processes of planning and policies for staff development. In this way the development of inclusive schooling comes to be seen as a process of school improvement (Ainscow, 1995b).

There is now considerable evidence that norms of teaching are socially negotiated within the everyday context of schooling (e.g. Rosenholtz, 1989; Talbert and McLaughlin, 1994). It seems that the culture of the workplace impacts upon how teachers see their work and, indeed, their pupils. However, the concept of culture is rather difficult to define. Schein (1985) suggests that it is about the deeper level of basic assumptions and beliefs that are shared by members of an organization, operating unconsciously to define an organization's view of itself and its environment. It manifests itself in norms that suggest to people what they should do and how. In a similar way, Hargreaves (1995) argues that school cultures can be seen as having a reality-defining function, enabling those within an institution to make sense of themselves, their actions and their environment. A current reality-defining function of culture, he suggests, is often a problem-solving function inherited from the past. In this way today's cultural form created to solve an emergent problem often becomes tomorrow's taken-for-granted recipe for dealing with matters shorn of their novelty. Hargreaves concludes that by examining the reality-defining aspects of a culture it should be possible to gain an understanding of the routines the organization has developed in response to the tasks it faces.

Certainly my impression is that when schools are successful in moving their practice forward this tends to have a more general impact upon how teachers perceive themselves and their work. In this way the school begins to take on some of the features of what Senge (1989) calls a learning organization, i.e. 'an organization that is continually expanding its capacity to create its future' (p. 14). Or, to borrow a useful phrase from Rosenholtz (1989), it becomes a 'moving' school, one that is continually seeking to develop and refine its responses to the challenges it meets.

It seems possible that as schools move in such directions the cultural changes that occur can also impact upon the ways in which teachers perceive pupils in their classes whose progress is a matter of concern (i.e. those nowadays referred to as having special needs). What may happen is that, as the overall climate in a school improves, such children are gradually seen in a more positive light. Rather than simply presenting problems that have to be overcome or, possibly, referred elsewhere for separate attention, such pupils may be perceived as providing feedback on existing classroom arrangements. Indeed, they may be seen as sources of understanding as to how these arrangements might be improved in ways that would be of benefit to all pupils. If this is the case, it might be argued that the children referred to as having special needs are hidden voices that could inform and guide improvement activities in the future. In this sense, as my colleague Susan Hart has suggested, special needs are special in that they provide insights into possibilities for development that might otherwise pass unnoticed (Hart, 1992).

It is important to recognize, of course, that the cultural change necessary to achieve schools that are able to hear and respond to the 'hidden voices' is in many cases a profound one. Traditional school cultures, supported by fixed organizational arrangements, teacher isolation and high levels of specialisms among staff who are geared to predetermined tasks, are in trouble when faced with unexpected challenges. On the other hand, the presence of children who are not suited to the existing 'menu' of the school provides some encouragement to explore a more collegiate culture within which teachers are supported in experimenting with new teaching responses. In this way, problem-solving activities may gradually become the reality-defining, taken-for-granted functions that are the culture of the inclusive school, i.e. a school that is attempting to reach out to all pupils in the local community.

How, then, can schools be helped to organize themselves in ways that encourage the development of such a culture? Once again I will draw on findings from a series of our school improvement studies (i.e. Ainscow et al., 1998; Ainscow and Hopkins, 1992, 1994; Ainscow et al., 1994; Ainscow and Southworth, 1996; Hopkins et al., 1994). All of these findings point to ways in which the restructuring of schools can impact upon organizational culture and, in turn, create the conditions within which experiments in classroom practice might occur.

By and large, schools find it difficult to cope with change (Fullan, 1991). In this respect they face a double problem: they cannot remain as they now are if they are to respond to new challenges, but at the same time they also need to maintain some continuity between their present and their previous practices. There is, therefore, a tension between *development* and *maintenance*. The problem is that schools tend to generate organizational structures that predispose them towards one or the other. Schools (or parts of schools) at the development extreme may be so over-confident of their innovative capacities that they take on too much too quickly, thus damaging the quality of what already exists. On the other hand, schools at the maintenance extreme may either see little purpose in change or have a poor history of managing innovation. Moving practice forward, therefore, necessitates a careful balance of maintenance and development.

Attempting to move practice forward also leads to a further area of difficulty which is experienced at both an individual and an organizational level. This involves forms of turbulence that arise as attempts are made to change the status quo. Turbulence may take a number of different forms, involving organizational, psychological, technical or micro-political dimensions. At its heart, however, it is frequently about the dissonance that occurs as people struggle to make sense of new ideas. It is interesting to note that there is evidence to suggest that without a period of turbulence, successful, long-lasting change is unlikely to occur (Hopkins et al., 1994). In this sense turbulence can be seen as a useful indication that the school is on the move. The question is, how can teachers be supported in coping with such periods of difficulty? What organizational arrangements are helpful in encouraging the development of practice?

From our experience of a range of schools that have made tangible progress towards more inclusive policies, we note the existence of certain arrangements that seem to be helpful in dealing with periods of turbulence. These provide structures for supporting teachers in exploring their ideas and ways of working, while at the same time ensuring that maintenance arrangements are not sacrificed. More specifically, they seek to support the creation of a climate of risk-taking within which these explorations can take place. In attempting to make sense of such arrangements my colleagues and I have formulated a typology of six 'conditions' that seem to be a feature of moving schools. These are:

- effective leadership, not only by the headteacher but spread throughout the school;
- involvement of staff, students and community in school policies and decisions;
- a commitment to collaborative planning;
- co-ordination strategies, particularly in relation to the use of time;
- attention to the potential benefits of enquiry and reflection;
- a policy for staff development that focuses on classroom practice.

The presence of these conditions seems to provide the basis for a climate that supports teacher development and, in so doing, encourages teachers to explore new responses to pupils in their classes. This goes well beyond the traditional patterns by which teachers attend external courses or, more recently, the use of one-shot school-based events. More than anything, it seems that if staff development is to have a significant impact upon thinking and practice it needs to be linked to school development (Fullan, 1991). As such it should be concerned with the development of the staff as a team, while not ignoring the learning of individuals.

It is helpful to think of two elements of staff development: 'the workshop and the workplace' (Joyce, 1991). The workshop is where understanding is developed, demonstrations provided and there are opportunities for practice. However, our experience suggests that ability to transfer into everyday class-room practice requires 'on-the-job' support. This implies changes to the workplace and the way in which we organize staff development in schools. In particular, it means there must be opportunity for immediate and sustained practice, collaboration and peer coaching, and conditions that support experimentation. We cannot achieve these changes in the workplace without, in most cases, drastic alterations in the ways in which we organize our schools. In particular, it requires that time is set aside for teachers to support one another within teams and to establish partnerships in order to explore and develop aspects of their practice. All of this implies new roles for learning support staff, who, through their involvement in mainstream class-rooms, can make a significant contribution to such activities (Cohen, 1997).

Conclusion

In summary, then, my reflections have suggested ingredients that seem to be relevant to those working to create schools that can become more effective in reaching out to all learners.. As we have seen, these ingredients are overlap-ping and interconnected in a number of ways. Perhaps more than anything, they are connected by the idea that attempts to reach out to all learners within a school have to include the adults as well as the pupils. It seems that schools that do make progress in this respect do so by developing conditions within which every member of the school community is encouraged to be a learner. In this way, responding to those who are experiencing barriers to learning can provide a means of 'raising standards' within a school.

Of course, I do not pretend that any of this is easy. As I have argued, deep changes are needed if we are to transform schools that were designed to serve a minority of the population in such a way that they can achieve excellence with all children and young people. Some may argue that before investing in such a project we need more evidence that it is possible. For myself, having seen what has happened in the schools referred to in this chapter, I see no need for further evidence. I have no doubt that among us we already have the knowledge that is necessary to teach successfully all the children in our country. The big question is, do we have the will to make it happen?

Note

This chapter is based on a keynote presentation given at the North of England Education Conference, Bradford, 5–7 January 1998.

References

Ainscow, M. (ed.) (1991) *Effective Schools for All*. London: Fulton.

Ainscow, M. (1994) *Special Needs in the Classroom: A Teacher Education Guide*. London: Jessica Kingsley/UNESCO.

Ainscow, M. (1995a) 'Education for all: making it happen', *Support for Learning*, 10(4), 147–57.

Ainscow, M. (1995b) 'Special needs through school improvement; school improvement through special needs', in C. Clark, A. Dyson and A. Millward (eds) *Towards Inclusive Schooling?* London: Fulton.

Ainscow, M. (1996) 'The development of inclusive practices in an English primary school: constraints and influences'. Paper presented at the American Education Research Association, New York, April 1996.

Ainscow, M. (1998a) 'Would it work in theory? Arguments for practitioner research and theorising in the special needs field', in C. Clark, A. Dyson and A. Millward (eds) *Theorising Special Education*. London: Routledge.

Ainscow, M. (1998b) 'Developing links between special needs and school improvement', *Support for Learning*, 13(2), 70–5.

Ainscow, M. (1999) *Understanding the Development of Inclusive Schools*. London: Falmer.

Ainscow, M. and Hopkins, D. (1992) 'Aboard the "moving school"', *Educational Leadership*, 50(3), 79–81.

Ainscow, M. and Hopkins, D. (1994) 'Understanding the moving school', in G. Southworth (ed.) *Readings in Primary School Development*. London: Falmer.

Ainscow, M. and Southworth, G. (1996) 'School improvement: a study of the roles of leaders and external consultants', *School Effectiveness and School Improvement*, 7(3), 229–51.

Ainscow, M. and Tweddle, D.A. (1979) *Preventing Classroom Failure*. London: Fulton.

Ainscow, M. and Tweddle, D.A. (1984) *Early Learning Skills Analysis*. London: Fulton.

Ainscow, M., Barrs, D. and Martin, J. (1998) 'Taking school improvement into the classroom'. Paper presented at the International Conference on School Effectiveness and Improvement, Manchester, UK, January 1998.

Ainscow, M., Hopkins, D., Southworth, G. and West, M. (1994) *Creating the Conditions for School Improvement*. London: Fulton.

Ballard, K. (1995) 'Inclusion, paradigms, power and participation', in C. Clark, A. Dyson and A. Millward (eds) *Towards Inclusive Schools?* London: Fulton.

Barth, R. (1990) *Improving Schools from Within*. San Francisco: Jossey-Bass.

Bartolome, L.I. (1994) 'Beyond the methods fetish: towards a humanizing pedagogy', *Harvard Education Review*, 64(2), 173–94.

Booth, T. and Ainscow, M. (1998) (eds) *From Them To Us: An International Study of Inclusion in Education*. London: Routledge.

Booth, T., Ainscow, M. and Dyson, A. (1998) 'Understanding inclusion in a competitive system,' in T. Booth and M. Ainscow (eds) *From Them To Us: An International Study of Inclusion in Education*. London: Routledge.

Centre, Y., Ward, J. and Ferguson, C. (1991) *Towards an Index to Evaluate the Integration of Children with Disabilities into Regular Classes*. Sydney, Australia: Macquarie Special Education Centre.

Cohen, M. (1997) 'A workshop in the workplace: a study in school-based teacher development', *Support for Learning*, 12(4), 152–7.

Department for Education and Employment (1997) *Excellence for All Children: Meeting Special Educational Needs*. London: The Stationery Office.

Dyson, A. (1990) 'Special educational needs and the concept of change', *Oxford Review of Education*, 16(1), 55–66.

Eichinger, J., Meyer, L.H. and D'Aquanni, M. (1996) 'Evolving best practices for learners with severe disabilities', *Special Education Leadership Review*, 1–13.

Elmore, R.F., Peterson, P.L. and McCarthy, S.J. (1996) *Restructuring in the Classroom: Teaching, Learning and School Organisation*. San Francisco: Jossey-Bass.

Fulcher, G. (1989) *Disabling Policies? A Comparative Approach to Education Policy and Disability*. London: Falmer.

Fullan, M. (1991) *The New Meaning of Educational Change*. London: Cassell.

Fuller, B. and Clark, P. (1994) 'Raising school effects while ignoring culture? Local conditions and the influence of classroom tools, rules and pedagogy', *Review of Educational Research*, 64(1), 119–57.

Hargreaves, D.H. (1995) 'School culture, school effectiveness and school improvement', *School Effectiveness and School Improvement*, 6(1), 23–46.

Hart, S. (1992) 'Differentiation. Part of the problem or part of the solution?' *Curriculum Journal*, 3(2), 131–42.

Heshusius, L. (1989) 'The Newtonian mechanistic paradigm, special education and contours of alternatives', *Journal of Learning Disabilities*, 22(7), 403–21.

Hopkins, D., Ainscow, M. and West, M. (1994) *School Improvement in an Era of Change*. London: Cassell.

Hopkins, D., West, M. and Ainscow, M. (1996) *Improving the Quality of Education for All: Progress and Challenge*. London: Fulton.

Hopkins, D., West, M. and Ainscow, M. (1997) *Creating the Conditions for Classroom Improvement*. London: Fulton.

Huberman, M. (1993) 'The model of the independent artisan in teachers' professional relations', in J.W. Little and M.W. McLaughlin (eds) *Teachers' Work: Individuals, Colleagues and Contexts*. New York: Teachers College Press.

Iano, R.P. (1986) 'The study and development of teaching: with implications for the advancement of special education', *Remedial and Special Education*, 7(5), 50–61.

Johnson, D. W. and Johnson, R.T. (1994) *Learning Together and Alone*. Boston: Allyn and Bacon.

Joyce, B. (1991) 'Cooperative learning and staff development : Teaching the method with the method', *Cooperative Learning*, 12(2), 10–13.

Joyce, B. and Showers, B. (1988) *Student Achievement Through Staff Development*. London: Longman.

Lipman, P. (1997) 'Restructuring in context: a case study of teacher participation and the dynamics of ideology, race and power', *American Educational Research Journal*, 34(1), 3–37.

Louis, K.S. and Miles, M. (1990) *Improving the Urban High School: What Works and Why*. London: Teachers College.

MacBeith, J., Boyd, B., Rand, J. and Bell, S. (1996) *Schools Speak For Themselves*. London: National Union of Teachers.

Oliver, M. (1988) 'The political context of educational decision making: the use of special needs', in L. Barton (ed.) *The Politics of Special Educational Needs*. Lewes: Falmer.

Rosenholtz, S. (1989) *Teachers' Workplace: The Social Organisation of Schools*. New York: Longman.

Schein, E. (1985) *Organisational Culture and Leadership*. San Francisco: Jossey-Bass.

Schon, D.A. (1987) *Educating the Reflective Practitioner*. San Francisco: Jossey-Bass.

Sebba, J. and Ainscow, M. (1996) 'International developments in inclusive education: mapping the issues', *Cambridge Journal of Education*, 26(1), 5–18.

Senge, P.M. (1989) *The Fifth Discipline: The Art and Practice of the Learning Organisation*. London: Century.

Skrtic, T.M. (1991) 'Students with special educational needs : Artifacts of the traditional curriculum', in M. Ainscow (ed.) *Effective Schools for All*. London : Fulton.

Slee, R. (1996) 'Inclusive schooling in Australia? Not yet', *Cambridge Journal Of Education*, 26(1), 19–32.

Talbert, J.E. and McLaughlin, M.W. (1994) 'Teacher professionalism in local school contexts', *American Journal of Education*, 102, 120–59.

Udvari-Solner, A. (1996) 'Theoretical influences on the establishment of inclusive practices', *Cambridge Journal of Education*, 26(10), 101–20.

Wang, M.C. and Reynolds, M.C. (1996) 'Progressive inclusion: meeting new challenges in special education', *Theory into Practice*, 35(10), 20–5.

West, M. and Ainscow, M. (1991) *Managing School Development*. London: Fulton.

7   Baseline Assessment

How Can It Help?

Geoff Lindsay

A perennial issue in special needs education concerns early identification. In the past, even some children with major impairments, for example a significant hearing loss, were identified late in their childhood. The impact is obvious: late identification results in lost opportunity for appropriate intervention. At best this may limit development, but in addition children may suffer secondary problems including frustration leading to behavioural problems.

As practice improved, major disabling conditions were identified at birth or in early infancy. The focus then shifted to children with mild to moderate difficulties which may not be identifiable until early childhood or school age. There was interest in developing screening at the age of 7–8 years, particularly for reading difficulties, and then screening programmes for children during their early infant schooling. Primarily, these initiatives, popular in the UK in the 1970s and early 1980s, were designed to attempt to identify children with developmental difficulties, and as a result to provide information to teachers which might lead to appropriate interventions.

Further development came with the Code of Practice (DfE, 1994) which set out a systematic approach to the identification of children's special educational needs, and the nature of those needs. This built upon the stages of assessment proposed in the Warnock Report (DES, 1978). Over this period individual schools and LEAs have developed their own approaches to early identification, with a small number subject to systematic evaluation (e.g. Lindsay, 1981; Desforges and Lindsay, 1995).

These local developments have now been brought into a government initiative which has the status of a statutory requirement. From September 1998, all schools with children entering compulsory education in England have been required to have in operation a scheme of 'baseline assessment'. In this chapter I shall review the recent origins of baseline assessment, describe the statutory basis and current implementation, and examine its usefulness as a means of improving the education of children with special educational needs (SEN).

Baseline Assessment – a Review

Baseline assessment, in its current guise, has been on the educational scene for only a few years. Although the early identification of children with SEN has been in practice in schools for at least 10–20 years, the term 'baseline assessment' started to appear only in the early to mid-1990s. 'Baseline' in this context refers to school entry, and indeed an alternative term has been 'school entry assessment'. In this sense it becomes a specific example of the wider use of the term 'baseline' to refer to a measure taken at the beginning of an intervention or experiment, which will produce a score against which a later score will be compared. On the basis of the relationship between the scores, inferences may be made about the effectiveness of the action taken during the intervening period.

The impetus to use this term, rather than 'school entry assessment', for example, came from one of the purposes to which the results would be put. With school entry assessment, or early screening, the purpose is one of identification, which should then be followed by action. However, the measure itself is not needed again as a comparison. For example in a screening test to identify conditions such as Down's syndrome or phenylketonuria, the screening procedure classifies the child. Other screening procedures may result in a probabilistic rather than discrete categorical designation. For example, children with very low reading scores at 7 years are more likely to have later reading difficulties than those with very good scores, but the relationship is not perfect. But, again, screening systems which identify such difficulties have not really used those scores as a baseline measure in the usual scientific sense given above. Screening is followed by action, but later performance or status is not compared with baseline measures (other than in validity trials).

A second development from school entry assessment concerned curriculum planning. Here the assessment provides a baseline against which a teacher may plan and monitor teaching. This is more similar to the traditional use of the concept of baseline assessment. Also, evidence on the success of identification processes had raised doubts about the accuracy of prediction of developmental pathways of children with patterns of underachievement or difficulty which were less marked than severe impairments (e.g. Lindsay, 1995). Consequently, a number of researchers and practitioners urged that early identification procedures should be part of a continuing process of monitoring children's development. That is, there should be a process which combined the purposes set out by Blatchford and Cline (1992).

Third, baseline assessment came to be used as a result of a very different set of interests. Rather than the identification of children with SEN, or curriculum planning, a further purpose concerned the progress of children over time primarily as a means of measuring *school* factors. That is, the purpose was one of accountability.

Lindsay (1998) has reanalysed the purposes of baseline assessment into eight types, which may be grouped into two main categories: child-focused and school-focused, with analysis of pre- and post-intervention measures cutting across this dichotomy – see Table 7.1. For example, items 1, 2 and 4 under *Child focus* are essentially about decision-making concerning action, whereas in item 3, 'Monitoring progress of all pupils', baseline assessment is implicitly a pre-intervention measure. In this case 'intervention' may refer to normal teaching, or an individually tailored programme for a specific child. Similarly, under *School focus*, the items 'Resource planning' and 'Budget determination' essentially use baseline assessment as a single measure, while 'Value-added' and 'School improvement' include it as the first assessment, to be compared with later measures – to allow assessment of change – see Lindsay and Desforges (1998) for a fuller discussion of the eight purposes. (A further, ninth purpose was allegedly suggested by the Minister, Charles Clark, at the publicity launch for baseline assessment in September 1998, but rapidly denied: the setting of children, at 4–5 years, into ability groups.)

Thus, baseline assessment is now a term used in conjunction with at least eight or nine processes, with the early identification of SEN now representing only part of this suite.

The Government's Scheme

From September 1998, all schools with children starting compulsory schooling have been required to have a baseline assessment scheme in place. The statutory basis is the Education Act 1997, Part 4, Chapter 1, para 15, which states: ' "baseline assessment scheme" means a scheme designed to enable pupils at a maintained primary school to be assessed for the purpose of assisting the future planning of their education and the measurement of their future educational achievement.'

This element of legislation is only part of an Education Act put together from components of the Education Bill with which the main political parties could agree in the last months of the previous Conservative government. It comprises a mere three clauses. However, the groundwork for the introduction of baseline assessment had been under way for several years, with pilot schemes, surveys of opinion and other activities. During this period (see Lindsay and Desforges 1998 for a review) there developed a

Table 7.1 Purposes of baseline assessment

Child focus	*School focus*
Early identification of pupils with SEN	Resource planning
Early identification of pupil's SEN	Accountability: value-added
Monitoring progress of all pupils	Budget determination
Identify learning objectives and teaching strategies for individual pupils	School improvement

generally positive support for the introduction of baseline assessment, including that of teachers, politicians and parents. Voices of caution were few (Lindsay, 1998).

By the time the legislation was passed, in early 1998, the School Curriculum and Assessment Authority (SCAA), later to become the Qualifications and Curriculum Authority (QCA), had commissioned research studies and published technical reports on baseline assessment. One initiative had been to trial three different forms of potential baseline assessment schemes, the results of which led to the National Foundation for Educational Research (NFER) being commissioned to produce a scheme drawing upon this research (see Lindsay and Desforges, 1998, for a review).

During 1997, SCAA produced the National Framework for Baseline Assessment (SCAA 1997). This adopted an interesting position. Rather than develop one measure, as with the National Curriculum assessment at the end of Key Stages, SCAA was required to accredit baseline assessment schemes which met criteria set out in the framework, which built upon principles set out in an earlier consultation document (SCAA, 1996). During 1997–8 schools and LEAs were encouraged to trial baseline assessment schemes, to prepare for the statutory introduction in the 1998–9 school year. Potential providers were required to submit their schemes to SCAA for review against the framework.

Belatedly, QCA published a pack for schools in the summer term 1998. This set out the framework with the accreditation criteria (QCA, 1998a) and also listed the schemes which had been accredited for 1998–9. At this point there were over eighty schemes. LEAs had adopted a variety of strategies: produced their own schemes; used the SCAA/QCA scheme (Baseline Assessment Scales, SCAA, 1997b); incorporated this scale into their own system; adopted the scheme developed by another LEA; adopted a scheme from an independent developer; adopted a local version of an independent scheme. All of these approaches met the accreditation criteria and consequently were acceptable to QCA.

The 1997–8 Trials

An evaluation of the trials of the SCAA/QCA scales was commissioned by SCAA/QCA and conducted during the first half of the autumn term 1997. The results (Pentecost and Betteridge, 1998) are drawn from a nationally representative survey of 458 schools through England (with 232 responding), a survey of all LEAs (78 responded) and case study visits to 42 schools, 14 LEAs and 3 non-LEA scheme providers.

Pentecost and Betteridge report that baseline assessment was viewed positively. Schools varied in their reports of manageability of the schemes they were using at that time. Pentecost and Betteridge (1998: 10) also reported variations:

- among schools across the country using different schemes;
- among schools using the same scheme in different LEAs; and
- among schools located in the same LEA, and using the same scheme.

Teachers hoped and expected that the data collected would help by informing planning, teaching and learning. However, arrangements for data collection and analysis were 'very diverse'. The majority of LEAs, on the other hand, had plans for using the outcomes. However, these did not include the identification of children with SEN. These uses are presented in Table 7.2, taken from Table 21 in Pentecost and Betteridge (1998).

The percentages sum to over 100 as respondents could presumably select or were allowed to submit more than one item (no example of the question-naire is provided). Even so, apart from resource allocation for SEN funding, there is no mention of SEN. The emphasis is clearly on whole school issues, including value-added analysis (23 per cent), school target-setting (23 per cent) and benchmarking (14 per cent).

Table 7.2   Use of outcomes of baseline assessment by LEAs

Use of outcomes of baseline assessment by LEAs	Percentage of LEAs' responses to questionnaire
To help school target-setting	23
Basis for value-added analysis	23
To focus LEA support for schools	18
To compare the value of pre-school experience	18
Benchmarking	14
To evaluate scheme in preparation for statutory baseline assessment in 1998	13
To compare schools	10
To contribute to the discussion on value-added analysis	10
To feed into LEA's pupil-profiling system	8
To establish pupil-tracking system	3
Detailed data analyses	3
To help calculate SEN funding	1
To inform discussion on record-keeping	1
For school improvement	1
Prediction to Key Stage 1	1
National comparisons	1
Overall profile of reception class children	1

Source: Pentecost and Betteridge, 1998.

This survey was primarily concerned with manageability and opinion. No attempt was made to examine the technical quality of the schemes in use, although one of the recommendations urges that there should be detailed guidance on data reliability and the potential of multivariate analysis, for example, but there is no recommendation that schemes should be judged and accredited relative to such factors. The closest recommendation is that research should be conducted into a possible 'common core' for all accredited schemes which 'should aim to provide numerical outcomes' (Pentecost and Betteridge 1998: 30).

Children with Special Educational Needs

The Draft Proposals for Baseline Assessment (SCAA, 1996) were clear. Sir Ron Dearing's foreword mentions the purpose of baseline assessment only in terms of helping children's learning. This reflects the views of teachers that 'the primary purpose of baseline assessment schemes should be to provide corrective and diagnostic information to the teacher' (p. 6). Four requirements of the assessment were then stated, starting with 'identify the child's strengths and learning needs' (p. 6). A similar focus was taken in the publicity leaflet published by SCAA in October 1997, *Is your child about to start school?*. The two answers to 'Why are schools doing baseline assessment?' specified finding out about children's knowledge and abilities in order that teachers can plan effectively, and checking that children are achieving as well as they might be.

Clearly, these statements pertain to the child focus in the typology presented above. They do not, however, focus on early identification of special educational needs as such, in contrast with some earlier screening schemes. However, this approach does fit with the view that the task is to identify and meet the learning needs of all children, and that any 'special needs' must be conceptualized, identified and met within the context of monitoring all children's learning (e.g. Lindsay, 1995).

Scale Construction

Nonetheless, there are implications for the development and implementation of schemes. Some, for example the Infant Index (Desforges and Lindsay, 1995), were originally conceptualized with the early identification of children with SEN as a key aim. Others have been designed specifically to assess the status of all children. These two approaches have implications for construction of instruments. A scale whose primary aim is to distinguish a group of 15–20 per cent (or even 2–5 per cent) of children with developmental difficulties from the rest will typically have items where discrimination is greatest around this cut-off. Hence, one of the criteria against which baseline assessment schemes might be judged is the discriminative power in this area.

The scheme developed by SCAA was not designed with this purpose. As stated in Caspall et al. (1997) the four items in each scale were selected with the aims of the following match:

first item: achieved by the majority of children (above 80 per cent)
second item: achieved between 40 and 80 per cent of children
third item: representing the *Desirable Outcomes* standard, achieved by between 20 and 60 per cent of children
fourth item: achieved by less than 20 per cent of children.

(Caspall et al., 1997: 1–2)

The item scores actually demonstrate a more varied set of distribution (see Caspall et al., 1997: Figure 2.3).

Subsequently, an extension scale was designed for optional use with children with learning difficulties (Caspall, 1998). This added downward extensions to change the 4-point to 7-point scales, and was trialled in schools where 'the nature of the children's special needs within the schools trialling the material tended to be moderate, severe or profound and multiple learning difficulties, rather than sensory or physical impairment or behavioural difficulties' (p. 1). The trial, resulting in data on 91 children in 12 special schools, has led to the optional additional scale, with generally much finer discrimination available at the lower end. For example, the Language and Communication Scale shows that no children scored 6 or 7, 1 per cent scored 5, 2 per cent scored 4 (the item in the standard scheme), whereas 11 per cent, 19 per cent, 46 per cent and 20 per cent scored 3, 2, 1, and 0 respectively.

These optional scales, therefore, provide a more suitable approach to assessment of children with intellectual impairment. Some evidence for the validity of this scale is provided by Caspall (1998), with mean scores of children in the categories of learning difficulty showing significant differences in the expected directions (e.g. children with moderate learning difficulties having higher scores than those with severe learning difficulties). In addition, significant differences in mean score were also found according to ethnic background, nursery education, means of communication and stage of learning English. As with the standard scales, data are presented on the item facilities, which allow judgements on relative difficulty and hence the coherence of the scales. On the other hand, no information is provided on inter-rater or test–retest reliability.

QCA Accreditation

The position currently is that schemes do *not* necessarily provide a sound basis for the identification of children with special needs. While some schemes were developed with this as a key purpose, most were not, and the new QCA Optional SEN scale is just becoming available. Also, the guidance published by QCA states that schools can expect all accredited schemes to include guidance on, among other matters, 'how the scheme *links with* [emphasis added] identification of children with special needs and more able children' (QCA, 1998a: Part 2, 3).

On the next page, this is restated, requiring the scheme to 'link to more detailed assessments which identify children's special educational needs and more able children' (p. 4).

The shift of focus, as far as the QCA is concerned, is clear. The focus of baseline assessment is not the identification of children with SEN but to link with other processes which assess the nature of those needs.

Implications

In this chapter I have traced a development which was at one time central to the SEN field – early identification. The interest in this increased and many local schemes grew up, but the development of the national initiative moved steadily away from this set of concerns. The reason for this can be traced to the growing interest in analysis of value-added measures whereby schools' contributions to children's educational development might be assessed. The purpose here is clearly accountability of schools. The main pressure came from league tables of GCSE, A level and Key Stage results, which were rightly criticized for using raw score data which did not allow comparisons to take account of the input characteristics of children entering the school, so leading to unfair comparisons.

The national scheme has been developed to require that a value-added analysis can be undertaken, using numerical data from baseline assessment schemes. No requirement is made that children with SEN should be identified. But does this matter? Could early identification be undertaken in any case? The following issues must be addressed.

Model of Early Identification

I have argued in the past that psycho-educational difficulties cannot usefully be conceptualized in the same way as physical ailments. Various genetic and chromosomal abnormalities, for example, can be identified with a high degree of accuracy. However, in areas including intellectual development, language, reading, personal and social behaviour, the child's characteristics at any one time are the result of an interaction of several factors, and progress is uncertain to varying degrees. The model of compensatory inter-action is used to describe these influences (Wedell, 1995; Wedell and Lindsay, 1980). Consequently, any form of screening must be part of a more comprehensive system.

Baseline assessment has the potential for contributing to early identification, but only if certain conditions are met.

Baseline assessment as screening   An irony in the development of the national baseline assessment initiative is that it is based upon a misnomer. The schemes accredited are of insufficient detail to allow an *assessment* of a child's developmental profile. Rather, the schemes are designed to provide a quick, easily administered general overview of a child's development. As such, decisions that may be reached are necessarily general. Some children may appear to be developing in a generally satisfactory manner; others may appear to have a difficulty in only one domain, e.g. language; others may appear to have difficulties in most or all areas. The exploration of these difficulties requires more in-depth assessment, which may also require the involvement of a specialist, including psychologist, audiologist, and language therapist.

Even a screening instrument may provide information which has analytic properties. The requirements for baseline assessment help in this sense as each scheme must address personal and social development, language, literacy and mathematics. However, there is a balance to be achieved between broad as opposed to in-depth coverage. For example, a scheme with four items covering one domain can provide more detail of that domain than a scheme which has the four items each covering different domains.

Lengths and structure of schemes vary. The QCA scheme has just 8 scales, each with 4 items. The Infant Index/Baseline-Plus (Desforges and Lindsay, 1995, 1998) has 15 scales, also with 4 items per scale. Some schemes are built around computer-based assessments of the children rather than teacher-administered rating scales or tasks (e.g. PIPs: Tymms et al., 1997; CoPS: Singleton et al., 1998). The later instruments provide longer measures, and have characteristics of assessment rather than screening procedures.

An identification and monitoring system   The Code of Practice (DfE, 1994) provides very useful guidance on a five-stage model of identification and assessment. The Infant Index/Baseline-Plus, for example, was designed so that teachers might use the data derived as part of Stage 1 of the Code of Practice. In principle, all baseline assessment, whether designed for this purpose or not, could be so linked. However, the scheme must provide information which is useful.

Technical quality   The structure of the measures should determine its purpose, but in any case the procedure must meet basic technical requirements. In fact, the SCAA/QCA criteria do not even require that a scheme can demonstrate that its technical quality has been examined, let alone that it reaches appropriate standards.

Some schemes have been subject to a programme of evaluation, so allowing judgements to be made of their quality. In their review, Lindsay and Desforges (1998) show that while several schemes have evidence for their technical quality, the amount and type of evidence is variable. For example, the scheme developed by SCAA/QCA has evidence on its internal coherence, based on analysis of the facility values of items within scales. The latest version of the scales now contains further data on the percentage of children scoring at each point on the eight scales, for the whole sample, and for boys and girls separately, but there is no measure of inter-rater or test–retest reliability, for example. Also, the manual (QCA, 1998a: Part 3) reports age-standardized score transformation from raw scores of children aged 3.06 to 3.11 when the standardization only covers children as young as 4.0. There is no information on predictive validity.

Data on a small number of schemes are more plentiful. Subsequent to the review by Lindsay and Desforges, a special issue of the *Journal of Research in Reading*, edited by Wolfendale and Lindsay (1999) presents further information on the Infant Index (Lindsay and Desforges, 1999), PIPs (Tymms, 1999) and Wandsworth scheme (Strand, 1999) and CoPS scheme (Singleton et al., 1999). However, the current accreditation criteria allow for poorly constructed, unevaluated schemes to be in use, providing they meet other criteria (e.g. manageability).

Age allowance   Baseline assessment is aimed at children in their first term of compulsory schooling. This may vary according to local practice, so that one child may be assessed when about 4:0, if an August birthday but admitted in September and assessed within that month. A child with an April birthday, admitted in April and assessed in May, may be 5:01. When determining whether a child's development is within normal limits, account must be taken of age. The new QCA scales' use of standardized scores is to be welcomed, and all scales should be required to provide scores which allow for age.

Research by Sharp and Hutchison (1997) has indicated that there are significant age effects with Key Stage 1 results, which have a complex relationship with terms of entry into school. The trend is for September entrants and older children (who are often the same) to score higher on KS1 assessments; and younger children and Easter entrants tend to score lowest. However, there is an interesting interaction effect suggesting that young children (birthdays April–August) who are admitted early in the year do not necessarily benefit from the extra schooling as expected. Studies of baseline assessment have shown clear age effects, with older children scoring higher (e.g. Birmingham City Council, 1996; Lindsay and Desforges, 1998). However, Lindsay and Desforges (1999) report an interaction between age and gender for the infant Index, which was administered in the term children became 5, irrespective of term of entry, with a significant term of entry effect for boys, with summer entrants scoring highest, but not for girls.

This is clearly an area for further research to investigate the interaction between age, gender, term of entry and other effects (e.g. social disadvantage, and English as an additional language). There are implications for special needs if a status of having SEN is incorrectly attributed without taking such variables into account.

Co-ordinating information   Children come into school from home only, or also from nurseries or other pre-school experience. In each setting there is a fund of knowledge about the child's development which should be linked into the school system. This may include discursive reports from teachers or parents, or detailed checklists or developmental scales completed over time.

Furthermore, there is potential, albeit hardly realized, for linking the educational database being created with earlier medical databases. In a pilot study, birth data, including characteristics of the mother (e.g. depression score) as well as the child (e.g. birth weight) were compared with Infant Index scores of a cohort of 4,487 children at school entry (Rigby et al., 1999). The study demonstrated that these two computer databases could be combined, while safeguarding the confidentiality of each child's data. The integration of such databases may be useful in adding to the information contributing to monitoring a child's progress.

Early identification and compensatory interaction   The model of compensatory interaction noted above challenges the view that a learning difficulty or a disability is fixed in its nature and impact. On the contrary, a child's difficulty in learning to read, for example, is viewed as the result of an interaction between the child's strengths and weaknesses, those of the environment, and the interaction of both over time.

With respect to baseline assessment, any child is assessed early in their school career – the influence of environment at this point, therefore, may be attributed mainly to that of the home and pre-school provision. As a consequence, a child's ability to perform the kinds of tasks contained in typical baseline assessment schemes will be influenced not only by their intrinsic developing capacities but also by their previous learning opportunities. Also, the former will be related to the child's age at the time of assessment (see 'Co-ordinating information' above).

As a consequence, there are dangers as well as positive opportunities in trying to use baseline assessment as a means of identifying children with SEN. Provided the results are seen as statements about current functioning, the dangers are reduced, but if they are seen as diagnostic evidence of inherent 'learning difficulties' there is a significant likelihood of inappropriate labelling and provision. In addition, this assumes the instruments and procedures are reliable and valid: inadequate instruments will lead to even less accuracy.

But it is also important to look forward from around 5 years to the rest of Key Stage 1, and beyond. The child's baseline assessment result at this stage may underestimate his or her later performance (e.g. at end of KS1) either because the initial assessment used inadequate measures: the measures were accurate, but the child's status had been limited by earlier pre-school experiences; or because the child's developmental trajectory up to 5 years either improved or diminished significantly during KS1, such that later performance was much better or worse than seemed likely at 5 years of age. In any of these instances, the child's performance at 7 years (end of KS1) will not be predicted so well from the baseline assessment data.

The evidence from recent studies of the predictive power of baseline assessment measures confirms the results achieved by Lindsay in the 1970s with similar measures for early identification (e.g. Lindsay, 1979). While a well-constructed baseline assessment measure may be expected to show correlations with KS1 National Curriculum assessments around 0.7 across a cohort of 5-year-olds (e.g. Strand, 1999), the predictive power of the baseline assessment instrument for the subgroup of lower scorers is much reduced, and may be close to 0 and non-significant (e.g. Singleton et al., 1999; Tymms, 1997). This raises questions about the technical quality of the baseline assessment instruments, with particular respect to predictive power, but also and more importantly indicates the importance of taking account of compensatory interaction.

Will Baseline Assessment Help Children with SEN?

The national baseline assessment scheme has potential for aiding children with SEN, but the current indications are that unless there is a re-emphasis, this potential will be squandered. The problem is the current focus on schemes for the purpose of assessing value added by schools. This favours simple measures, preferably a unitary score, or at best a very small number. Understanding and planning for development of all children, on the other hand, requires a richer understanding of the child's developmental status at a point in time, its change over a specified period, and the relative impact of within-child and environmental factors, and of their interaction.

Teachers and others who responded to the various surveys conducted on behalf of SCAA/QCA demonstrated a variety of opinion. For example, Pentecost and Betteridge (1998) report that, while for most reception teachers their prime interest is a diagnostic and formative assessment to contribute to planning and implementing learning programmes for the children, headteachers and LEAs are also concerned with standards, effectiveness and value added. Until this confusion is resolved, schemes will be designed to meet different objectives, with a very real danger of failing to meet any one satisfactorily.

There is confusion also in allowing a diversity of schemes. This continues to be the QCA position, hence the framework approach, and reflects the strong views held in schools and LEAs in support of local initiatives. However, diversity cannot be matched by appropriate value-added analyses, which require common measures. To address this, there appears to be growing support for a 'common core' (Pentecost and Betteridge, 1998) and QCA reply (1998b: Para 4). But what does this mean? If the QCA scales are to form the common core, they must be used by all and presumably become statutory. What would be the non-core elements? These could be extensions of scales for children requiring more detailed assessments, but replication of elements would be wasteful of resources.

What is missing from this discussion is a distinction between *diversity* and *quality*. It is possible to have a variety of scales if each could be shown to be fit for the purpose. For example, it is common practice for a small number of well-produced and evaluated tests of cognitive ability and reading to be used. The problem with the baseline assessment approach at present is that the QCA has a system which does not require schemes to have instruments of appropriate quality, and those which have been evaluated carefully are in danger of falling by the wayside. Of course, if the primary aim against that declared in statute is to enable value-added analyses of schools, then a *single* scheme will be necessary for national comparisons and league tables. Is this to be the primary purpose?

This initiative will require technically robust assessment procedures with satisfactory levels of reliability and concurrent measures of validity, especially construct validity. Measures of predictive validity for the scales across whole populations of children should demonstrate significant and respectable correlations, but these measures are of less importance given the argument presented above with respect to compensatory interaction. Rather than use baseline assessment results as *diagnostic* or *classificatory*, they should be regarded as *hypothesis-generating*. That is, children who score poorly should be monitored more closely, and be considered for the school's SEN register, with possible referral, at a later stage, to outside professionals (e.g. psychologists).

If this is to be a major emphasis of baseline assessment, it will be necessary to research further the accuracy of the baseline assessment data, the use made of the data, and the usefulness of baseline assessment as linked to the Code of Practice five stages of assessment. My own view is that there is great potential for baseline assessment to provide useful information, which will inform the school in its dealing with children with developmental difficulties, alerting teachers to the need to modify their teaching by differentiations and amending expectations, without lowering them unrealistically.

My present analysis, therefore, is that the national baseline assessment initiative will *not* be as helpful to children with SEN as it might have been. This can be prevented by a reorientation by QCA, and if those practitioners and researchers who are developing baseline assessment schemes ensure that identification of children with SEN, and subsequently the assessment and clarification of this needs, are central aims of the schemes.

It seemed at one time that the government's interest in baseline assessment was a significant marker. It is referred to positively in the Green Paper (DfEE, 1997). But, regrettably, the development and implementation have resulted in this purpose being downgraded along the way. We should not, therefore, be over-optimistic about the national scheme. However, looking at it positively we should see the initiative as an opportunity, a vehicle which we can ride to further our objectives. This will require political and scientific action, to maintain and develop the SEN element in the national scheme, and to develop and evaluate instruments which are of appropriate quality.

References

Birmingham City Council (1996) *Baseline Assessment for the Primary Phase – Autumn 1995*. Report of the Chief Education Officer to Education (Service Review and Monitoring) Sub-Committee, 25 June 1996, Birmingham: Local Education Authority.

Blatchford, P. and Cline, T. (1992) 'Baseline assessment for school entrants', *Research Papers in Education*, 7, 247–69.

Caspall, L. (1998) *Trials of Baseline Assessment Scales for Children with Special Educational Needs*. Slough: NFER.

Caspall, L., Sainsbury, M. and Cropper, A. (1997) *Trials of Baseline Assessment Scales: Report 3*. Slough: NFER.

Department for Education (1994) *The Code of Practice on the Identification and Assessment of Pupils with Special Educational Needs*. London: HMSO.

Department for Education and Employment (1997) *Excellence for All Children: Meeting Special Educational Needs*. London: The Stationery Office.

Department of Education and Science (1978) *Special Educational Needs* (The Warnock Report). London: HMSO.

Desforges, M. and Lindsay, G. (1995) *Infant Index*. London: Hodder and Stoughton.

Desforges, M. and Lindsay, G. (1998) *Baseline-PLUS*. London: Edexcel/ Hodder and Stoughton.

Lindsay, G. (1979) 'The early identification of learning difficulties and the monitoring of children's progress', unpublished PhD thesis. University of Birmingham.

Lindsay, G. (1981) *The Infant Rating Scale*, Sevenoaks: Hodder and Stoughton.

Lindsay, G. (1995) 'Early identification of special educational needs', in I. Lunt, B. Norwich and V. Varma (eds) *Psychology and Education for Special Needs: Recent Developments and Future Directions*. London: Arena, Ashgate Publishing.

Lindsay, G. (1998) 'Baseline assessment: a positive or malign initiative?' in B. Norwich and G Lindsay (eds) *Baseline Assessment*. Tamworth: NASEN.

Lindsay, G. and Desforges, M. (1998) *Baseline Assessment: Practice Problems and Possibilities*. London: David Fulton.

Lindsay, G. and Desforges, M. (1999) 'The use of the Infant Index/ Baseline-PLUS as a baseline assessment measure of literacy', *Journal of Research in Reading*, 22, 55–66.

Pentecost, A. and Betteridge, J. (1998) *Report of the Evaluation of the National Arrangements for Baseline Assessment During the Pilot Year, vol. I; The Autumn Term 1997*. (no location): Benchmark Educational Services (Midlands). Also available from Qualifications and Curriculum Authority.

QCA (Qualifications and Curriculum Authority) (1998a) *The Baseline Assessment Information Pack*. London: QCA.

QCA (Qualifications and Curriculum Authority) (1998b) 'Commentary on the evaluation report of baseline assessment during the pilot year in the autumn term 1997'. London: QCA.

Rigby, A., Sanderson, C., Desforges, M., Lindsay, G. and Hall, D.(1999) 'The Infant Index: a new outcome measure for pre-school children's services', *Journal of Public Medicine*, 21, 172–8.

SCAA (Schools Curriculum and Assessment Authority) (1996) *Baseline Assessment: Draft Proposals.* London: SCAA.

SCAA (Schools Curriculum and Assessment Authority) (1997a) *The National Framework for Baseline Assessment: Criteria and Procedures for the Accreditation of Baseline Assessment Schemes.* London: SCAA.

SCAA (Schools Curriculum and Assessment Authority) (1997b) *Baseline Assessment Scales.* London: SCAA.

Sharp, C. and Hutchison, D. (1997) *How Do Season of Birth and Length of Schooling Affect Children's Attainment at Key Stage 1? A Question Revisited.* Slough: NFER.

Singleton, C., Horne, J. and Thomas, K. (1999) 'Computerised baseline assessment in literacy', *Journal of Research in Reading*, 22, 67–80.

Singleton, C., Thomas, K. and Horne, J. (1998) *CoPS Baseline Assessment System.* Beverley, East Yorkshire: Lucid Research Ltd.

Strand, S. (1999) 'Baseline assessment results at age 4: associations with pupil background factors', *Journal of Research in Reading*, 22, 14–26.

Tymms, P. (1997) 'PIPs Baseline and Value Added', unpublished paper, CEM Centre, University of Durham.

Tymms, P. (1999) 'Baseline assessment, value-added and the prediction of reading', *Journal of Research in Reading*, 22, 27–36.

Tymms, P., Merrell, C. and Henderson, B. (1997) 'The first year at school: a quantitative investigation of the attainment and progress of pupils', *Education Research and Evaluation*, 3, 101–18.

Wedell, K. (1995) *Putting the Code of Practice into Practice: Meeting Special Needs in the School and Classroom.* London: Institute of Education, University of London.

Wedell, K. and Lindsay, G. (1980) 'Early identification procedures: what have we learned?', *Remedial Education*, 15, 130–5.

8 Transition

How Can It Be Improved?

Lesley Dee

Introduction

Tucked away at the end of the 1994 *Code of Practice on the Identification and Assessment of Special Educational Needs* (DfE, 1994a) are twenty paragraphs on the management of the transition of young people with special educational needs from school to their post-school destination. Yet, as several commentators have remarked, the Code's guidance on transition has been largely neglected by policy-makers, researchers, the Schools' Inspectorate and sometimes by schools themselves (Wilenius, 1996; Derrington et al., 1996). Behind this helpful, though neglected, advice and guidance are complex issues and dilemmas which challenge its interpretation as well as the nature of some of the guidance itself. The purpose of this chapter is to attempt to unravel some of these complexities to inform both policy and practice and to suggest how the management of transition, during the final years of schooling, might begin to reflect the true complexity of the process.

In this chapter, I intend to argue that transition planning at the school-leaving stage needs to be seen much more broadly than currently is generally the case. The decisions that are made during this phase of a young person's life need to be understood in the context of an individual's total life span, as just one step in a much longer and gradually evolving process of deciding who they are and who they want to become. These processes in turn need to be placed within the context of their families, cultures and communities. If planning is driven by such considerations, then we may genuinely begin to support the process of the transition to adulthood by reducing the danger of the official procedures – e.g. 14+ annual reviews[1] and the completion of transition plans – becoming merely bureaucratic exercises.

Transition and its Meaning

The final years of secondary schooling are seen by the Centre for Educational Research and Innovation (CERI) (1986) as the first part of the transition of young people towards adulthood. More broadly, according to McGinty and Fish, transition is:

... a *phase* or period of time between the teens and twenties which is broken up educationally and administratively. During the phase there are changes of responsibility from child to adult services, from school to further and higher education and from childhood dependence to adult responsibility.

... a *process* by which the individual grows through adolescence to adulthood and achieves the balanced state of dependence and independence which a particular community expects of its adult members.

(McGinty and Fish, 1992: 6)

Using McGinty and Fish's definition of transition, the focus of this chapter is on the interface between the final years of schooling and post-school options. During this period, there are shifts of responsibility for young people's education from local education authorities to the further or higher education sectors. Some young people may, by design or default, fall outside the remit of any of these services (Armstrong and Davies, 1995; Wilkinson, 1995). The procedural management of this phase for young people with identified special educational needs is governed by the guidance set out in the 1994 Code of Practice as well as various pieces of associated legislation including the 1986 Disabled Persons Act, 1989 Children Act, 1990 NHS and Community Care Act, 1992 Further and Higher Education Act and the 1995 Disability Discrimination Act.

The Code proposed that planning for transition should begin at the young person's 14+ annual review meeting and that an individual transition plan should be drawn up. The meeting should be convened by the local education authority and parents and the careers service must be invited. The plan should address the young person's aspirations and likely support needs, the contribution that each service and parents will make and the nature of the school curriculum. The Code stressed the involvement of young people and their parents in the decision-making process, noting in particular the need for young people to be given information about their options so that they could make informed choices. Young people should be supported to participate in the process by programmes of self-advocacy. Other services, including future providers of education or training, should be informed of any relevant information that would be useful in planning to meet the students' future requirements. The Code also reiterated the existing relevant legislation on inter-agency planning, described above. Finally, the Code proposed that guidance could be extended to include pupils without statements but who might benefit from some more planned support as they prepare to leave school.

As the result of a survey of LEAs, schools, parents and careers officers, Bowers et al. (1998) reinforced the perception that the Code's guidance on transition is neglected, noting that 60 per cent of respondents in their questionnaire survey of 55 secondary schools did not complete the section on transition. Among the problematic issues identified by respondents were the quality of participation and involvement by parents and young people in the transition planning process, the timing of the first transitional review, and the relationship between this and subsequent reviews.

Some of these issues relate to the gap between policy and practice, how professionals interpret the guidance and how young people and their families experience the process of transition from adolescence to adulthood described by McGinty and Fish (1992). According to Erikson (1968), during this period young people begin to formulate goals for themselves based on their beliefs about who they are and who they might become. At the same time families are having to adjust to and deal with the impact of these changes on the dynamics of the family and family relationships. When the young person has a disability or learning difficulty these processes are likely to be even more complex and stressful. Yet little is known about these experiences. Beresford (1995) in a survey of 1,000 parents of severely disabled children found that their second most pressing need was help with planning their child's future, and there were consistently higher levels of unmet needs among the parents of older children. Gascoigne (1995: 138), herself a parent of three disabled children, eloquently describes the feelings of many parents as their child approaches the school-leaving stage.

> Parents are torn by conflicting wishes for and on behalf of their children as they approach the end of their formal school education and begin to consider the range of future options. On the one hand they want their child to become as independent as possible, and on the other hand they wish to extend their protection of them. This is true of all parents, whether or not their child has special needs. The feelings are exaggerated however where the pupil has special needs. The parents have probably fought many battles both within the home and with external agencies over the years to maximise their child's independence. The approach of adulthood in their child may be a time when early hopes are finally dashed, or where the hopes being realised cause an onset of panic.

To understand more about these processes, it is worth examining some of the mainstream thinking on career learning, which, unfortunately, has generally ignored the experiences of young disabled people and their families. According to Szymanski (1994), discussions on transition have been limited in their scope, concentrating mainly on the school-leaving stage and the transition into employment. She refers to the work of Super (1980, 1994), for example, who challenged his own earlier thinking which saw career paths as being set during adolescence and instead suggested that who we are and our roles are influenced by our life-space – that is, the contexts of home, community, education and work – and this in turn influences our changing roles –

e.g. child, student, spouse, carer, citizen, etc. Furthermore, our roles change throughout our life span. By adopting a life-span or life-history approach, Hodkinson et al. (1996) believe that we can begin to see the school-leaving stage as merely one step in the process of career development which continues throughout our lives. In addition, most commentators also now define career more broadly than just relating to work. Banks et al. (1992) define career as the 'progress through domains of education, employment, leisure and domestic life'.

These are helpful ideas. Not only do they address many of the dilemmas faced by professionals working in special education by proposing a much broader notion of career which is thus more inclusive, but these ideas also provide a much clearer rationale for careers education and guidance in the school environment. They also help us to see that the so-called unrealistic ideas of many young people with learning difficulties and/or disabilities are part of a natural process of exploration which may take longer for some than others, as young people come to terms with their own strengths, needs and interests. Here is an extract from an interview conducted as part of some research into young people's aspirations. Sam is 15 and a wheelchair user.

> I would like to be a police officer. I know that it's going to be too diffi-
> cult but I mean that is something that I have always wanted to be since
> I was a little kid ... I don't like being behind desks, I have to be active.
> I like to move about as much as possible. ... Now I am coming to terms
> with that, I won't be able to do that sort of thing, I will have to think of
> something that I can do because as I have grown up, I have got more
> used to being in a wheelchair but I still feel that I would like to get out
> of this and start walking on my own, get out of this and run off, but
> that is not going to be possible either.

It is also important to recognize that the period of transition from school to adult life is a relative concept influenced by cultural and contextual variables. Indeed, this transitional phase is becoming both more extended and more complex for many young people (Jones, 1995) as their entry into the labour market is increasingly delayed and they remain dependent on their families for longer. Thus, although the problems and difficulties associated with the transition phase are likely to be more complex and last well into their twenties and thirties for some young people, particularly if they have severe or complex learning difficulties and/or disabilities, their needs during this period will not be fundamentally different from their peers. In the long term they will require support, advice, economic independence, opportunities to develop social networks and friendships and, above all, recognition as an adult and citizen with equal rights and responsibilities.

Before exploring the practical implications of these ideas during the final years of schooling, I want to consider one further aspect of the transition process, that of the relationship between the key decision-makers and the effects of these relationships on the decisions that are made. Most career learning theorists emphasize the explicit or implicit influence on individuals of the family, culture, friends, schooling, community and the availability of local opportunities in determining post-school destinations and eventual lifestyles. Arguments exist about the relative importance of each of these factors although most agree on the significance of families. While Foskett and Hesketh (1997) found, in a study of non-disabled school leavers, that young people are more instrumental in making choices at 16 than some earlier studies would suggest, these decisions are framed or circumscribed for them by their family circumstances and attitudes. Thus parents and children are both 'decision-makers' but the final decision is 'the product of internal processes within that partnership. The balance between the two partners will clearly vary from case to case and from issue to issue' (p. 307).

Following on from this and given the nature of the relationship between parents and their disabled child which Gascoigne describes above, it is not surprising parents are likely to have a substantial influence on the decisions that are made. Very little is known about the effect of feelings and emotions on decision-making (Mellers et al., 1998), yet it is self-evident that parental love for their child is bound to engender powerful feelings. For example, when asked about their aspirations for their child in a study of parental experiences of the transition process (Dee, 1997), parents found it easier to describe their fears than their aspirations: e.g. concern for their child's safety, being forced to leave school, unemployment. The emotions which these fears can generate may lead parents to resist thinking about the future or alternatively rushing to make a decision without weighing up the options. Either way, such emotions are likely to make the transition process a complex and difficult time for parents, their child and the professionals involved in supporting them.

The part played by professionals in making decisions about post-school destinations has been highlighted by Hodkinson et al. (1996). They suggested that professionals play an equally important and influential role through virtue of the power that they have over policy and resources and which may in the end become the defining factors in what and how decisions are made. For example, a local education authority may decide that special schools only accept pupils up to 16, or the Further Education Funding Learning and Skills Council may endeavour to shift resources from specialist to sector provision, thereby reducing the choices that are available to parents and young people. Within special education there are numerous examples of the unequal power relationships that exist, for example, between parents and professionals (Harry, 1992; Sandow, 1994), between professional and professional (Weatherley, 1979) and between disabled students and professionals (Corbett and Barton, 1992). We have already seen that many people are sceptical about the genuine involvement of young people and their parents in the decision-making processes. For instance, Derrington (1997) found considerable variation in the practice of pupils' attendance at 14+ annual reviews between the schools in three LEAs, and even where pupils do express an opinion they are not always heard. Why is this the case?

Corbett and Barton (1992) locate the barriers to the full involvement of disabled people in decision-making within structural inequalities in the economy and society. Real choice does not exist, because options are manipulated to accommodate changes in the labour market and funding levels. For example, access to training or further education may be increased or decreased according to government or local priorities.

This could lead to the conclusion that the ostensibly rational, participatory decision-making procedures described by the Code of Practice are therefore used to 'cloak' an essentially political process (Weatherley, 1979). Like Weatherley, Hudson (1989) uses Lipsky's idea of the 'street level bureaucrats' (Weatherley and Lipsky, 1977), and maintains that public sector workers are accorded considerable power and discretion in how they conduct their professional roles because they are required to make decisions about other people. Hudson notes, 'It is through street level bureaucrats that society organises the control, restriction and maintenance of relatively powerless groups' (Hudson 1989: 397). In examinations of the conduct of transitional review meetings, both Tisdall (1996) and Wood and Trickey (1996) concluded that annual review meetings are generally focused around the needs of professionals to meet their procedural obligations rather than a concern to involve young people and their parents in the process.

Whatever the underlying motives, failure to involve parents and young people in processes which affect their lives is at worst a denial of their human rights and at best thoughtless. The conduct of meetings and their length appear to be important factors in the degree of satisfaction with meetings felt by students and their parents. Tisdall found that where professionals had met beforehand and meetings were longer, parents and students felt a greater degree of satisfaction, while Miner and Bates (1997) found levels of satisfaction were more related to organizational factors than whether or not students and parents had been prepared for meetings.

So far, then, I have argued that, by broadening our understanding of transition during the final years of secondary schooling, we can increase our capacity to manage the process more effectively and improve the support that is offered to young people and their parents or carers. I turn now to examining in more detail the practical implications of these ideas in an attempt to close the potential gap between processes and procedures. A set of underlying principles are proposed and the practical implications of each are described. Four elements of practice are considered: the curriculum, parent partnerships, annual reviews and individual transition plans.

Implications for Practice

Curriculum

*Inclusive Education Policies Should Take Account of the Transitional Needs
of All Pupils, Including those with Special Educational Needs*

The reduction in the amount of time that has to be spent on the National Curriculum at Key Stage 4 has enabled schools to pay more attention to careers education and guidance. That said, there is now considerable evidence to suggest that pupils with special educational needs in special schools are likely to receive more extensive careers education and guidance than their peers in mainstream schools (CERI, 1986; OFSTED, 1995; Derrington, 1997). Bowers et al. (1998) found that careers officers believed that special schools teachers had a better understanding of their role as careers educators than their mainstream colleagues, a possible indication of the contribution made by them to the special schools' leavers programmes.

The quality and access to information and guidance also differs markedly between schools (Taylor, 1992). The kind of opportunities that may be provided include work experience, mini-enterprise schemes, link courses, business visits, residentials and community work. While Taylor did not include special schools in her study, she did find that differences existed not only between schools but within schools, and that boys and higher-attaining pupils were more likely to participate in career-related activities. This supports the OECD's (CERI, 1986) finding that lower-attaining pupils are less likely to experience careers education programmes in mainstream secondary schools than in special schools. As more young people begin to be included in general provision, due regard must be paid to ensuring the access of all pupils to a comprehensive and supportive careers education programme.

*Inclusive Education Policies Should Acknowledge that All Pupils,
Including Those with Learning Difficulties and/or Disabilities, are Likely
to Experience an Extended Period of Exploration and Floundering*

Some teachers complain that young people with special educational needs are often unrealistic in their aspirations. Yet this is an essential part of career learning (Krumboltz, 1979; Gottfriedson, 1981). Individuals need to fantasize and try out ideas about who they are and who they might become as part of the natural process of growing up. Indeed, the OECD (CERI 1988) argued that disabled people are limited in this process by being socialized into their role as a 'handicapped' member of society. Families and society at large may perpetuate the myth of the ' dependent child'. Young people with disabilities can therefore be inhibited from ever seeing themselves as adults, adopting adult roles and responsibilities, and will not be encouraged to speculate about the adult they 'might become'.

Part of this process of exploring possibilities may include having to come to terms with having a disability, as Sam had to, and the effect that this may have on individual aspirations. This has important implications for the role of guidance in the curriculum, which needs to enable young people with special educational needs to explore their feelings and concerns as well as to experiment and try out other ideas.

Through this exploration clues can be gleaned about how best to support a student's learning. For example, John, who attends a school for pupils with moderate learning difficulties, wanted to work as a driver's mate, delivering catering equipment with his cousin. When asked what he thought might prevent him from doing this, he said simply, 'Maps,' meaning his inability to read anything, including maps. To build on his motivation, an individual programme was designed to help him overcome this problem and gradually he began to be able to read simple maps.

Inclusive Education Policies Should Develop Students' Sense of Achievement and Self-efficacy through the Curriculum

The Code of Practice emphasizes the importance of pupil involvement in the decisions that are made during the transition process. The Code goes on to list a number of ways that the curriculum can promote pupil involvement by encouraging students to review and reflect on their own experiences and express their own views. An important vehicle for this process is the Progress File (formerly Record of Achievement) which can link the pupil's individual education plan and the individual transition plan. Some schools ensure that pupils take their Progress Files to the annual review meetings, and use them as a means of involving the pupil by getting them to talk through their achievements. For pupils with severe or complex learning difficulties, videoed Progress Files provide an immediate and powerful reminder for them of their interests and strengths as well as evidence of progress to parents and other professionals.

The Code also stresses the need to develop students' self-esteem. However, what seems more at issue for young people with learning difficulties and/or disabilities is not simply their self-esteem, which is important, as much as their self-efficacy and the extent to which they feel that they have control over events. A number of studies have drawn this distinction, including Jahoda et al. (1988), Fox and Norwich (1992), Ridell et al. (1993) and Ward et al. (1994). Hirst and Baldwin (1994) compared feelings of self-esteem among disabled young people to those of a control group. They concluded that those attending regular schools had higher self-esteem than those who had attended special schools but lower than others attending regular schools. While some pupils scored higher than the general population on self-esteem, fewer felt a sense of personal control which, according to Oyserman and Markus (1990), may be a more important factor in realizing aspirations. They argued that self-efficacy is just as important as having positive self-esteem in negotiating a way through choices and options.

Strategies for promoting self-advocacy and the skills to make choices are well documented elsewhere (see, for example, Crawley, 1983; Clare, 1990; Flynn and Ward, 1991; Derrington, 1997). What seems harder to achieve is really allowing young people to be heard in the process of making complex decisions as opposed to the more mundane everyday choices with which they are often presented.

Being aware of our own professional practice and how we can unwittingly manipulate decisions is an important part of critical reflection on practice and can assist service providers in becoming more alive to the needs of young people and their parents or carers. For example, beliefs about an individual can help to form the implicit 'rules' which can govern decision-making. Where a young person goes on leaving school may be influenced by the destinations of other leavers from the same school: for example, common patterns may be seen in progression routes from special schools for the deaf to specialist colleges for the deaf. These decisions may be based on unspoken rules exercised by the professionals involved in providing information to students or parents about the options available to them – information based on custom and practice.

Choices can also be influenced through tone of voice, through the choices that are presented, through the order of choices and through the nature of the dialogue (Jenkinson, 1993; Mellers et al., 1998). Jenkinson's research is particularly relevant to the kind of decisions that have to be made during the school-leaving years. She found that individuals are more likely to be influenced by others in complex decision-making situations, particularly where they experience stress or where choices are so controlled that they feel helpless.

Parent and Carer Involvement

Ensure that Parents are Provided in Good Time with Information about the Procedures for Deciding Post-school Destinations as well as about the Options that are Available

How soon should discussions about leaving school start? To some extent, it depends on the individual needs of parents as well as the purpose of the discussions. Parents are not a homogeneous group. Some parents want discussions to start as soon as their child enters secondary school. Others cannot bear to think about the future. Some professionals argue that to begin discussing post-school options three or four years before they predict the child will leave school is too soon and creates unnecessary distress and alarm, particularly to parents. Yet, in a study conducted by Bowers et al. for the DfEE, a parent noted,

> It [the transition plan] gives us a clear guide to the future and plenty of time for parents and children to plan, i.e. look at every option. At first I thought it was too early but not now, having been through the system.
>
> (Bowers et al., 1998: 100)

Furthermore, if we accept that the decision-making processes are not logical and rational but messy, with the potential to cause stress and anxiety, then the kind of support that is required will not just be about what options are available. Wertheimer (1989: 40) cites a mother who said,

> life outside the boundaries that we and the school system have created in the past terrifies us. All our earlier feelings are reactivated. We may once again experience grief and upset, guilt and sadness, fear and despair. These feelings need to be acknowledged by the people who work with us.

Families have been identified as one of the main influences on the post-school destinations of all young people. Yet more often than not they rely for their information on informal rather than formal sources (Dee, 1997). An analysis of data gathered from three sets of parents showed that their main sources of information were other family members, neighbours and friends, the media, other parents, and their own experiences.

This informally gleaned information was sometimes positive and helpful but it could also be negative, helping to build up negative perceptions about a particular type of provision. Such perceptions, then, influence the choices that parents and carers make. They are not irrational decisions, but are based on their own experience and knowledge. Here is the mother of James, a deaf student, talking about their local college.

> Going back to the local colleges, I know nothing about them. There is a bit of a blockage because there is one place in Barchester that's not bad. Then I began to hear different stories about it and it is a normal college but there is a group of people my friend works with and a few of them are deaf and the rest aren't but they are all what you might call mature students, I think, not 16 to 18 ones. I think they all tend to be 20 up to 30 and they are all mentally retarded and some of them happen to be deaf as well ... I don't agree with them all being in a class together. ... There's nothing wrong with James. We don't hold anything against mentally retarded people but I've met these people she works with and they are pretty severely retarded.

So what do parents want to know? Sometimes they may not know what they want to know, and only in retrospect are they able to describe what would have been helpful at the time. Requirements will clearly vary, and it is important for schools in particular not to assume knowledge on the part of parents such as, for example, that the school has a post-16 section, what the role of the careers service is or what link courses are. The following list is derived from what parents have said would be helpful to them.

- A checklist of what happens, and when, with respect to school-leaving procedures, including parental rights and responsibilities. While the Code emphasizes the need for parents to know where to get practical help, they also want to know how decisions are made and over what period of time. The parents' guide to the Code is helpful (DfE, 1994b) but information will need to be customized to account for local differences.
- A list of the range of options available, including local and residential options and who to contact. Parents or carers require objective information with the opportunity for visits so that they can find out for themselves what the provision is like.
- A list of service providers, their responsibilities, names, telephone numbers and addresses.
- A mentor, that is, someone who is objective and whom they feel is outside the formal agencies and systems. Some parents feel, rightly or wrongly, that different professionals have particular agendas and may be operating under constraints which prevent them from passing on or processing certain information. While the concept of the named person or independent parental supporter is now a well-accepted part of the statutory assessment procedures, it has yet to be adopted during the transition years, when it arguably becomes even more important as parents and their child attempt to navigate a path between child and adult services and school and post-school provision.

Improving Procedures

Work with Other Professionals to arrive at an Agreed Understanding of the Purpose of the 14+ Annual Review as well as Subsequent Annual Review Meetings

It is important that professionals spend time clarifying how they see the purpose of these meetings. Decisions about what to do after school involve making plans, the outcomes of which are often uncertain. Thus the purpose of the 14+ review will be to begin the process of exploration rather than making a definite decision. Plans are made over a period of time and may involve making a number of smaller decisions which may or may not lead towards the desired goal – e.g. I want to become an electrician, but I want to be with other deaf students and the specialist college doesn't offer the right course for me. If we place the 14+ and subsequent annual reviews in the context of Hodkinson's argument, that the school-leaving stage is just one step in a lifelong process of career development, then this allows us to begin to see the reviews as part of an incremental process of decision-making through which young people and their parents can explore ideas about the future and pursue different options as they change their minds. For example, the student in the above example might explore what a different residential college has to offer, try out a link course at the local further education college or change his mind about what he wants to do. The Code, as it stands, rather neglects the later stages of the transition process and the conduct of subsequent annual reviews. If the purpose of transitional reviews is seen more broadly than making decisions about post-school destinations, then this may help to resolve some of the current debates about the timing of the first transitional review.

Develop a Planning Cycle to Ensure that as far as possible the Different Activities Associated with Transition follow in a Logical Sequence

Schools, often in conjunction with the careers service, undertake numerous activities which help students and their parents to explore their options – parents' evenings, careers conventions, work experience, visits to colleges or workplaces, providing written guides, inviting speakers into the school. As far as possible, annual reviews need to be planned to take account of these, so that students and parents, as well as other professionals, have some basis of knowledge and experience to draw on in the meetings.

In preparing for meetings, it is also important to ensure that, where possible, careers service colleagues have had the opportunity to meet the student beforehand and have made at least telephone contact with parents, so that there has been some opportunity to begin to explore roles and make some initial contact. There will probably need to be some negotiation with careers colleagues to take account of the constraints under which they operate as well as the expectations of their role. Equally, medical or other reviews need to be borne in mind so that as far as possible the outcomes of one review or meeting can inform the other.

Ensure that the Conduct of Meetings Facilitates Contributions from All

As Tisdall (1996) points out, the presence of young people and their parents at annual review meetings does not guarantee their active involvement in the procedures. Indeed, Tisdall questions whether such meetings are the best way of ensuring young people's involvement. My own research into the experiences of parents during the transition phase revealed the power of professionals in controlling events at meetings. When asked beforehand about his expectations of his daughter's annual review, a father replied,

> When we go for the review we will be asking a lot more questions. What does happen, you know, when they leave school? What do you think Grace will be capable of? What sort of college will she be able to go to?

In the event, Grace's parents only made three interventions which related to post-school placements before the class teacher changed the course of the discussion. When asked about the meeting afterwards, both the deputy headteacher and the occupational therapist felt that the meeting had failed to consider any plans for Grace's future.

That said, there are steps which can be taken to support the involvement of both young people and their parents. First, it is important to ensure that review reports and other relevant documentation are circulated beforehand, so that less time is taken up during the meeting on going through reports, enabling at least one third or more of the total meeting time to be given to immediate and longer-term plans. Second, effective meetings tolerate silences, allowing participants to process information and formulate their ideas. Third, using open as well as closed questions is more likely to encourage contributions and exploration of options.

Most important of all is the willingness of professionals to attach credence to the views and wishes of young people and their parents. Despite her severe communication disorder, Kim had already made a number of contributions about her achievements, prompted by questions from the chair. However, towards the end of the meeting she raised her wish to attend a youth club, something her parents had forbidden.

Chair:	Is there anything else?
Kim:	Club, don't go to club on Thursday.
Father:	Not really, we're only getting [involved] with our fears.
Mother:	Not really.
Kim	Club … don't go to club on Thursday.

While her request was originally ignored, Kim's persistence made sure she was eventually heard and her mother agreed to explore the possibilities. The decision was recorded on the action plan and this was then followed up at the subsequent meeting.

Transition Plans

Use Transition Plans to Keep Track of the Decision-making Journey

Most LEAs provide a proforma for transition planning on which schools are expected to, in the words of the Code, 'build on the conclusions reached and targets set at previous annual reviews'. The Code provides helpful guidance on the kind of information that will need to be recorded. The design of such proformas needs to allow for the fact that they will need to be updated and changed over the course of the students' final years of schooling.

Ensure that Copies of Plans are Passed between Year Groups as well as into Further Education

It is all too easy to file transition plans away and ignore what they say about what the school or other professionals should be doing to enable young people and their parents to make up their minds about the future. The Code also stresses the importance of passing this information on to further education and social services, provided that permission has been obtained from the young person and their parents, again emphasizing the longitudinal nature of the transition process reaching well beyond the school gate.

Information contained in transition plans is important, not only for individual planning purposes but for strategic planning as well. Some local authorities have developed concordats between local providers, including child and adult services, colleges and training providers, so that gaps in local opportunities are identified collectively and agreements made about how best these should be met. This has been particularly useful in identifying the likely needs of young people returning from residential schools to their home areas.

Conclusion

I began this chapter by suggesting that the guidance on transition has been largely overlooked and yet it is, arguably, one of the most important and complex aspects of the Code's guidance. For parents, the transition of their child from adolescence to adulthood is certainly one of the most stressful and worrying periods. To close the gap characterized by McGinty and Fish (1992) between the educational and administrative procedures and the psycho-social processes that the young person experiences, the school-leaving stage should be seen as just one step in an individual's total life span and part of a much longer journey. The decisions that are made are often tentative and incremental, and the process itself is often difficult and messy. Furthermore, decisions cannot be separated from the influences of family, culture and community. The services and the official procedures need, as best they can, to support the twists and turns of young people's lives, working with and respecting the inherent informal support networks that exist within the family and community.

Note

1   At the time of writing the transitional review takes place at the first annual review after the pupil's fourteenth birthday, and responsibility for convening meetings rests with the local education authority. It is likely that new guidance will shortly be issued by the DfEE which standardizes this to Year 9 and transfers responsibility for convening meetings to the school.

References

Armstrong, D. and Davies, P. (1995) 'The transition from school to adulthood: aspiration and careers advice for young adults with learning and adjustment difficulties', *British Journal of Special Education*, 22(2), 70–5.

Banks, M., Bates, I., Breakwell, G., Bynner, J., Emler, N., Jamieson, L. and Roberts, K. (1992) *Careers and Identities*. Milton Keynes: Open University Press.

Beresford, B. (1995) *Expert Opinions*. Bristol: Policy Press.

Bowers, T., Dee, L., West, M. and Wilkinson, D. (1998) *Evaluation of the User-Friendliness of the Special Educational Needs Code of Practice*. London: DfEE.

Centre for Educational Research and Innovation (1986) *Young People with Handicaps: The Road to Adulthood*. Paris: OECD.

Centre for Educational Research and Innovation (1988) *Disabled Youth: The Right to Adult Status*. Paris: OECD.

Clare, M. (1990) *Developing Self-Advocacy Skills with People with Disabilities and Learning Difficulties*. London: FEU.

Corbett, J. and Barton, L. (1992) *A Struggle for Choice*. London: Routledge.

Crawley, B. (1983) 'Self-advocacy manual'. Paper no. 49, Habilitation Technology Project, Hester Adrian Rehabilitation Centre, University of Manchester.

Dee, L. (1997) 'Whose decision? Factors affecting the decision-making progress at 14+ for students with learning difficulties and/or disabilities'. Unpublished paper presented at the British Educational Research Association Conference, September.

Department for Education (1992) *Further and Higher Education (FHE) Act*. London: HMSO.

Department for Education (1994a) *Code of Practice on the Identification and Assessment of Special Educational Needs*. London: Central Office of Information.

Department for Education (1994b) *Special Educational Needs: Guide For Parents*. London: HMSO.

Department of Health (1986) *Disabled Persons (Services, Consultation and Representation) Act*. London: HMSO.

Department of Health (1989) *Children Act*. London: HMSO.

Department of Health (1990) *NHS and Community Care Act*. London: HMSO.

Disability Discrimination Act (1995) London: The Stationery Office.

Derrington, C. (1997) *In on the Planning? Professionals' Approaches to Involving Young People with Special Educational Needs in Transition Planning*. Slough: NFER.

Derrington, C., Evans, C. and Lee, B. (1996) *The Code in Practice: The Impact on Schools and LEAs*. Slough: NFER.

Erikson, E. (1968) *Identify: Youth and Crisis*. London: Faber and Faber.

Flynn, M. and Ward, L. (1991) 'We can change the future: citizen and self-advocacy', in S. Segal and V. Varma (eds) *Prospects for People with Learning Difficulties*. London: Fulton.

Foskett, N. and Hesketh, A. (1997) 'Constructing choice in contiguous and parallel markets: institutional and school leavers' responses to the new post-16 market place', *Oxford Review of Education*, 23(3), 299–319.

Fox, P. and Norwich, B. (1992) 'Assessing the self-perception of young adults', *European Journal of Special Needs Education*, 7(3), 193–203.

Gascoigne, E. (1995) *Working with Parents as Partners in Special Education*. London: Fulton.

Gottfriedson, L. S. (1981) 'Circumspection and compromise: a developmental theory of occupational aspirations', *Journal of Counselling Psychology*, 28(6), 545–79.

Harry, B. (1992) *Cultural Diversity, Families and the Special Education System: Communication and Empowerment*. New York: Teachers College Press.

Hirst, M. and Baldwin, S. (1994) *Unequal Opportunities: Growing Up Disabled*. London: HMSO.

Hodkinson, P., Sparkes, A. and Hodkinson, H. (1996) *Triumphs and Tears: Young People, Markets and the Transition from School to Work*. London: Fulton.

Hudson, B. (1989) 'Michael Lipsky and street level bureaucracy: a neglected perspective', in L. Barton (ed.) *Disability and Dependency*. London: Falmer Press.

Jahoda, A., Markova, I. and Cattermole, M. (1988) 'Stigma and the self-concept of people with a mild mental handicap', *Journal of Mental Deficiency Research*, 32, 103–15.

Jenkinson, J.C. (1993) 'Who shall decide? The relevance of theory and research to decision-making by people with an intellectual disability', *Disability, Handicap and Society*, 8(4), 361–75.

Jones, G. (1995) *Leaving Home*. Buckingham: Open University Press.

Krumboltz, J. (1979) 'A social learning theory of career decision-making', in A.M. Mitchell, G.B. Jones and J.D. Krumboltz (eds) *Social Learning and Career Decision-Making*. Cranston: Carroll.

McGinty, J. and Fish, J. (1992) *Learning Support for Young People in Transition: Leaving School for Further Education and Work*. Buckingham: Open University Press.

Mellers, B., Schwartz, A. and Cooke, A. (1998) 'Judgement and decision-making', *Annual Review of Psychology*, 49, 447–77.

Miner, C. and Bates, P. (1997) 'The effect of person centred planning activities on the IEP/transition planning process', *Education and Training in Mental Retardation and Developmental Disabilities*, June, 105–11.

OFSTED (Office for Standards in Education) (1995) *The Implementation of the Code of Practice for Pupils with Special Educational Needs: A Report from Her Majesty's Chief Inspector of Schools*. London: HMSO.

Oyserman, D. and Markus, H. (1990) 'Possible selves and delinquency', *Journal of Personality and Social Psychology*, 59(1), 112–25.

Riddell, S., Ward, K. and Thomson, G. (1993) 'Transition to adulthood for young people with SEN', in A. Closs (ed.) *Transition to Adulthood for Young People With Special Educational Needs*. Edinburgh: Moray House Publications.

Sandow, S. (1994) 'They told me he would be a vegetable: parents' views', in S. Sandow (ed.) *Whose Special Need? Some Perceptions of Special Educational Needs*. London: Paul Chapman Publishing.

Super, D. (1980) 'A life-span, life-space approach to career development', *Journal of Vocational Behaviour*, 16, 282–98.

Super, D. (1994) 'A life-span, life-space perspective on convergence', in M.L. Savickas and R.W. Lent (eds) *Convergence in Career Development Theories: Implications for Science and Practice*. Palo Alto, CA: Consulting Psychologists Press.

Szymanski, E.M. (1994) 'Transition: life-span and life-space considerations for empowerment', *Exceptional Children*, 60(5), 402–10.

Taylor, M.J. (1992) 'Post-16 options: young people's awareness, attitudes, intentions and influences on their choice', *Research Papers in Education*, 7(3), 301–34.

Tisdall, E. (1996) 'Are young disabled people being sufficiently involved in their post-school planning? Case studies of Scotland's future needs assessment and Ontario's educational–vocational meetings', *European Journal of Special Needs Education*, 11(1), 17–36.

Ward, K., Thomson, G. and Riddell, S. (1994) 'Transition, adulthood and special educational needs: an unresolved paradox', *European Journal of Special Needs Education*, 9(2), 125–44.

Weatherley, R. (1979) *Reforming Special: Policy Implementation from State Level to Street Level*. London: The MIT Press.

Weatherley, R. and Lipsky, M. (1977) 'Street-level bureaucrats and institutional empowerment: implementing special-education reform', *Harvard Educational Review*, 47 (2 May), 171–97.

Wertheimer, A. (1989) *Self-Advocacy and Parents: The Impact of Self-Advocacy on the Parents of Young People With Disabilities*. London: FEU.

Wilenius, F. (1996) *Experiencing Transition: The Impact of the Code of Practice*, Occasional Paper no. 13. London: University of London Institute of Education.

Wilkinson, C. (1995) *The Drop-Out Society: Young People on the Margin*. Leicester: Youth Work Press.

Wood, D. and Trickey, S. (1996) 'Transition planning: process or procedure?', *British Journal of Special Education*, 23(3), 120–5.

Section 3

Individuals and Groups

Learning Together

9 Multidisciplinary Work

Challenges and Possibilities

Penny Lacey

There have been several decades of exhortations and initiatives in multidisciplinary and multi-agency working for children who have special educational needs. Recent legislation in the human services encourages (but does not compel) co-operation between agencies. Local projects have been set up with joint funding, services have combined under a single manager and professionals have been gathered together under the same roof. There are many examples of good practice, ranging from child development and family centres to child protection teams and specific projects such as Leeds Early Years Partnership, Portage (Dessent, 1996) or the Pen Green Centre for families and young children in Corby (Audit Commission, 1994).

So, with all this good practice in evidence, why are there still many reports of poor or non-existent joint work between agencies? Recent studies show that either there was no joint work between relevant agencies supporting single mothers of children with learning disabilities (Cigno and Burke, 1997; Middleton, 1998) or there was a lack of coherence and integration of services, especially at the point of diagnosis, as was the case in Bamford et al.'s (1997) survey of consumer satisfaction in cerebral palsy care and Roaf and Lloyd's (1995) study of agencies working with youth in Oxford. Joseph Rowntree Foundation (1995) found similar problems in their study of young people in difficulty, as did Dyson et al. (1998) when reporting on communication between agencies working within the Code of Practice in Special Educational Needs. The Audit Commission report on *Misspent Youth* (1994) concludes that enormous sums of money are wasted when agencies do not work together.

According to the conclusions of a five nations study by CERI (1996) and a survey of 55 LEAs in England and Wales by Derrington et al. (1997), professionals and agencies on the whole see the benefits of working together, so what are the challenges that they face? And, more importantly, what can be done in the future to alleviate these and encourage good practice right across the country? In this chapter, there will be a discussion of these questions and some suggestions for ways to move forward as the new millennium is approaching.

What is Multidisciplinary Work in Special Education?

Many children have special needs deriving from roots which are not specifically educational, although many of the solutions to those needs are in the hands of teachers who can adjust the school environment or the curriculum to remove those difficulties (Ainscow, 1991). Children with physical or sensory disabilities, speech difficulties, medical problems, social or behavioural difficulties need the support of professionals other than teachers. The more complex the needs, the more professionals are likely to be involved. A Royal National Institute for the Blind survey (1992) revealed that 27 different professionals were involved with a group of 45 children with multiple disabilities. These professionals included some who came from a variety of different medical disciplines from paediatrics, orthoptics and orthopaedic surgery to speech therapy, physiotherapy and dietetics. There were several different educationists involved, including peripatetic teachers for the visually impaired, educational audiologists and Portage workers. There was also a group of professionals with semi-medical roles, for example an aromatherapist, a music therapist and a chiropodist. Social services were represented by a residential social worker and the voluntary sector through the Barnados fostering team. The Community Mental Handicap Team were also involved, and they are themselves a multidisciplinary body.

There was certainly a phenomenally large number of professionals found in this study and there is a pressing need to organize them in some way to prevent children and their families from being totally overwhelmed by their ministrations. Although there are a variety of ways to harness the expertise offered by the diverse professionals, the general term used by many is 'multidisciplinary teamwork'. This has almost as many meanings as groups who use the term. Youngson-Reilly et al. (1995) suggest there are three types of multidisciplinary teams identifiable from the literature: 'practice', 'assessment' and 'discussion' teams. 'Assessment' and 'discussion' teams are made up of professionals from a number of agencies who meet periodically, either for assessment purposes or merely for case discussion purposes, whereas the 'practice' team is formed in a fixed location such as a school and is concerned with the day-to-day management of the needs of children with special needs.

In relationship to 'practice' teams in school, whether special or mainstream, there appears to be a difference between the classroom or home multidisciplinary *team* and the multidisciplinary *network*, as this distinction helps to make sense of the sheer number of people who could be involved. Those with daily contact could be said to belong to the *team* who work closely with the child and family, while all others have a consultative role and could be said to belong to a wider *network*. They will sometimes have 'hands on' contact with the child, but their main task is to help problem-solve and pass on expertise to those who can carry out programmes daily (Lacey, 1995). Again, although this is an accepted way of defining the multidisciplinary team, it certainly does not represent all examples. There are still many members of the *network* who would claim they are part of the *team* but who visit the classroom once a week, withdraw the child for intensive work, which is not shared with the classroom staff and parents, and write a report once a year for the annual review of the statement of special educational needs.

The most advanced practice, however, can be clearly related to 'transdisciplinary teamwork' (Orelove and Sobsey, 1991; McCormick and Goldman, 1988; Rainforth et al., 1992) or 'collaborative teamwork' (Lacey and Lomas, 1993; Gregory, 1989; Hart, 1991). These two terms seem to be largely synonymous, the first emanating from the United States of America and the second from the United Kingdom. McCormick and Goldman (1988) suggest that in the transdisciplinary model the respective disciplines are directly responsible for initial assessment in their own areas and then are expected to contribute to a comprehensive individual programme for the child. The responsibility for the carrying out of the programme is, however, in the hands of one or two team members utilizing the others as consultants. There are examples of parts of the initial assessment being carried out by more than one team member, such as the practice at the Wolfson Centre where speech, occupational and physiotherapists collaborate very closely using video and direct observation as the stimulus for combined assessment (Joleff et al., 1994).

Why Collaborate?

It can be said that the arguments that it is desirable for members of different agencies and disciplines to work in a collaborative manner are largely based on common sense. These arguments will be rehearsed here as they are a vital part of the underpinning of the most advanced practice in this country.

Fragmentation

A common-sense approach offers many examples of the perceptions of professionals concerning the efficacy of collaborative teamwork. One area of interest to many writers is that of counteracting fragmentation (McCormick and Goldman, 1988; Orelove and Sobsey, 1991). It is very easy for each agency or professional involved with individual children to concentrate only on the small aspect of the child's needs for which they are directly responsible. The physiotherapist is only interested in gross motor movement, the speech therapist in communication, the occupational therapist in hand function and the teacher in intellectual development. With such a fragmentary view it is perfectly possible for individual children to be working in completely different and even conflicting ways with different people. Any advice following assessment can be contradictory and far from the holistic and ecological ideal of educationists such as Bronfenbrenner (1979), Fish (1985) and Linder (1990).

One of the reasons for fragmentation can be attributed to the fact that services for children with special needs have grown up piecemeal. Education actually had very little interest in children with disabilities at the beginning of the century. The growth of the educational psychology service heralded a new era, but this new attention meant disability and difficulty were segregated and marginalized in the education world. Medicine had a close grip and, although the 'medical model' of care has now largely been superseded by an educational model, medicine is still an important discipline within the lives of children with physical or complex disabilities. Alongside education and medicine can be placed the relatively new social services, who must be involved with every young person with disabilities as they leave school and are often involved with families 'in need'. A fourth agency may be involved. Increasingly the triangle of services (Freeman and Gray, 1989) has become a rectangle (Lacey and Lomas, 1993) as voluntary bodies have grown in the attempt to fill in the gaps left by constant cost-cutting and rationalization in the public sector.

There have long been calls for one agency to be responsible for and respond to the needs of children (Swan and Morgan, 1993; Evans et al., 1989; Pugh, 1992). In the absence of a Ministry for Children (Rafferty, 1997), there have been many ideas and attempts to draw together the different agencies under a single council or committee. Some local authorities, such as Strathclyde, have integrated their education and social services and allocated management responsibility to education during the childhood years (Pugh, 1992) but this new department does not include health authorities, which are not the responsibility of local authorities.

The fact that health authorities have a direct relationship with national government rather than through the local authorities contributes to their difficulties in working together with education and social services. Health funding comes from a different source and their geographical boundaries are rarely coterminous with those of local authorities, which can make relationships complicated. Management structures across all three agencies are different, as are salaries, arrangements for training and promotion. Their philosophies and values are often at odds with each other and result in fundamental differences which need skill and perseverance to overcome (Evans et al., 1989; Gregory, 1989; Davie, 1993). Davie (1993) is particularly strong in his language concerning the difficulties besetting professionals who desire to work together. He writes of 'internecine relationships' and 'empire' building and of power struggles between the different departments.

Holistic View

It can be argued that if everyone in the team is aware of the holistic needs of individual children, it is possible for each person to identify changes in needs as they arise. If transfer of skills and understanding is effective, new needs can be responded to immediately by any one of the team. For more intractable difficulties specialist help will be needed, but it will be offered within the team umbrella so that everyone is advised similarly. There is little discussion in the literature of how this can be achieved in a school setting to ensure that the curriculum received by individual children is as holistic as their care or assessment of needs. Curriculum issues generally have been little explored, but Lacey and Lomas (1993) suggest a greater equality of sharing of expertise between education and health professionals so that school-based therapists have a fuller understanding of the demands of the curriculum and teachers know more of the therapy needs of individual children. They promote a 'collaborative curriculum' where therapists and members of support services are fully part of the curriculum rather than on the periphery, as they so often are.

It is suggested that not only could a collaborative curriculum ensure an holistic view of the child's learning and care needs, but it could also help to prevent the unnecessary overlap of provision. Common-sense arguments can be offered to suggest that there must be savings if duplication of activities can be eliminated. It is not the case that collaboration always means a reduction in the number of people involved, just that they are managed in a more co-ordinated manner. For example, it may be desirable for a young child to have the services of a teacher, nursery nurse, physiotherapist, speech therapist and occupational therapist while her needs are being assessed and individual programmes written. These five people may be best managed through the co-ordination of one who takes overall responsibility and ensures the smooth running of the team. Members can agree on who does what and joint work can be planned and implemented (Linder, 1990; Starr and Lacey, 1996).

Research carried out by Kersner (1996) lends some support to the importance of teachers and therapists carrying out assessments and writing educational programmes together. Results of Kersner's questionnaire, to discover the extent of the collaboration between speech and language therapists and teachers, found that almost half carried out assessments together, over 70 per cent jointly implemented programmes, and 95 per cent said that therapy programmes were carried out by classroom staff when the therapist was not present. Kersner (1996) suggests that the collaboration experienced in the assessment and programme planning and implementation contributed to the commitment towards the therapy, whoever carried it out.

Discussion leading to collaborative problem-solving is cited on many occasions as being a very clear advantage to professionals working together (Orelove and Sobsey, 1991; Losen and Losen, 1985; Handy, 1985; Payne, 1982). The word used is 'synergy', and the implication is that a team of people can achieve more together than each could as individuals. Balanced against this is the very real criticism that many teams find it difficult to use meetings profitably. They waste time that could be spent on solving problems, and make decisions through petty power struggles, withholding information or pure ineptitude.

Challenges and Possibilities

Some of the challenges of collaboration have already been discussed, but unfortunately there are several more that beset the best intentions of professionals who genuinely desire to combine their work efforts. Returning to the fundamental differences between agencies, one of the intractable challenges appears to be that surrounding confidentiality. Despite several well-publicized cases – such as that concerning Maria Colwell – where children have been placed in danger because services did not share information, there is still a great reluctance for professionals from different services to consider modifications to their confidentiality codes. Social services, in particular, have very strict rules governing confidentiality, and although it is possible to understand the origins of these rules it is hard to justify them when professionals are trying to work in a collaborative team. The Warnock Report (DES, 1978) uses the term 'extended confidentiality' and the Home Office et al. (1991: 13) suggest that 'confidentiality may not be maintained if the withholding of information will prejudice the welfare of the child'. From their research into identifying models of inter-agency working, Maychell and Bradley (1991: 39) report that some of their respondents suspected that information of a non-confidential nature was withheld in the interest of maintaining power and control over others. One of their examples concerned the reluctance of social workers to pass on case history information on a student to his new college in the name of confidentiality. College staff felt that unfortunate incidents that had arisen could have been avoided had they known the student's background, and that withholding the information was unnecessary.

It can be argued that members of collaborative teams should trust each other to the point of feeling that confidences can be shared among them and remain within that group of people. There may be some cases where this is not in the interest of the child and his or her family. When this happens, the agency in question must be very clear about why the confidence is not to be shared. Many writers discuss trust and sharing, suggesting that these are central to effective teamwork (Hornby, 1993; Rainforth et al., 1992; Rouse, 1987). Trust is difficult to build up, especially as so many writers mention problems with territorial disputes between agencies and professionals (Clough and Lindsay, 1991; Solity and Bickler, 1994), power struggles (Fish, 1985; Gregory, 1989) and feelings of job insecurity (Maychell and Bradley, 1991; Thomas, 1992). The present climate of dividing the 'purchaser' from the 'provider' within the human services may be adding to these difficulties and encouraging competition rather than collaboration (Lupton and Khan, 1998).

Another area of difficulty is that relating to the roles that individuals have within teams. It is recommended that roles should be very clearly defined so that there is no doubt concerning the experience, expertise and guiding values of each person (Dyson et al., 1998; Clough and Lindsay, 1991; Home Office et al., 1991; HMI, 1991). This does not necessarily mean that everyone's role has to be completely separate from any other. There are times when roles should actually be overlapping so that children receive the same input from each person who works with them (Bowers, 1987; Orelove and Sobsey, 1991; Rainforth et al., 1992). For example, if everyone who works with a particular child with physical disabilities knows how to position that child so that she can be comfortable and well-supported, she will be able to join in all activities to the optimum degree. This implies the willingness on the part of individuals to share expertise with each other in a form of 'role release' – that is, that they are prepared to 'release' part of their roles to others, trusting them to carry out those roles in their places. This is very demanding and implies that professionals feel secure in their roles and have confidence in their own abilities (Fish, 1985; Hart, 1991).

Miller's (1996) research points to the importance of professionals from different disciplines sharing a language and understanding each other's point of view. Her study, of the outcomes of training speech and language therapists and teachers on the same course, shows that both sets of professionals felt that they could communicate more effectively, plan and work together more closely, and generally experience a better professional working relationship after being on the course. She does, however, point to some negative results which suggest that some participants felt threatened by sharing knowledge.

The sharing of expertise is implicit in the way in which a collaborative team works. Through natural observation of each other at work, joint problem-solving and professional discussion, skills and understanding are exchanged and put into practice (Bailey, 1991; Connolly and Anderson, 1988; Hanko, 1990). Like all teamwork, it is relatively easy to find isolated examples of good practice but very difficult to find evidence that this trust and sharing is the norm in multidisciplinary teams who work with children with special needs. It is a difficult and demanding thing to achieve and there are so many factors militating against it in schools today, particularly the demands of a crowded curriculum, inspection and league tables.

Research by Wright (1996) has contributed something to the understanding of the challenges and possibilities for collaboration across disciplines. Wright looked specifically at pairs of speech and language therapists and teachers working together to try to ascertain what each felt they gained from the partnership. From her interviews, she found several ways in which the pairs felt they had gained from working together. These included benefits to the child, such as less fragmentation; personal benefits such as sharing concerns, support and reducing stress; and professional gains, such as new knowledge in specific areas ('cognitive gain'). Challenges included the difficulties in finding time to collaborate, the added strain of working with another person, and loss of autonomy. Wright (1996) recommends the use of a facilitator when teachers and therapists first start to work together as a strategy to help them to identify their own personal and professional benefits from working together, as well as the disadvantages.

Strategies for Enabling Collaboration

Wright's suggestion is one strategy that can assist effective collaboration to become more likely. From the literature it is possible to build up a picture of other possibilities. Many service managers seem to believe that if you exhort people to work together and call them 'teams', they will automatically collaborate. Tomlinson (1982: 31) is sceptical of this and suggests that it 'assumes an unrealistic degree of communication, co-operation and absence of professional conflicts and jealousies'. There is also an assumption that the structures exist to support team members both personally and in their efforts to work together. In many cases this is just not so.

Legislation

Legislation underpinning multidisciplinary and multi-agency work is largely facilitative and encouraging rather than demanding. The Code of Practice on the Identification and Assessment of Special Educational Needs attached to the Education Act 1993 is a good example of this. One of its principles is: 'There must be close cooperation between all the agencies concerned and a multidisciplinary approach to the resolution of issues' (Department for Education, 1994: 3).

However, in the detail that follows, it appears that agencies who support schools can choose not to respond to demands for assessments and reports if they feel the request is unreasonable in terms of their own available resources. The Children Act (1989) has a similar let-out sentence.

> District Health Authorities, LEAs, grant maintained schools and City Technology Colleges must comply for a request from a social services department for assistance in providing services for *children in need*, so long as the request is compatible with their duties and does not unduly prejudice the discharge of their functions.
>
> (Children Act 1989: Section 27)

Even though the legislation lacks compulsion, there is evidence to suggest that agencies are committed to working together and have devised certain strategies to facilitate this. Joint committees and departments have already been mentioned. It would be useful to look in some detail at a documented attempt at local government level to provide a structure to support collaboration. Swan and Morgan (1993) write of local interagency councils which have been set up in certain parts of the United States of America in the effort to counteract the complexity and fragmentation in existing services for young children and their families, particularly in terms of the legislation governing the education of children with disabilities.

Interagency Council

Swan and Morgan (1993: 4) suggest that a state interagency co-ordinating council (ICC) can provide 'a mechanism for discussion of issues and implementation of necessary services among groups of parents, lawmakers, educators and policymakers'. There is an emphasis on problem-solving at a local level and on networking between agencies. It is claimed that ICCs can achieve results in terms of:

- general co-ordination
- multidisciplinary assessment
- a child-find and referral system
- public awareness
- a local directory of services
- personnel development and training
- written contracts
- generation of revenue

Interagency co-ordination can be achieved through the development of a formal working team of agency representatives who have authority within their own services. They meet regularly with the following aims:

1 to develop a common information base and communication;
2 to eliminate unnecessary duplication of services;
3 to co-ordinate existing agency programs;
4 to identify gaps in services;
5 to determine agency roles and responsibilities;
6 to shift resources to create a complete continuum of services;
7 to develop an interagency case management function;
8 to ensure appropriate services to all identified children.

(Swan and Morgan, 1993: 27)

Swan and Morgan (1993) voice various cautions, for example that the council should not become another layer of bureaucracy, that hierarchy within the council should be avoided and that every member should be committed to the ideal of working collaboratively. Throughout the account there is awareness of the difficulties of working in this way, but there are many extremely useful strategies that could be adopted by agencies wishing to work together.

Contracts and Job Descriptions

One of the strategies explored by several writers is that of written contracts and service agreements (Bowers, 1991a, 1991b; Clough and Lindsay, 1991; Swan and Morgan, 1993). Clough and Lindsay's (1991) research into the support services in 'City LEA' reveal that contracts can vary in their format but are basically a tool to aid clarity of purpose in relationships between services and schools. They were in no way legal documents but agreements concerning the way in which schools and services could work together. The results of the research suggest that contracts are useful 'milestones' in an evolutionary process of affecting change in schools, but that their usefulness is largely governed by the success with which individuals interact with each other while fulfilling the contract. The researchers suggest that relying on contracts could have the effect of ensuring that special educational needs continues to be seen as the responsibility of outside services rather than of the school itself.

Contracts and service agreements can aid in the delineation of the roles individuals have within the team or the network. It is important to know exactly what is expected from any one person and how each person's role fits into the others. Job descriptions can contribute to feelings of security, as can time spent exchanging information concerning the experience and expertise of team members. Rainforth et al. (1992) give a sample-therapy job description which includes processes as well as tasks. For instance, there are several references to collaboration, to team meetings, to ecological assessments and to joint planning of programmes. Lacey and Lomas (1993) argue that discussing these issues and having a written document summarizing them can be a useful strategy for enabling effective collaboration.

Meetings

Meetings of all kinds have also been seen as having the potential to support collaborative teamwork. Rainforth et al. (1992) suggest that interaction is particularly important when teams are setting up. But throughout their lives teams need time to talk together and to work together. This includes time allocated to carry out joint assessments, plan programmes together and actually work side by side (Linder, 1990; Losen and Losen, 1985). This implies support from management, who must facilitate time spent together. Cocker (1995) points to the importance of non-contact time for class teachers and special educational needs co-ordinators (SENCOs) to work together. She claims that she could not carry out her role as SENCO without being given time to meet with other people.

To facilitate meetings and general communication, several writers and researchers suggest the importance of close proximity to collaborative work (Yerbury, 1997; Wright, 1996). Common sense would also suggest that those who have offices under the same roof are more likely to be in regular communication than those whose bases are on opposite sides of the locality, although this cannot be assumed. There is evidence to suggest that more services are convinced of the need to place side by side those who are trying to collaborate. This is particularly so in the under-5s or under-8s services, such as those in the Leeds Early Years Partnership.

Structure

Generally, there is the need for a structure to promote collaboration if teams of professionals are to be effective in their work (Joseph Rowntree Foundation, 1995). Facilitating time for meetings and joint work is one aspect, and encouraging the imaginative use of time is another. Traditionally, support from outside services or therapists has been in regular, short bursts. This works quite well while there is generous staffing, but in the age of diminishing resources it leads to frustration as parents and class teachers feel that they are being short-changed. Where once the speech therapist could offer time to work directly with individual children, now often she has an increased caseload and responsibilities elsewhere in the service and consequently can offer less time to individuals (Wright, 1996). Rainforth et al. (1992) argue for the blocking of time, not just as an expediency but because it makes sense to use therapists as consultants rather than expect them to give small amounts of time to individual children for direct work. This might result in the therapist making an initial assessment of several children and jointly writing programmes with other team members within one block of time, then leaving the classroom staff to carry out the programmes for a few weeks. Later the therapist returns to monitor the programme and help with adjustments or further assessments. This could be done in several classrooms or schools, with the effect that the needs of more children are discussed, and those needs can be met daily by classroom staff instead of twice weekly for ten minutes by the therapist.

Blocking of time reflects a fundamental difference in structure which relates directly to the shift in response to special needs from the medical to the educational model and from a fragmentary to an holistic view of the child. Philosophy and structure are intrinsically bound in that, if education and health professionals believe sufficiently in the power of the collaborative team, it could be argued that they will have to change the structures that support them in their work or it will be impossible to enable these teams to be effective.

Keyworker Systems

One of the structures which requires examination is that pertaining to the keyworker system. Collaborative teamwork implies the use of a keyworker or core member who takes the main responsibility for meeting the needs of individual children (Orelove and Sobsey, 1991; Rainforth et al., 1992; Linder, 1990). This is not quite synonymous with 'team leader' in the sense found in industry, but appears to be more of a co-ordinator's role combined with an advocate's role. Any member of the team can take the lead or core role in terms of planning and implementation of programmes, using other members in a consultative role. Several writers refer to the importance of understanding role transition to appreciate the changes needed if professionals are to use the core-consultant structure of collaborative teams (Woodruff and McGonigal, 1988).

Difficulties faced by professionals prepared to go through role transition have been alluded to earlier in this chapter. It is suggested that professional and personal threats stir up strong feelings and should not be underestimated. Training others, and being trained, places individuals under considerable scrutiny which may be uncomfortable. There may also be feelings of diminished professional status. If it is possible to pass on skills and understanding to colleagues in different disciplines, then how can professional status be maintained? Orelove and Sobsey (1991) suggest that in fact status can be enhanced through the fostering of greater respect and interdependence.

Providing structures to support the changes implicit in this manner of working appears to be important, and it is likely that they are the responsibility of both the team members themselves and of the management facilitating the team. This points to the need for time together to be used carefully so that training, observation and discussion can be built in. A system of audit and review will contribute considerably to this and encourage team members to use its formality to address challenges and possibilities for which they do not normally have time (Lacey and Lomas, 1993).

Conclusions

In this chapter, there has been a catalogue of challenges facing individuals and agencies who are trying to work together to meet special educational needs. Possibilities have also been discussed, and at an agency level these can be summed up in the results of a recent study by Dyson et al. (1998). Dyson et al. examined communication between school, LEAs and health and social services, particularly as they fulfilled their duties in relation to the Code of Practice (DfE, 1994). They found a number of factors which seemed to sustain effective co-operation between services. These include efficient information management within and between agencies; specific projects as opportunities for developing co-operation; a clearly defined focus which is significant to each agency; shared aims and agreed definitions; and proactive individuals to provide the stimulus for joint work.

Dessent (1996), in looking to the future, suggests eight options for improving the effectiveness of interagency working. These are not mutually exclusive and elements from several could work together. The suggestions range in complexity from a kind of 'heroic big bang' of restructuring local authority services into one organization and creating stronger legislation to compel co-operation, through to providing corporate funding, clustering schools, agreeing project areas for collaboration or merely clarifying boundaries for working together. Although the more radical suggestions made by writers and researchers, such as local authority reorganization, could be realized, the immediate future is more likely to contain more conservative changes, such as extending regional co-ordination of special educational needs, introducing new duties for partnerships with more flexible funding, improving provision of speech and language therapy and transitions to adult life, as have been promised in the *Programme for Action* (DfEE, 1998) following the Green Paper *Excellence for All Children* (DfEE, 1997). What is clear is that good practice exists and can be disseminated across the country so that every child with special educational needs can experience effective multidisciplinary and multi-agency work.

References

Ainscow, M. (1991) *Effective Schools for All*. London: David Fulton.

Audit Commission (1994) *Seen but not Heard: Co-ordinating Community Child Health and Social Services for Children in Need*. London: HMSO.

Audit Commission (1996) *Misspent Youth: Young People and Crime*. London: HMSO.

Bailey, T. (1991) 'Classroom observation: A powerful tool for teachers?', *Support for Learning*, 6(1), 32–6.

Bamford, D., Griffiths, H., Long, S. and Kernoham, G. (1997) 'Analysis of consumer satisfaction in cerebral palsy care', *Journal of Interprofessional Care*, 11(2), 187–93.

Bowers, T. (1987) 'Human resources and special needs: some key issues', in T. Bowers (ed.) *Human Resource Management and Special Educational Needs*. Beckenham: Croom Helm.

Bowers, T. (1991a) *LMS and SEN Support Services Resources and Activity Pack*. Cambridge: Perspective Press.

Bowers, T. (1991b) *Schools, Services and Special Educational Needs. Management Issues in the Wake of LMS*. Cambridge: Perspective Press.

Bronfenbrenner, U. (1979) *The Ecology of Human Development*. Cambridge: Harvard University Press.

Centre for Educational Research and Innovation (CERI) (1996) *Integrating Services for Children at Risk*. Paris: OECD.

Cigno, K. and Burke, P. (1997) 'Single mothers of children with learning disabilities: an undervalued group', *Journal of Interprofessional Care*, 11(2),177–86.

Clough, P. and Lindsay, G. (1991) *Integration and the Support Services: Changing Roles in Special Education*. Windsor: NFER Nelson.

Cocker, C. (1995) 'Special needs in the infant school', *Support for Learning*, 10(2), 75–8.

Connolly, B. and Anderson, R. (1988) 'Severely handicapped children in the public schools: a new frontier for the physical therapist', in P. Jansma (ed.) *The Psychomotor Domain and the Seriously Handicapped* (third edition). New York: Universal Press of America.

Davie, R. (1993) 'Implementing Warnock's multi-professional approach', in J. Visser and G. Upton (eds) *Special Education in Britain after Warnock*. London: David Fulton.

Department for Education (1994) *The Code of Practice on the Identification and Assessment of Special Educational Needs*. London: HMSO.

Department for Education and Employment (1997) *Excellence for All Children: Meeting Special Educational Needs*. London: The Stationery Office.

Department for Education and Employment (1998) *Meeting Special Educational Needs: A Programme for Action*. London: HMSO.

Department of Education and Science (1978) *Special Educational Needs* (The Warnock Report). London: HMSO.

Department of Health (1986) *Children Act*. London: HMSO.

Derrington, C., Evans, C. and Lee, B. (1997) *The Code in Practice: The Impact on Schools and LEAs*. Slough: NFER.

Dessent, T. (1996) 'Meeting special educational needs – options for partnership between health, social and education services', in NASEN (ed.) *Options for Partnership Between Health, Social and Education Services*. Tamworth: NASEN.

Dyson, A., Lin, M. and Millward, A. (1998) *Effective Communication between Schools, LEAs and Health and Social Services in the Field of Special Educational Needs*. London: DfEE.

Evans, J., Everard, B., Friend, J., Glaser, A., Norwich, B. and Welton, J. (1989) *Decision Making for Special Educational Needs*. Loughborough: Tecmedia.

Fish, J. (1985) *Special Education: The Way Ahead*. Milton Keynes: Open University Press.

Freeman, A. and Gray, H. (1989) *Organising Special Needs: A Critical Approach*. London: Paul Chapman.

Gregory, E. (1989) 'Issues of multiprofessional co-operation', in R. Evans (ed.) *Special Educational Needs: Policy and Practice*. Oxford: Blackwell/NARE.

Handy, C. (1985) *Understanding Organisations*. Harmondsworth: Penguin.

Hanko, G. (1990) *Special Needs in Ordinary Classrooms: Supporting Teachers* (second edition). Oxford: Blackwell.

Hart, S. (1991) 'The collaborative dimension: risks and rewards of collaboration', in C. McLaughlin and M. Rouse (eds) *Supporting Schools*. London: David Fulton.

Her Majesty's Inspectorate (1991) *Interdisciplinary Support for Young Children with SEN*. London: DES.

Home Office, Department of Health, Department of Education and Science, Welsh Office (1991) *Working Together under the Children Act 1989*. London: HMSO.

Hornby, S. (1993) *Collaborative Care: Interprofessional, Interagency and Interpersonal*. Oxford: Blackwell Scientific.

Joleff, N., Price, K. and Wisbeach, A. (1994) 'An approach to combined therapy assessment', unpublished conference paper for 'Practical Teamwork for Children with Multiple Disabilities', Wolfson Centre, London.

Joseph Rowntree Foundation (1995) *Multi-Agency Work with Young People in Difficulty*. York: Joseph Rowntree Foundation.

Kersner, M. (1996) 'Working together for children with severe learning disabilities', *Child Language Teaching and Therapy*, 12(1), 17–28.

Lacey, P. (1995) 'In the front line: special educational needs co-ordinators and liaison', *Support for Learning*, 10(2), 57–62.

Lacey, P. and Lomas, J. (1993) *Support Services and the Curriculum: A Practical Guide to Collaboration*. London: David Fulton.

Linder, T. (1990) *Transdisciplinary Play-based Assessment*. Baltimore: Paul Brookes.

Losen, S. and Losen, J. (1985) *The Special Education Team*. Boston: Allyn and Bacon.

Lupton, C. and Khan, P. (1998) 'The role of health professionals in the UK child protection system: a literature review', *Journal of Interprofessional Care*, 12(2), 209–21.

McCormick, L. and Goldman, R. (1988) 'The trans-disciplinary model: implications for service delivery and personnel preparation for the severely and profoundly handicapped', in P. Jansma (ed.) *The Psychomotor Domain and the Seriously Handicapped* (third edition). New York: University Press of America.

Maychell, K. and Bradley, J. (1991) *Preparing for Partnership: Multi-Agency Support for Special Needs*. Slough: NFER.

Middleton, L. (1998) 'Consumer satisfaction with services for disabled children', *Journal of Interprofessional Care*, 12(2), 223–31.

Miller, C. (1996) 'Relationships between teachers and speech and language therapists', *Child Language Teaching and Therapy*, 12(1), 29–38.

Orelove, F. and Sobsey, D. (1991) *Educating Children with Multiple Disabilities: A Transdisciplinary Approach*. Baltimore: Paul Brookes.

Payne, M. (1982) *Working in Teams*. London: Macmillan.

Pugh, G. (1992) 'A policy for early childhood services?' in G. Pugh (ed.) *Contemporary Issues in the Early Years: Working Collaboratively for Children*. London: Paul Chapman.

Rafferty, F. (1997) 'Integrated services praised', *Times Educational Supplement*, 20 June 1997.

Rainforth, B., York, J. and McDonald, C. (1992) *Collaborative Teams for Students with Severe Disabilities*. Baltimore: Paul Brookes.

Roaf, C. and Lloyd, C. (1995) *Multi-Agency Work with Young People in Difficulty*. York: Joseph Rowntree Foundation.

Rouse, M. (1987) 'Bringing the Special Needs Department out of the cupboard', in T. Bowers (ed.) *Special Educational Needs and Human Resource Management*. Beckenham: Croom Helm.

Royal National Institute for the Blind (1992) *Curriculum Materials Used with Multi-handicapped Visually Impaired Children and Young People: Report from the Working Party*. London: RNIB.

Solity, J. and Bickler, G. (eds) (1994) *Support Services: Issues for Education, Health and Social Service Professionals*. London: Cassell.

Starr, A. and Lacey, P. (1996) 'Multidisciplinary assessment: a case study', *British Journal of Special Education*, 23(2), 57–61.

Swan, W. and Morgan, J. (1993) *Collaborating for Comprehensive Services for Young Children and their Families*. Baltimore: Paul Brookes.

Thomas, G. (1992) *Effective Classroom Teamwork: Support or Intrusion?*. London: Routledge.

Tomlinson, S. (1982) *A Sociology of Special Education*. London: Routledge and Kegan Paul.

Woodruff, G. and McGonigal, M. (1988) 'Early intervention team approach: the transdisciplinary model', in J. Jordan, P. Gallagher, P. Hutinger and M. Karnes (eds) *Early Childhood Special Education: Birth to Three*. Reston: Council for Exceptional Children.

Wright, J. (1996) 'Teachers and therapists: the evolution of a partnership', *Child Language Teaching and Therapy*, 12(1), 3–15.

Yerbury, M. (1997) 'Issues in multidisciplinary teamwork for children with disabilities', *Child Care, Health and Development*, 23(1), 77–86.

Youngson-Reilly, S., Tobin, M. and Fielder, A. (1995) 'Multidisciplinary teams and childhood visual impairment: a study of two teams', *Child Care, Health and Development*, 21(1), 3–15.

10 Supporting Collaborative Problem-Solving in Schools

Harry Daniels, Angela Creese and Brahm Norwich

In a recent issue of *Educational and Child Psychology*, Phil Stringer (1998) responded to an article by Sara Meadows (1998) in which it was suggested that neo-Vygotskian accounts of cognitive development are now influencing educational theory and policy. Stringer contends that approaches to peer group work in schools, including some of our own recent work on collaborative problem-solving among teachers, can be given a 'Vygotskian reading'. That we as writers/researchers did not undertake the work with a Vygotskian model in mind perhaps reveals something of the way in which psychological accounts are seen to and/or do influence theory, research, policy and practice.

In this chapter we will attempt to provide the absent 'Vygotskian writing' of our work on Teacher Support Teams (TSTs). A TST is an organized system of peer support which consists of a small group of teachers who take referrals from individual teachers on a voluntary basis. The referring teacher brings concerns about classes, groups or individuals in order to discuss and problem-solve with their peers. Follow-up meetings are held as necessary. The process is as confidential as the requesting teacher wants it to be.

TSTs are novel in that they are an example of a school-based development designed to give support and assistance to individual teachers. In this way, TSTs address a significant but neglected area of school development which has the potential to enhance the working conditions of teachers. They involve a sharing of expertise between colleagues, rather than some teachers acting as experts to others. They also provide an opportunity to support students indirectly by supporting teachers. As a form of group problem-solving, they have the potential of extending staff involvement in the development of SEN policy and practice. They can help focus on the balance between addressing students' individual needs and bringing about change within school systems. TSTs aim to complement existing structures for supporting teachers at work. They do not intend to replace them.

The role of a collaborative professional culture in schools is an important but under-researched aspect of school effectiveness and improvement literature. What there is points to the positive benefits of collaborative cultures (Rosenholtz, 1989; Fullan and Hargreaves, 1992; Nias, 1989). However, creating such an ethos is not without its problems. Professional individualism has been seen as an obstacle to collaboration and has been attributed to the organization of schools, especially in secondary schools (Nias, 1993).

The literature suggests that schools which aim to develop support structures allowing for professional interaction and shared knowledge with fellow teachers are likely to have positive outcomes. This is partly a question of providing teachers with the opportunity to be reflective practitioners, (Pollard, 1988, in Woods, 1993: 76), extended professionals (Hoyle, 1989, in Woods, 1993: 265), or teacher-researchers (Cochran-Smith and Lytle, 1993), but also of allowing the school to reallocate its time and resources as problems are solved in-house.

Teachers can collaborate and support one another in many different ways, both formally and informally, within the classroom and outside it. Within class, research on partnership teaching (Bourne and McPake, 1991), team teaching (Cohen, 1981), advisory/support teaching (Biott, 1991), classroom assistants (Martin-Jones and Saxena, 1989), individual support teachers and SEN co-ordinators (Dyson, 1990; Garnett, 1988; Hart, 1986) has highlighted the advantages of bringing teachers with different expertise together in mutually beneficial ways. Models of teaching and learning which focus on an inclusive and differentiated pedagogy also involve collaborative working as a key element in interaction with staff development, flexible resource management and the management of change (Clark et al., 1997).

Teacher collaboration outside the classroom is less well researched. This has been looked at in the work of Hanko (1989, 1990), Mead (1991), the Newcastle educational psychology service (Stringer et al., 1992) and in our own work (Norwich and Daniels, 1997; Creese et al., 1997). These researchers, although differing in their focus, have developed and evaluated collaborative problem-solving schemes. Study of group peer support systems in the UK and USA show positive results. American research has indicated that Teacher Support Teams (TSTs) can contribute to a drop in the number of inappropriate referrals to outside services and other benefits (Chalfant and Pysh, 1989; Harris, 1995).

TSTs may be seen as a form of intervention which seeks to alter the socio-cultural context of schooling through the development of a culture of collaborative peer problem-solving. In this way, TSTs aim to enhance the capacity of the school to respond to diverse student populations. It is thus an intervention which seeks to alter the context in order to enhance collective thinking. Teachers are, as Stringer (1998) suggests, 'seen as the target and agent of change'. Given this interpretation of TSTs we will now attempt to provide that which was absent but perhaps implicit in some of our original thoughts.

Vygotsky developed an account of the social formation of mind within which discourse mediates children's formal and informal learning (Daniels, 1996). The essence of this developmental model advanced a dialectical conception of the relations between personal and social life. Specific social practices may be associated with modes of discourse and modes of personal thinking. (See Olson and Torrance, 1996.) The key concept of 'mediation' opens the way to a non-deterministic account in which 'psychological tools' serve as the means by which the individual acts upon and is acted upon by social, cultural and historical factors. Thus the potential for understanding cultural and social factors as they impact on individual understanding and learning is afforded. However, a good deal of the post-Vygotskian research conducted in the west has focused exclusively on the effects of interaction at the interpersonal level, with insufficient attention paid to the form of collective social activity with specific forms of interpersonal communication interrelations between interpersonal and socio-cultural levels. There is clearly a need for such a theoretical orientation, given that the training which teachers receive and the organizational structure of schools seem to discourage cultures of professional interaction and knowledge sharing. The reasons for this professional individualism, as Nias points out, 'are also profoundly cultural' (1993: 141).

The ways in which schools are organized and constrained to organize themselves are seen to have an effect on the possibilities for teacher peer collaboration and support. However, the theoretical tools of analysis of this kind of organizational effect are somewhat underdeveloped within the post-Vygotskian framework. 'As a rule, the socio-institutional context of action is treated as a (largely unanalysed) dichotomised independent variable – or left to sociologists' (Cole 1996: 340).

The consequences of this restricted concept of context are made manifest in the interpretation of one of the key Vygotskian terms – the Zone of Proximal Development (ZPD). Lave and Wenger (1991) argue that the operational definition of ZPD has itself undergone many differing interpretations. These differences may be seen to reveal the more general theoretical drift towards a broader, more cultural and historical view of the 'social' which is theorized as being progressively and more intimately a part of the 'individual'. Thus, Lave and Wenger (1991: 48) distinguish between a 'scaffolding', a 'cultural' and a 'collectivist' or 'societal' of the original formulation of the ZPD. The 'scaffolding' interpretation is one in which a distinction is made between support for the initial performance of tasks and subsequent performance without assistance: 'the distance between problem-solving abilities exhibited by a learner working alone and that learner's problem-solving abilities when assisted by or collaborating with more experienced people.'

The 'cultural' interpretation is based on Vygotsky's distinction between scientific and everyday concepts. It is argued that a mature concept is achieved when the scientific and everyday versions have merged. However, as Lave and Wenger (1991) note, no account is taken of 'the place of learning in the broader context of the structure in the social world'.

the distance between the cultural knowledge provided by the socio-historical context – usually made accessible through instruction – and the everyday experience of individuals calls this the distance between understood knowledge, as provided by instruction, and active knowledge, as owned by individuals.

(Lave and Wenger, 1991: 48)

In the 'collectivist', or 'societal' perspective, Engeström defines the zone of proximal development as the 'distance between the everyday actions of individuals and the historically new form of the societal activity that can be collectively generated' (Engeström et al., 1997: 174). Under such societal interpretations of the concept of the zone of proximal development, researchers tend to concentrate on processes of social transformation. This involves the study of learning beyond the context of pedagogical structuring, including the structure of the social world in the analysis, and taking into account in a central way the conflictual nature of social practice (after Lave and Wenger, 1991: 48–9).

Here, then, is *a* theoretical position which has more than a passing resonance with the TST development process. TSTs seek to alter the communicative practices of teachers in schools. They engage with the tensions, dilemmas and even conflicts which teachers experience in the social worlds of the schools they inhabit. Vygotsky attached the greatest importance to the formative effect of the school itself as an institution. His particular interest lay in the structuring of time and space and the related system of social relations (between pupils and teacher, between the pupils themselves, between the school and its surroundings, and so on) (Ivic, 1989).

We know from our own work on TSTs that teachers come to value and enjoy collaboration with their peers in team settings. The overly cognitive interpretation of much of Vygotsky's work should not detract from affective and regulative considerations. Recent contributions have drawn attention to the need develop a model of social formation of mind that extends beyond constraints of the cognitive domain.

Educationally significant human interactions do not involve abstract bearers of cognitive structures but real people who develop a variety of interpersonal relationships with one another in the course of their shared activity in a given institutional context ... modes of thinking evolve as integral systems of motives, goals, values, and beliefs that are closely tied to concrete forms of social practice (after Minick et al., 1993: 6).

They argue that the concept of the ZPD should be redefined from a broader social and cultural perspective. Taken together, the positions established by del Rio and Alvarez (1995) along with that of Minick et al. point towards the need for more holistic and coherent development: inclusive in that it should seek to take account of cognitive and affective domains, coherent in that it should handle these domains as highly interrelated and/or embedded matters. The outcomes of our work on TSTs suggests that such theoretical development is necessary. The changes in the context TSTs bring about lie in both cognitive and affective outcomes.

In order to try and discuss innovation and improvement of specific forms of multiprofessional activity, Engeström et al. (1997) develop a three-level notion of the developmental forms of epistemological subject–object–subject relations within a Vygotskian framework. They call these three levels 'co-ordination', 'co-operation' and 'communication'. Within the general structure of co-ordination actors follow their scripted roles, pursuing different goals (see Figure 10.1).

Within the general structure of co-operation actors focus on a shared problem. Within the confines of a script the actors attempt both to conceptualize and to solve problems in ways which are negotiated and agreed. (See Figure 10.2.) The script itself is not questioned. That is, the tacitly assumed

Figure 10.1   The general structure of co-ordination

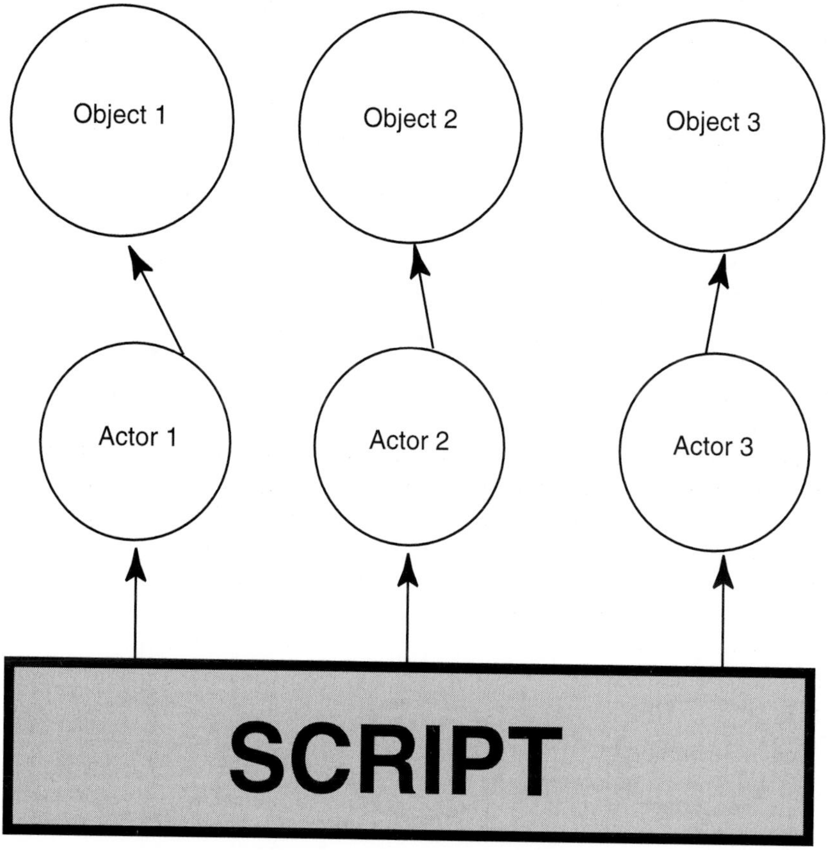

traditions and/or the given official rules of engagement with the problem are not challenged.

Rogers and Whetton (1982) define and compare co-operation and co-ordination as follows:

- *Co-operation* is defined as deliberate relations between otherwise autonomous organizations for the joint accomplishments of individual goals. This definition stresses more informal relations, autonomy and individual goals.
- *Co-ordination*, by contrast, is the process whereby two or more organizations create and/or use existing decision rules that have been established to deal collectively with their shared task environment.

Eraut (1994) drew an important distinction between reflection 'in action' and reflection 'on action'. While reflection in action may well occur in co-operative and co-ordinated systems, reflection on action is more difficult to attain. Engeström et al. (1997: 373) discuss reflective communication

Figure 10.2   The general structure of co-operation

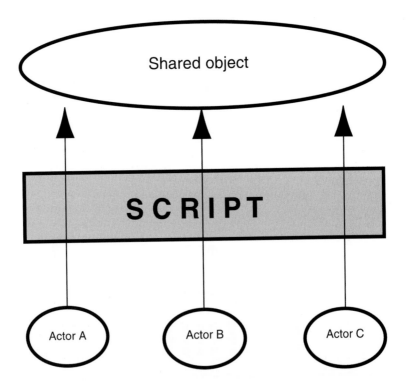

in which the actors focus on reconceptualizing their own organization and interaction in relation to their shared objects and goals [see Figure 10.3]. This is reflection on action. Both the object and the script are reconceptualized, as is the interaction between the participants.

Implicit in this general structure of communication is a version of Vygotsky's (1978) concept of the Zone of Proximal Development (ZPD). That is the 'area that is beyond one's full comprehension and mastery, but that one is still able to fruitfully engage with, with the support of some tools, concepts and prompts from others' (Bazerman, 1997: 305). The concept has also been to consider the way that peers prompt each other dialogically. The emphasis is on reciprocal support for mutual understanding. Newman et al. (1989) describe this form of activity in the classroom: 'The multiple points of view within a ZPD are not seen as a problem for analysis but rather the basis for a process of appropriation in which children's understandings can play a role in the functional system' (Newman et al., 1989: 136).

Lave and Wenger's (1991) definition of a scaffolding approach to the concept of ZPD could be argued as the theoretical underpin for activity in teams which resembles the co-ordination model outlined above. Their collectivist definition leads to a view of activity as envisaged in the communication

Figure 10.3   *The general structure of communication*

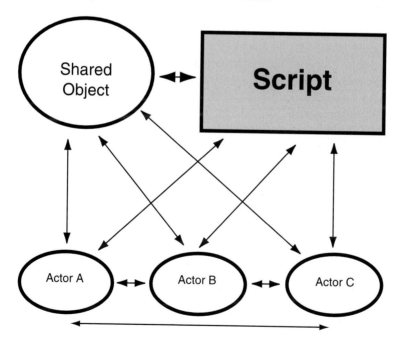

model. This envisages activity systems that contain a variety of different viewpoints or 'voices', as well as layers of historically accumulated artifacts, rules and patterns of division of labour. This multivoiced and multilayered nature of activity systems is both a resource for collective achievement and a source of compartmentalization and conflict. Contradictions are the engine of change and development in an activity system, as well as a source of conflict and stress (Cole et al., 1997: 4). TSTs can function in such a way as to bring differences and alternative views (constructive contradictions) into the working lives of teachers in schools.

We originally conceived of TSTs as a system of support from a team of peers for class teachers experiencing teaching difficulties in relation to special educational needs (SENs). Our model was that individual teachers request support on a voluntary basis from a team which usually includes the SEN co-ordinator, a senior teacher and another class teacher. The team, along with the referring teacher, collaborate in order to understand the problem(s) and design appropriate forms of intervention related to learning and behaviour difficulties.

From a Vygotskian perspective, these mediating communicative patterns constitute tools for action and cognition. Though each participant in a discursive field need not think alike – indeed the discursive activities of disciplines largely rely on people not thinking precisely alike – each must draw on a common body of resources, cope with the same body of material and symbolic artifacts, master the same tools, and gain legitimacy for any new resources they want to bring into the field, by addressing the same mechanisms of evaluation by which new concepts, tools, or phenomena gain standing in the discourse (Bazerman, 1997: 305).

Research about the outcomes of peer support in the schools studied is encouraging. Two recent studies, a pilot project in three primary schools (Daniels and Norwich, 1992) and an ESRC project in a further eight primary schools (Norwich and Daniels, 1994) looked at the processes and outcomes of the setting up of TSTs. Researchers and schools collaborated to evaluate the operation and impacts of TSTs at the schools. This involved collecting information about the frequency of the meetings, the number of requests, the nature of the concerns expressed, what action was recommended and what follow-up meetings were organized. This information was analysed within the context of each particular school with a view to understanding how a school's culture can contribute to supporting new schemes and how new schemes can contribute to a school's need to deal with and shape change.

In the primary school projects mentioned above (Daniels and Norwich, 1992; Norwich and Daniels, 1994), the outcomes of the TST's work was positive. Both the teachers who were members of the team and the teachers who referred to the team for help reported that they felt their professional development was enhanced through the discussion and acquisition of strategies – either new, forgotten or not previously used – to deal with situations personal to them at that particular time. These included:

- *Strategies for collaborating with other staff*   this involved the direct involvement of the SEN co-ordinator or a TST member covering for a teacher.

- *Strategies for the teacher to use in-class*   examples included the use of conduct charts, contracts and report books, the development of individual programmes, and class management changes, such as use of group work and seating rearrangements.

- *Strategies for lunchtime*   for example, play materials were made available to some pupils to encourage more constructive play.

- *Parental involvement*   arranging specific meetings with parents and reaching agreement for parents to help their children in specific ways at home.

- *Communication with external support services*   this involved writing to educational psychologists about statutory assessment or about bringing forward the date for the Statement review.

The TST members were very positive about the value of their TST work for themselves as teachers. All were keen to continue as members. For the SEN co-ordinator in particular, TSTs were seen as positively affecting their work by promoting linking across the school and preventing isolation.

Overall, it was found that there were fewer requests in relation to girls than boys, and to older than younger children. At the end of a two-term period, only a small proportion of the requests dealt with were judged as closed in the sense that improvement was sufficient to merit the withdrawal of support. However, there was some improvement in about two-thirds of the requests overall, as judged by the TSTs. In all schools the requesting teachers were mostly positive about the value for themselves of going to the team. The headteachers corroborated these views. Requesting teachers' perceptions of the nature of the support offered by the TSTs can be grouped under the following themes:

- enabled them to distance themselves from problems and re-examine their activities;
- enabled problems to be aired;
- enabled them to form their own strategies;
- provided an opportunity to let off steam legitimately, with it being cathartic to talk to sympathetic colleagues with a non-judgemental attitude;
- enabled them to confirm approaches already being used;
- provided an opportunity to discuss school policy which could then be raised at staff meetings.

Below are examples of typical comments by teachers about TSTs.

Staff feel now that they do not have to struggle on single-handed.

A joint approach to handling the child was agreed upon. There was open and frank dialogue with colleagues.

Teachers feel they are not alone with a problem. More people to share ideas with — more team spirit and sharing of experiences.

In particular, the study showed how the TST supported teachers' perceptions of the difficulty of a situation. A validation of the teachers' perceptions led to an enhancement in the utility of their own intervention strategies, which were reaffirmed (Norwich and Daniels, 1994).

We employed the concepts of 'teacher tolerance' and 'active engagement' as means of theorizing the relationship between TST activity and the outcomes we observed.

There is much prescription about managing schools which is relevant to SEN as well as much prescription about teaching pupils with SEN, but few specific theories about the conditions which affect the tolerance, capability and engagement of class teachers and schools in doing so. Gerber and Semmel (1985) and Gerber (1988) have developed a theoretical position on the costs to class teachers of extending their range of tolerance, which takes account of the purpose of class teaching, structural constraints and teaching resources. They suggest that, in the context of limited resources, tolerance conditions the relation between equity and excellence. In using the concept of teacher tolerance we proposed a number of theoretical assumptions. First, we suggested that pupils come to be seen by teachers as varying in their difficulty to teach and manage, and that teachers have a range of teaching tolerance for variations in attainment and social behaviour. Beyond the limits of tolerance, pupils come to be seen as unresponsive to teaching and can come to lower the teacher's perception of her/his teaching competence and therefore her/his professional self-evaluation. This can lead to feelings of insecurity and anxiety, which in turn can result in less appropriate teaching and even further unresponsiveness from pupils. By this process teachers come to see certain pupils as beyond their teaching tolerance.

Ironically, those teachers with the most effective teaching strategies for low-achieving students might be those who report that they tolerate less maladaptive behaviour in their classrooms, and that they may actively resist placement of students with SEN in their classrooms (Gersten et al., 1988: 433). Studies undertaken in the USA suggest that there is a dilemma concerning quality of instruction and access to the mainstream classroom.

> The 'effective' teachers – those with high standards and low tolerance for deviant behaviour – are those most likely to seek help in dealing with these problems. Moreover, the most successful teachers are those who efficiently use their instructional time. Therefore, one reason for the type of resistance identified in this study may be the effective teacher's attempt to guard against inefficient use of academic instructional time, which could result in an overall decreased level of student performance. If the necessary technical assistance could be provided to implement teaching models that are effective for all students, it is likely that these skilled teachers with high standards would be the first to accept students with SEN into their classrooms.
>
> (Gersten et al., 1988: 437)

What is needed to increase teaching tolerance, given the social psychological, structural, functional and resource conditions, is an organizational strategy to extend and make good use of existing teaching resources. TSTs, by enabling teachers to support each other and share their teaching competence, can provide one way to increase the range of teaching tolerance and enhance active engagement in providing quality teaching for pupils with SEN.

Our own research suggests that TSTs actually function in a much broader way than we originally thought would be the case. In some schools they may well function as supports for teachers' problem-solving far beyond the original SEN remit. TSTs utilize the sadly underused resource of the potential support that consultation and collective problem-solving can offer teachers. They also provide a way in which a school may structure and organize its response to the Code of Practice. In so doing, they may well enhance and refine the role and effectiveness of the SEN co-ordinator. TSTs may support the formulation and review of IEPs as part of the practice of offering more general support to teachers. They may help schools to establish priorities in their negotiation for external support services. Issues raised in TSTs may also feed back into the institutional and SEN policy development planning process.

Meadows (1998: 7) argued that 'collaboration with others … may make things achievable which were not – and indeed still are not – achievable by the individual acting alone. There can of course be many reasons for this social facilitation of development.' Our evaluation of TSTs reveals a range of outcomes associated with collaboration between teacher peers. As such, it can be seen to provide support for some of the more recent developments in post-Vygotskian theory. Intervention in the cultural context of the institution which seeks to alter teachers' communicative practices can make a difference to the instructional practices in classrooms. Collaborative problem-solving between teachers can provide an engine for development in schools.

References

Bazerman, C. (1997) 'Discursively structured activities', *Mind, Culture and Activity*, 4(4), 296–308.

Biott, C. (ed.) (1991) *Semi-Detached Teachers: Building Support and Advisory Relationships in Classrooms*. London: Falmer Press.

Bourne, J. and McPake, J. (1991) *Partnership Teaching: Co-operative Teaching Strategies for English Language Support in Multilingual Classrooms*. London: HMSO.

Chalfant, J.C. and Pysh, M. (1989) 'Teacher assistance teams: Five descriptive studies on 96 teams', *Remedial and Special Education*, 10(6), 49–58.

Clark, C., Dyson, A., Millward, A.J. and Skidmore, D. (1997) *New Directions in Special Needs: Innovations in Mainstream Schools*. London: Cassell.

Cochran-Smith, M. and Lytle, S.L. (1993) *Inside Outside: Teacher Research and Knowledge*. New York: Teachers College, Columbia University.

Cohen, E. (1981) 'Sociology looks at team teaching', *Research in Sociology of Education and Socialization*, 2, 163–93.

Cole, M. (1996) *Cultural Psychology: A Once and Future Discipline*. Cambridge, Mass.: Belknap Press of Harvard University.

Cole, M., Engeström, Y. and Vasquez, O. (1997) Introduction, in M. Cole, Y. Engestrom, and O. Vasquez (eds) *Mind, Culture and Activity: Seminal Papers from the Laboratory of Comparative Human Cognition*. Cambridge: Cambridge University Press.

Creese, A., Daniels, H. and Norwich, B. (1997) *Teacher Support Teams in Secondary Schools*, DfEE Report. London: Fulton.

Daniels, H. (ed.) (1996) *An Introduction to Vygotsky*. London: Routledge.

Daniels, H. and Norwich, B. (1992) *Teacher Support Teams: An Interim Evaluation Report*. London: Institute of Education, London University.

Daniels, H. and Norwich, B. (1996) 'Supporting teachers of children with special needs in ordinary schools', in G. Upton and V. Varma (eds) *Stresses in Special Educational Needs Teachers*. Aldershot: Arena.

del Rio, P. and Alvarez, A. (1995) 'Directivity: the cultural and educational constructions of morality and agency', *Anthropology and Education Quarterly*, 26(4), 384–409.

Dyson, A. (1990) 'Effective learning consultancy: a future role for special needs co-ordinators', *Support for Learning*, 5(3), 116–27.

Engeström, Y., Brown, K., Christopher, L.C. and Gregory, J. (1997) 'Co-ordination, co-operation and communication in the courts: expansive transitions in legal work', in M.C. Cole, Y. Engestom and O. Vasquez (eds) *Mind, Culture and Activity*. Cambridge: Cambridge University Press.

Eraut, M. (1994). *Developing Professional Knowledge and Competence*. London: Falmer.

Fullan, M. and Hargreaves, A. (1992) *What's Worth Fighting in Your School?* Buckingham: Open University Press/OPSTE.

Garnett, J. (1988) 'Support teaching: taking a closer look *British Journal of Special Education*, 15(1), 15–18.

Gerber, M.M. (1988) 'Tolerance and technology of instruction: implication for special education reform', *Exceptional Children*, 54(4), 309–14.

Gerber, M.M. and Semmel, M.I. (1985) 'The micro-economics of referral and re-integration: a paradigm for evaluation of special education', *Studies in Educational Evaluation*, 11, 13–29.

Gersten, R., Walker, H. and Darch, C. (1988) 'Relationship between teachers' effectiveness and their tolerance for handicapped students', *Exceptional Children*, 54(5), 433–8.

Hanko, G. (1989) 'After Elton – how to manage disruption', *British Journal of Special. Education*, 16(4), 140–3.

Hanko, G. (1990) *Special Needs in Ordinary Classrooms: Supporting Teachers*. Oxford: Blackwell.

Harris, K. (1995) 'School-based bilingual special education teacher assistance teams', *Remedial and Special Education*, 16(6), 337–43.

Hart, S. (1986) 'Evaluating support teaching', *Gnosis*, 9, 26–32.

Ivic, I. (1989) 'Profiles of educators: Lev S. Vygotsky (1896–1934)', *Prospects XIX*, 3, 427–36.

Lave, J. and Wenger, E. (1991) 'Practice, person and social world', Chapter 2 in J. Lave and E. Wenger *Situated Learning: Legitimate Peripheral Participation*. Cambridge: Cambridge University Press.

MacBeith, J., Boyd, B., Rand, J. and Bell, S. (1996). *Schools Speak for Themselves: Towards a Framework for Self-Evaluation.* London: National Union of Teachers.

Martin-Jones, M. and Saxena, M. (1989) 'Developing a partnership with bilingual classroom assistants', *Working Paper no. 16*. Lancaster: Centre for Language in Social Life, Lancaster University.

Mead, C. (1991) *A City-Wide Evaluation of PSG Training*. Birmingham: Birmingham Local Education Authority.

Meadows, S. (1998) 'Children learning to think: learning from others? Vygotskian theory and educational psychology', *Educational and Child Psychology*, 15(2), 6–13.

Miles, M.B. and Huberman, A. (1994) *Qualitative Data Analysis: An Expanded Source Book of New Methods*. London: Sage.

Minick, N., Stone, C.A. and Forman, E.A. (1993) 'Introduction: Integration of individual, social and institutional processes in accounts of children's learning and development', in E.A. Forman, N. Minick and C.A. Stone (eds) *Contexts for Learning: Sociocultural Dynamics in Children's Development*. Oxford: Oxford University Press.

Newman, D., Griffin, P. and Cole, M. (1989) *The Construction Zone: Working for Cognitive Change in Schools*. Cambridge: Cambridge University Press.

Nias, J. (1989) *Primary Teachers Talking*. London: Routledge.

Nias, J. (1993) 'Changing times, changing identities: grieving for a lost self', in R. Burgess (ed.) *Educational Research and Evaluation for Policy and Practice*. London: Falmer Press.

Norwich, B. and Daniels, H. (1994) 'Evaluating teacher support teams: a strategy for special needs in ordinary schools – final report to ESRC'. Award number R–000–23–3859.

Norwich, B. and Daniels, H. (1997) 'Teacher support teams for special educational needs in primary schools: evaluating a teacher-focused support scheme', *Educational. Studies*, 23, 5–24.

Olson, D.R. and Torrance, N. (eds) (1996) *Modes of Thought: Explorations in Culture and Cognition*. Cambridge: Cambridge University Press.

Rogers, D. and Whetton, D. (1982) *Interorganizational Coordination: Theory, Research and Implementation*. Iowa: Iowa State University.

Rosenholtz, S. (1989). *Teachers' Workplace: The Social Organization of Schools*. White Plains, NY: Longman.

Stringer, P. (1998) ' "One night Vygotsky had a dream": children learning to think ... and implications for educational psychologists', *Educational and Child Psychology*, 15(2), 14–20.

Stringer, P., Stow, L., Hibbert, K., Powell, J. and Louw, E. (1992) 'Establishing staff consultation groups in schools', *Educational Psychology in Practice*, 8(2), 87–96.

Visser, J. and Upton, G. (1993) *Special Education in Britain after Warnock*. London: Fulton.

Vygotsky, L.S. (1978) *Mind in Society: The Development of Higher Psychological Processes*. Cambridge, MA: Harvard University Press.

Woods, P. (1993) *Critical Events in Teaching and Learning*. London: Falmer Press.

11 School Support Services and School Improvement

Paul Timmins

Introduction

Special Educational Needs Co-ordinators (SENCOs) play a major role in the implementation of the Code of Practice (DfE, 1994) which informs the way in which schools support pupils with special educational needs. Research shows that responding to the requirements of the Code has not been without its problems for SENCOs. Surveys (Evans et al., 1996; Lewis et al., 1996; DfEE, 1997) indicate that SENCOs feel they are required to carry out their duties with insufficient time and resources and that their teacher colleagues have an inadequate understanding of the Code and its implications for their work in the classroom. Evans et al. (1996) also found SENCOs were most satisfied with their role where they received full support from their senior management team (SMT) for the implementation of the Code and a whole school approach to special educational needs (SENs). This chapter describes an approach to the improvement of SEN systems which attempted to address many of these difficulties.

A study designed to support a group of SENCOs in the development of their school SEN systems and the implementation of the Code of Practice was carried out in 1994. Approaches used in the study were informed by a whole school approach to SEN (Dessent, 1987; Ainscow and Florek, 1989) and concepts and practices informing the role of the SENCO presented in the literature (Dyson, 1990, 1991; DfE, 1994). These also incorporated insights from the school improvement literature which identified processes associated with effective change and development and mechanisms for improving the quality of teaching and learning in schools.

A novel feature of the study was the use of a cross-school support group approach. This involved SENCOs and local education authority (LEA) support service staff (educational psychologists and advisory teachers) in regular group meetings, in the course of a school year. This group provided a structure for the author and support service staff to introduce processes which informed the development of school SEN systems. Meetings also enabled participants to share their experiences of completing this work in schools. A review of the research on groups of this nature had indicated that they had the potential to enhance professional skills and reduce the stresses and strains associated with many work contexts (Mead and Timmins, 1993).

Part of the evaluation of the work carried out in schools is described in this chapter. This includes the impact of the study on the development of schools' SEN systems, and the extent to which the school improvement model developed to support SENCOs in their SEN system development was implemented (School Improvement Model for SEN – SIMSEN). The results of the evaluation are discussed in terms of the value of a support group approach as a vehicle for LEAs and support services to support school improvement; the strengths and weaknesses of SIMSEN in practice; and the range of SEN development work stimulated in schools as a result of participation in the study.

The section below outlines features of the whole school approach to SEN and the role of the SENCO. These aspects of the literature informed the development of SIMSEN.

The Whole School Approach to SEN and the Role of the SENCO

Dessent (1987) described the nature of the work to be carried out in mainstream schools to develop the whole school approach to SEN. One key principle he identified was the notion that all teachers needed to be responsible for teaching pupils with SENs in their classrooms. Dessent (1987) noted that in order to attain this ideal, schools needed a coherent plan which ensured that teachers received appropriate training and resources. Perhaps in response to Dessent's stimulus, there followed a flurry of publications which attempted to elaborate further the nature of support schools required to establish a whole school approach to SEN. Much of this identified the challenges and roles to be pursued by SENCOs, who had become identified as key players in the promotion of the whole school approach. For example, Dyson (1990) identified the need for Learning Consultants (SENCOs) who would determine the core teaching skills required to support pupils with SENs in the classroom, and ensure that teachers received training in these.

Prior to Dessent's work, the National Association for Remedial Education (NARE, 1985) developed an influential prescription for the role of the SENCO. This included a role in the management of SEN resources, planning educational programmes for pupils to enhance their access to the curriculum, and support and training for teachers to help them meet SENs in the classroom. The introduction of the Code of Practice (DfE, 1994) gave SENCOs a clear role in SEN resource management in schools; in particular, it provided guidance on essential elements of SEN policy. Subsequent appreciation of the difficulties SENCOs experienced implementing the Code and the whole school approach led to the notion of greater SMT involvement in

SEN system development and maintenance (Dyson and Gains, 1995; Clark et al., 1997).

The recently published Teacher Training Agency National Standards for SENCOs (TTA, 1998) will be used to inform training initiatives for SENCOs and reflect the notion that they need to be equipped to play a strategic role in SEN resource management and system development. It will also be used to help teachers to improve the quality of teaching and learning on a school-wide basis.

The SIMSEN approach, described in greater detail below, provides SENCOs with a framework for sharing SEN responsibilities with their SMTs and reinforces and encourages the further development of many of the key day-to-day aspects of the SENCO's role, as described in the Code (DfE, 1994) and by NARE (1985). It also includes a strategic process capable of improving the quality of teaching and learning in schools.

The next section introduces some of the principles of school improvement incorporated in the SIMSEN approach, particularly ones thought to stimulate improvements in the quality of teaching and learning in schools.

School Improvement: The Cambridge Institute of Education Approach

Writers and researchers at the Cambridge Institute of Education have been influential in the field of school improvement in the UK. They developed the School Development Planning approach which received the support of the government via a booklet sent to all schools (Hargreaves et al., 1989). This, and a later book (Hargreaves and Hopkins, 1994) provided schools with a 'how to do it' orientation to school improvement. The authors maintained that their approach enabled schools to manage change and development at a time when they were required to respond rapidly to a plethora of government guidance and legislation. Hargreaves and Hopkins described School Development Planning in the following manner:

> Development planning encourages governors, heads and staff (teachers and support staff) to ask four basic questions:
> * Where is the school now?
> * What changes do we need to make?
> * How shall we manage these changes over time?
> * How shall we know whether our management of change has been successful?

Development planning helps the school to provide practical answers to these questions. This will, of course, itself take time and energy; the gain is that the school is enabled to arrange what it is already doing and what it needs to do in a more purposeful and coherent way.

The distinctive feature of a development plan is that it brings together, in an overall plan, national and LEA policies and initiatives, the school's aims and values, its existing achievements and its need for development.

(Hargreaves and Hopkins, 1991: 3)

Phases of the school development planning cycle are shown in Figure 11.1.

In later work, as a result of applying their model in some thirty or so schools, the Cambridge group (Hopkins et al., 1994) presented further perspectives on school improvement. Their aim was to 'produce and evaluate a model of school development and a programme of support that strengthens a school's ability to provide high quality education for all its pupils by building upon existing good practice' (p. 7).

This aim was closely associated with their notion of school improvement which they defined as 'A distinct approach to educational change that enhances student outcomes as well as strengthening the school's capacity for managing change' (p. 3).

Figure 11.1   The development planning cycle

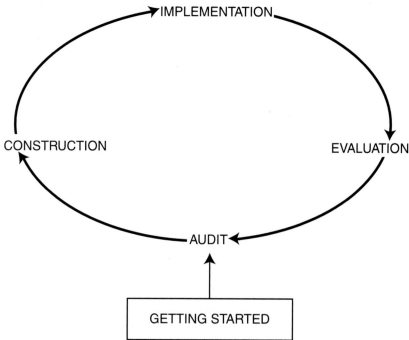

Source: Hargreaves et al., 1989: 5.

They recognized the role played by school structure and culture in improving schools and sought to influence these features through their notion of Management Arrangements, which they defined in the following manner:

> Management Arrangements [are divided] into three analytically distinct dimensions ... *Frameworks* consist of structures that any school has to establish, such as means of devising organizational aims and policies, a system for decision making and communication; mechanisms to allow members to meet and co-ordinate their activities. *Roles* refer to the relationships between members and partners – the expectations held by and towards people involved, the allocation of responsibilities, the groupings of people. *Working together* refers to the quality or character of relationships: the nature and extent of co-operation or conflict, the forms of leadership and styles of management.
>
> (Hopkins et al. 1994: 19)

Their model included further concepts felt to be important in shaping the school improvement process and bringing about an improvement culture, these being Priorities, Strategies and Conditions.

Priorities identified key areas for school improvement. Schools determined these by harmonizing the outcomes of internal audits of school need with external pressures for change stemming from legislation, etc. For example, an internal audit might suggest that teachers experience difficulty with differentiation for SEN in Maths; at the same time, there might be government pressure to introduce a Numeracy Hour in schools. In response, a school priority might be based on differentiation for SEN, in the context of the national Numeracy Hour.

Priorities are addressed through Strategies. Strategies are informed by knowledge of factors presumed to enhance a school's capacity to manage change. Aspects of internal organization which may be influenced by Strategies are highlighted in the five principles presented below and Management Arrangements. Strategies need to impact on the following levels of school life:

- *the whole school*   policy development; the management needs of the school; resources and approaches to staff development for school improvement;
- *the working group*   the development of collaborative working arrangements to plan, implement and review improvement activities;
- *the individual teacher* a focus on developing practice in the classroom.

The Conditions feature provides a framework for self-evaluation derived from the structures and processes associated with improving and effective schools. The Conditions review includes an analysis of leadership style, strategies for co-ordinating development initiatives, staff and student involvement in decision-making, staff development practices and the status given to inquiry and reflection in school. This analysis suggests further areas for school development within the framework provided by Priorities and Strategies.

The need for evaluation is stressed in the Cambridge model, and schools are encouraged to construct success criteria for their Priorities, with a particular focus on student and teacher outcomes. In addition, success criteria are necessary in relation to Conditions and Strategies, 'in order to monitor how well the school as a whole is building its capacity to manage change' (Hopkins et al., 1994: 207).

Hopkins et al. (1994: 102) describe five principles they feel give a sense of philosophical coherence to their model of school improvement and which they feel are 'likely to provide quality education and enhanced outcomes for pupils' (p. 101). These provide an additional framework for appreciating the association between core school improvement processes, staff development and the quality of the educational experience:

1   The vision of the school (the school in the future) should be one to which all members of the school community have an opportunity to contribute, and most will seek to.
2   The school, because it has its vision, will see in external pressures for change important opportunities to secure its internal priorities.
3   The school will seek to create and maintain conditions in which all members of the school's community can learn successfully.
4   The school will seek to adapt and develop structures which encourage collaboration and lead to the empowerment of individuals and groups.
5   The school will seek to promote the view that the monitoring and evaluation of quality is a responsibility in which all members of staff share.

The Need for External Support for School Improvement

School effectiveness and school improvement studies suggest that external support is an important factor in successful school improvement (Mortimore, 1991; Levine, 1992). This finding informed the stance taken by Hopkins et al. (1994) in their implementation of the school improvement model described above. They formed groups comprising LEA support service representatives and university and trained school staff, to support each school in their study. These facilitated the improvement process and provided INSET for school. Hopkins et al.'s (1994) approach suggests that relatively complex mechanisms are at work in the effective and improving school, and that development initiatives need to be based on a careful analysis of a school's internal functioning. They maintain that this work is best facilitated by external professionals with appropriate knowledge and skills, working in partnership with school staff.

Another strategy for supporting school improvement, equivalent to a whole LEA approach, was developed in Canada in the Halton Effective Schools Project (Stoll and Fink, 1996). This resulted in school board-wide support for schools. Here, school board administrators, school principals and an educational researcher worked collaboratively to examine the school improvement literature and from this to develop the Halton approach to school improvement. This model was used by schools to determine their priorities for development work. This was then supported in a variety of ways by school board administrators. Advantages of this approach included a language of school improvement shared by the entire school board and the enhanced ability of the board to make a strategic response to needs identified by its schools.

At the time of writing, the Secretary of State for Education and Employment is promoting the notion of LEA involvement in school improvement, and pragmatism at least may motivate them to consider their role in this area. LEAs considering how to work in this manner will need to give thought to ways in which effective forms of relating and communicating are to be engineered in order to best support schools in their work. The framework designed to introduce the SIMSEN approach to schools provides an example of how LEAs might support school improvement.

External Support for the Implementation of the SIMSEN Approach

At the time the SIMSEN approach was being planned, it seemed unlikely that many LEAs in the UK would have had the resources necessary to replicate the strategic approach taken in the Halton study. One factor here was the erosion in staffing levels associated with financial delegation. An effort was therefore made to identify the processes of support for school improvement likely to be effective under the conditions of stringency prevailing in LEAs at that time. (That is, approaches which could be implemented easily within the service delivery capacities of the educational psychology and advisory teacher services involved in the study.)

A form of support which could be organized relatively easily was a multi-professional support group involving educational psychologists (EPs), advisory teachers (ATs) and senior school staff. Mead and Timmins (1993) considered the research on similar groups (peer support groups) and their benefits to participants. Most of the studies they identified had the modest goal of supporting group members' professional development within a single institution, rather than being concerned with the development of the whole institution. The authors discussed the nature of the support processes operating in peer support groups, and noted the similarity between the findings for professional-skills oriented support groups and more traditional support groups, such as those attended by the bereaved, phobics, alcoholics, etc. They indicated that group members experienced improvements in personal confidence and their sense of agency and competence. These outcomes were associated with group processes which included sharing information, giving and receiving guidance and advice, social companionship and emotional support, these being facilitated by the level of open and shared communication attained in the groups.

An Overview of the SIMSEN Approach and its Introduction to Schools

The SIMSEN approach provided an annual cycle of activity for the development of school SEN systems. Each phase of the approach is described in Figure 11.2. Work associated with the phases was to be co-ordinated by SENCOs and their SMTs. Ideal dates for completing each phase are also given in Figure 11.2.

A survey for gathering information on staff and pupil development needs was an important feature of the SIMSEN approach. This was adapted from the System Supplied Information approach to school improvement (Myers et al., 1989). This allowed pupils' needs to be assessed in areas of functioning such as literacy, numeracy, communication and social skills, study skills, general behaviour and physical skills. Teachers were able to provide survey data on their class groups in 5–10 minutes when familiar with the survey schedule. The manner in which survey data were collated and prioritized allowed staff development needs and pupils in need of extra support to be identified.

Capitalizing on the anticipated value of a support group approach, the implementation of the SIMSEN approach was supported through a series of meetings (Special Needs Development Group – SNDG) attended by SENCOs and where possible by a member of their SMT. EPs and ATs attached to each SENCO's school also attended SNDG meetings and helped to facilitate them. An advantage of having school support staff present was that they were familiar with their 'patch school' contexts and were therefore well placed to support SENCOs and their SMTs in the implementation of the SIMSEN approach. The main content of each of the SNDG meetings is described in Table 11.1. There were mini-presentations for each topic listed in this table, and opportunities for SENCOs to discuss these and in particular the implementation of the Code of Practice. Eight SNDG meetings, lasting between 1.25 and 1.50 hours were held, these being well attended. Meetings were scheduled to allow the presentation and discussion of a particular phase of the SIMSEN approach, just before it was to be implemented in school. (See dates for SNDG meetings in Table 11.1.) Members of

Figure 11.2 The SIMSEN process

1 Planning the year's work (by June/September)
Time and resources protected for:
- setting, attaining and evaluating targets for SEN system development;
- implementing remaining six phases of SIMSEN
- meeting staff development needs identified by survey;
- meeting needs of individual pupils with SENs identified by survey.

2 Introducing all school staff to the 7-phase process (by late September)
Staff meeting held to:
- describe SIMSEN and discuss issues raised;
- introduce and describe survey;
- explain how survey would be used to identify staff development needs;
- explain how survey would help identify pupils' needs;
- reinforce and explain school SEN policy in particular staff roles in the school-based stages of the *Code of Practice.*

3 Conduct survey and retrieve survey sheets from all school staff (by early October)

4 Collate survey returns (by mid-October)
From collated survey data identify:
- potential areas for staff development;
- pupils who may be in need of SEN support;
- any need for staff working groups related to issues raised by survey data.

5 Discuss collated data in meeting with school staff (by end October)
Present collated data showing potential areas for staff development and pupils in need of SEN support. Discuss and agree:
- priorities for staff development and methods for addressing these (e.g. INSET or school improvement task-groups);
- pupils to receive additional SEN support and where possible approaches to be used.

6 • Prepare, then implement, plans for addressing staff and pupil needs agreed with staff in phase 5 (by mid-November)
Plans to include time-scales, methods and frameworks for evaluating:
- any staff development needs to be addressed;
- impact of SEN support provided for pupils with SEN.

7 Review use of SIMSEN process with school staff (by mid-June)
With future use of SIMSEN in mind, review:
- outcomes achieved through implementing phase 6 of SIMSEN:
- overall SIMSEN process;
- any outstanding aspects of school SEN policy.

the SNDG received a manual which described how to implement the approach in school and materials to support the introduction of the Code.

SENCOs were invited to secure the support of key senior staff for the implementation of the SIMSEN approach, this being a factor associated with successful school improvement. Specifically, they were encouraged to set up an SEN co-ordinating group in their schools to share planning and development work associated with the initiative. This group was to include a member of the school's SMT, the professional development tutor, the school SEN governor and possibly a member of the school support services.

Six primary and four secondary SENCOs opted to participate in the study

Table 11.1 The timing and content of SNDG meetings and examples of processes of school improvement

Time-scale for SNDG meetings	Content of SNDG meetings	Examples of school improvement processes introduced in study
June	Present and discuss phase 1 of SIMSEN including: • Overview of work to be carried out during study • Protecting time and resources • Process for determining targets for SEN system development • Enlisting SMT and school staff support for work in school	• Priorities, Strategies, Conditions • Protecting time and resources for audit, implementation and evaluation processes • Management Arrangements, particularly Working Together
Early September	Present and discuss phase 2 of SIMSEN and: • Share targets for SEN system development	• Priorities and linked Strategies • Evaluation • Management Arrangements
Mid September	• Discuss implementation of Code of Practice • Discuss development of SEN policy	• Management Arrangements, particularly Frameworks and Working Together
End September	Present and discuss phases 3 and 4 of SIMSEN including: • Prioritizing from survey data • SEN record-keeping	• Interpretation of survey data • Further consideration of Priorities, Strategies and Conditions
Early November	Present and discuss phases 5 of SIMSEN including: • Addressing prioritized staff and pupil needs • Effective methods for addressing pupils' SENs	• Staff development to improve quality of teaching and learning

Time-scale for SNDG meetings	Content of SNDG meetings	Examples of school improvement processes introduced in study
Mid November	Present and discuss phase 6 of SIMSEN including: • Evaluation of initiatives and SEN policy • Sharing action plans for staff and pupils • Further discussion of SEN policy	Evaluation of: • School improvement work carried out • Management Arrangements • SIMSEN process
Mid May	Present and discuss phase 7 of SIMSEN including: • Structure for staff meeting to review SIMSEN process and SEN policy • Sharing outcomes attained to date in each school	• Evaluation, Priorities, Strategies, Conditions and Management Arrangements
Early July	Discuss: • Strengths and weaknesses of SIMSEN as used in schools • Proposals for future use of SIMSEN in participants' schools	

after seeing it advertised in the LEA INSET booklet. There was no contract relating to the extent of each school's involvement with the SIMSEN approach, attendance at SNDG meetings or the level of support to be provided between SNDG meetings by EPs and ATs, although schools were encouraged to take advantage of these forms of support. This approach contrasted with the more time-intensive input provided in Hopkins et al.'s (1994) work. They required schools to agree to implement specific school improvement processes in return for training and ongoing support from themselves and other professionals.

The Evaluation of the SIMSEN Approach

The evaluation was based on information gained from questionnaires and interviews completed by SENCOs and members of the school support services involved in the study. Full details of the studies can be found in Timmins, 1998. An illuminative approach (Parlett, 1981) was taken to the design of the evaluation. The evaluation resulted in descriptions of the implementation of the SIMSEN approach in each school and explored SENCO and school support service staff perceptions of the strengths and weaknesses of this and the study processes used to support its implementation. The evaluation also explored the nature of SEN work carried out in schools and the extent to which SENCOs and support staff were able to work together to implement the SIMSEN approach. The section below describes some of the questions addressed in the study and associated findings. Here, a distinction is made between the implementation of each phase of the SIMSEN process and the structural changes in school SEN systems supported by the study. The latter work is taken to be SEN system development work, although of course the implementation of the approach could also be viewed as SEN system development.

The Implementation of the SIMSEN Approach and Improvements to the Quality of Teaching and Learning in Schools

Schools found it relatively easy to implement phases 1–6 of the SIMSEN process (see Figure 11.2). Phase 7, the evaluation of the SIMSEN process and outcomes, was least well implemented. Only two schools involved all school staff in this process, though four more of the schools recognized the importance of the review and two of these carried out a partial review. This finding suggested that discussion of the SIMSEN evaluation process in the SNDG and manual had not had sufficient impact on schools. Difficulties faced by schools in this respect were echoed in research on approaches to school development planning conducted by MacGilchrist et al. (1995). They found that even among schools nominated for their interest in school development planning there were only weak structures for evaluating development plans.

Of particular interest was the finding that all ten of the SENCOs had provided or intended to provide staff INSET based on survey results; these initiatives included differentiation, study skills for Key Stage 1, the teaching of spelling and reading, and behaviour management. In Hopkins et al.'s (1994) model of school improvement, staff development is organized in a manner which enhances the quality of teaching and learning in school and has a planned-for impact in classrooms. It represents an investment in a school's future ability to support pupils with SENs and underpins the whole school approach.

Eight SENCOs felt that the SIMSEN cycle repeated over a period of three years or so had the ability to improve the quality of teaching and learning in their schools, and all schools in the study used the survey data to determine SEN provision for pupils. These findings underline the potential of the SIMSEN approach for supporting school improvement and the whole school approach to SEN.

The Nature of SEN System Development Work Carried Out by Schools

A total of 29 targets for SEN system development were set by the ten schools. Each school worked on at least 2 targets, these being agreed with their SMT. There was clear documentary evidence that at least 19 of the targets had been attained by schools. The most common targets were Code of Practice-related, and included the development of SEN policy, Code-related record-keeping systems for individual education programmes, the development of SEN registers and raising staff awareness of the Code. Nine of the schools developed their SEN policy during the course of the year. SENCOs were also asked to complete rating scales which indicated the extent to which they felt that participation in the study had helped them to progress these targets and their degree of satisfaction with this work. For 19 of the 29 targets, SENCOs felt that they had made more progress through participation in the study than they would have made working alone. For 21 of the 29 targets, they were either satisfied or highly satisfied with the work they had carried out.

SENCOs' Perceptions of Benefits of the SNDG, the Manual and Implementing the SIMSEN Approach

The main benefit of implementing the SIMSEN approach was seen as its ability to support the development of school SEN systems and its compatibility with the Code of Practice. Nine SENCOs made comments concerning the support provided for SEN system development by the processes of the SNDG group. They valued the opportunities provided by the group for the discussion of SEN issues and for sharing concerns. They also felt they received support from other SENCOs. Many also mentioned the value of sharing SEN materials circulated by members of the group. In response to a direct question, eight SENCOs felt that they had increased their sense of competence in their ability to fulfil their role as a result of participation in the study. Additional responses to this question suggested that SNDG processes made a significant contribution to this feeling. Half of the SENCOs made comments in the interviews which revealed more personal benefits associated with participation in the study. Examples included increased feelings of confidence and an increased sense of confidence and status in relation to their roles in school.

The manual was viewed as being particularly useful for supporting SEN target-setting between SENCOs and their SMTs and for organizing the survey of staff and pupil needs.

SENCOs' Perceptions of Hindrances to the Implementation of the SIMSEN Approach

Six of the SENCOs perceived class teachers to be under too much pressure to implement the Code, a specific issue being a lack of availability of training relating to the implications of the Code for teachers and their role with pupils with SENs in the classroom. EPs also identified these issues. Four

SENCOs mentioned a lack of time and resources to complete SEN development work and to evaluate pupils' individual educational plans (IEPs). Three SENCOs mentioned problems in their communications with their SMT regarding the implications of the Code for school. EPs also commented on this difficulty.

Four SENCOs indicated that the survey identified too many pupils in need of SEN support. EPs also noted this difficulty. This issue was addressed in the manual and through an exercise introduced during an SNDG meeting. It was not clear whether these SENCOs had failed to take advantage of this support or had failed in spite of the guidance available. One of these SENCOs, who worked in a large secondary school, subsequently resolved this difficulty by using the prioritization process described in the manual. The problem of large numbers of pupils being identified by the survey was thought likely to be encountered in schools where class teachers had not accepted their responsibility for developing or sharing the development of IEPs (an important aspect of the whole school approach and the Code).

EP and AT Support for the Implementation of SIMSEN in Schools

Support for the introduction of phase 2 of the SIMSEN approach was provided for five schools. Of these, one school involved school support staff in INSET and another in phase 5. (This support was in addition to that provided through support service participation in SNDG meetings.)

EP and AT Perceptions of the Benefits of the SIMSEN Approach for Schools

Many of the benefits identified by SENCOs were echoed by the educational psychologists. In six schools they noted support for structuring and developing SEN systems, in three schools they noted an enhanced role and status for SENCOs, and in four schools there was an improved relationship between themselves and SENCOs.

What Part did SENCOs' School Colleagues Play in Supporting the Implementation of the SIMSEN Approach?

The most common form of support from school SMTs (in six schools) was for the implementation of phase 2. In three schools, SMTs were involved in phase 5. At the beginning of the study year, six SENCOs were already part of, or had set up as a result of the study, SEN co-ordinating groups in schools. Only two of these SENCOs provided information on how these groups supported the SIMSEN process in the course of the study. This suggests that the approach may provide a framework for sharing SEN management responsibility in schools.

Conclusions

Conclusions drawn from the study are limited by the illuminative nature of the evaluation (Parlett, 1981). Limited research resources prevented comparisons being made between schools participating in the study and those developing their SEN systems without this support. In addition, it was not possible to baseline features of schools' SEN systems and school improvement processes prior to their participation in the study. In spite of these limitations, the following conclusions were drawn.

SENCOs and school support service staff felt that the SNDG process supported the development of their school SEN systems and the implementation of the SIMSEN approach. The group also provided professional and personal support for participants. Given the relatively small amount of time taken by SNDG meetings, the approach was felt to be an effective vehicle for supporting the early stages of school improvement initiatives and involving school support staff in some aspects of school improvement. The general approach is therefore worthy of consideration when LEAs are planning their involvement in school improvement, though a more strategic approach, such as that employed in the Halton Schools project (Stoll and Fink, 1996), provides a further important dimension to this work.

In the study, in Hopkins et al.'s (1994) terms, there was clearly scope for more support for the improvement of the internal processes they associated with the improving school. A means of gaining this support would be to extend the life of the SNDG, with more attention being paid to school improvement processes, particularly the issue of evaluation, as this phase of the SIMSEN approach was least well implemented by schools. Further support was engineered in a more limited fashion at the end of the study, when SENCOs and support service staff were encouraged to set up their own school cluster meetings to discuss SEN issues. Many still hold these meetings.

Difficulties encountered in the study included a lack of staff training for SEN responsibilities and communication between some SENCOs and their SMTs regarding SEN issues. In future work of this nature, at phase 1 of the SIMSEN process, it would be useful for support service staff to work with participating schools to audit school Conditions, these being the processes which support successful school improvement (Hopkins et al., 1994). This approach would involve, among other things, an exploration of staff development issues and strategies and relationships in school. Developments in these areas could then become part of the Priorities set for school work through the SIMSEN process and be supported in a focused manner by school support service staff. Some of the relationship issues between SENCOs, their SMTs and school staff which surfaced in the study were thought to require skilled mediation. A Conditions audit might have identified these and enabled more effective SEN development work to be carried out. These issues suggest a need for more school support service involvement in school improvement work than was identified in the study, as the issues and support implied are likely to need sensitive handling. School support service staff, particularly educational psychologists, have the skills necessary to play a part in providing this support, by virtue of their training and close and frequent working in schools.

References

Ainscow, M. and Florek, A. (eds) (1989) *Special Educational Needs: Towards a Whole School Approach.* London: David Fulton.

Clark, C., Dyson, A., Millward, A. and Skidmore, D. (1997) *New Directions in Special Needs: Innovations in Mainstream Schools.* London: Cassell.

Department for Education (1994) *Code of Practice on the Identification and Assessment of Special Educational Needs.* London: DfE.

Department for Education and Employment (1997) *The SENCO Guide. Good Practice for SENCOs. Individual Education Plans. Developing SEN Policies in Schools.* London: HMSO.

Dessent, T. (1987) *Making the Ordinary School Special.* London: Falmer Press.

Dyson, A. (1990) 'Effective learning consultancy: a future role for special needs co-ordinators?' *Support for Learning*, 5(3), 116–27.

Dyson, A. (1991) 'Rethinking roles, rethinking concepts: special needs teachers in mainstream schools', *Support for Learning*, 6(2), 51–60.

Dyson, A. and Gains, C. (1995) 'The role of the special needs co-ordinator: poisoned chalice or crock of gold?' *Support for Learning*, 10(2), 50–6.

Evans, R., Docking, J. and Evans, C. (1996) 'Improving support for children with special needs', *Support for Learning*, 11(3), 99–104.

Hargreaves, D. and Hopkins, D. (1991) *The Empowered School: The Management and Practice of School Development Planning.* London: Cassell.

Hargreaves, D. and Hopkins, D. (1994) *Development Planning for School Improvement.* London: Cassell.

Hargreaves, D., Hopkins, D., Leask, M., Connolly, J. and Robinson, P. (1989) *Planning for School Development.*London: Department of Education and Science.

Hopkins, D., Ainscow, M. and West, M. (1994) *School Improvement in an ERA of Change.* London: Cassell.

Levine, D. (1992) 'An interpretive review of US research and practice dealing with unusually effective schools', in D. Reynolds and P. Cuttance (eds) *School Effectiveness: Research Policy and Practice.* London: Cassell.

Lewis, A., Neill, St J. and Campbell, J. (1996) *The Implementation of the Code of Practice in Primary and Secondary Schools: A National Survey of the Perceptions of Special Educational Needs Co-ordinators.* London: National Union of Teachers.

MacGilchrist, B., Mortimore, P., Savage, J. and Beresford, C. (1995) *Planning Matters: The Impact of Development Planning in Primary Schools.* London: Paul Chapman Publishing.

Mead, C. and Timmins, P. (1993) 'Peer-support groups and whole-school development', in K. Bovair, and C. McCloughlin (eds) *Counselling in Schools*. London: David Fulton.

Mortimore, P. (1991) 'The nature and findings of research on school effectiveness in the primary sector', in S. Riddell and S. Brown (eds) *School Effectiveness Research: Its Messages for School Improvement.* Edinburgh: HMSO.

Myers, M., Cherry, C., Timmins, P., Brzezinska, H., Miller P. and Willey, R. (1989) 'System supplied information (SSI): how to assess needs and plan effectively within schools/colleges', *Educational Psychology in Practice*, 5(2), 91–6.

National Association for Remedial Education (1985). *Guidelines 6: Teaching Roles for Special Educational Needs.* Stafford: NARE.

OFSTED (Office for Standards in Education) (1996) *The Implementation of the Code of Practice for Pupils with Special Educational Needs: A Report from the Office of Her Majesty's Chief Inspector of Schools.* London: HMSO.

Parlett, M. (1981) 'Illuminative evaluation', in P. Reason and J. Rowan (eds) *Human Inquiry: A Sourcebook of New Paradigm Research*. Chichester: John Wiley.

Stoll, L. and Fink, D. (1996) *Changing Our Schools*. Buckingham: Open University Press.

Teacher Training Agency (1998) *National Standards for Special Educational Needs Co-ordinators*. London: Teacher Training Agency.

Timmins, P. (1998) 'Developing schools' special educational needs support systems using a cross-school, multi-professional and peer-support group approach'. PhD thesis, University of Birmingham School of Education.

12 Peer and Cross-Age Tutoring and Mentoring Schemes

Francis Mallon

Introduction

World-wide there is evidently massive interest in the use of peer tutoring within education systems. An Internet search using the words 'peer tutoring' on the Altavista search engine recently resulted in 361,329 matches. A brief sample of the websites revealed entries from a huge number of countries. Similarly, academic library searches uncover a host of research programmes testifying to the efficacy of peer tutoring and to a wide variety of applications in primary, secondary and higher education, in business and commerce and in all the professions.

Yet as a practising educational psychologist, this author continues to cause surprise when advocating to teachers approaches which include peer tutoring as potential solutions to problems they refer. Reactions span from apparent surprise at the 'novelty' of the idea; through concerns about the practicalities, particularly with certain pupil populations; ethical considerations about 'education on the cheap'; to fears that while tutees might gain, tutors may be held back or miss out on aspects of the curriculum. Clearly not all are convinced. Yet the literature and research contain powerful evidence not only for the potency of peer tutoring as an approach but for the positive benefits to both tutors and tutees. In reviewing the literature and considering in detail one radical approach which specifically targets disaffected adolescents as tutors, the Valued Youth Program (Cardenas et al., 1992), it is hoped that more teacher colleagues will be stimulated to consider possible applications of peer or cross-age tutoring.

An Historical Perspective

The process of transferring skills or knowledge from peers who possess such to those who do not must date from the earliest days of humankind (see, e.g. Jenkins and Jenkins, 1987). It is our immense capacity to learn from one another, together with the power of language, that has made *Homo sapiens* the most successful and best adapted species on the planet. Descriptions of educational practice in ancient Rome and in early Judaism have features we might recognize as peer tutoring (Topping, 1988) and we know that monitors were used in Elizabethan classrooms (Seaborne, 1966).

Most authors, however, accept that the earliest systematic use of a system whereby peers were used in formal teaching was by Andrew Bell, a school superintendent in Madras, India, who saw the potential power of children teaching children (Bell, 1797). Bell established elaborate hierarchies whereby in each class there were pairings of tutors and pupils, typically twelve more able pupils paired with twelve less able, with an assistant teacher who instructed and supervised tutors. In turn, the assistants were overseen by teachers who had overall responsibility for pupil progress and classroom discipline. However, the assistants and teachers themselves were aged between 7 and 14 years of age! The hierarchies were completed by sub-ushers and ushers, who were ultimately responsible to schoolmasters. Thus we have in Bell's system both peer and cross-age tutoring. Bell was a truly remarkable educator who recognized the many advantages of peer tutoring, not only in terms of educational progress but in the improved self-esteem of all involved and the accruing improved discipline in classroom and school as a whole. Over two hundred years ago, he realized that, far from being held back in his studies, 'the tutor far more efficiently learns his lesson than if he had not to teach it to another. By teaching he is well taught' (Bell, 1797). As will be apparent from the research quoted below, this observation has since been confirmed empirically, time and time again.

Joseph Lancaster opened a school in Southwark in 1798, eventually catering for 350 boys. He adopted and developed Bell's system, establishing classes each of which had a monitor, an able pupil with superior knowledge of the subject matter (Lancaster, 1803). Large classes also had assistant monitors. Interestingly, Lancaster saw the monitor role as not being to teach so much as to ensure the pupils taught each other. Thus a monitor would not correct a mistake but would ensure another pupil offered a correction (Goodlad and Hirst, 1989). Lancaster grouped pupils by ability in individual subjects, further sub-dividing these into smaller groups, each with a monitor. Lancaster also reported improvements in behaviour among monitors, concluding that 'the best way to form them is to make monitors of them'.

From these beginnings the monitorial system flourished throughout the nineteenth century, but with the increasing professionalism of teaching and increased state aid to education, it waned in the early twentieth century. Topping (1988) comments that peer tutoring projects continued on a small scale but have made a great resurgence since the 1960s through concerns about under-achievement and the perceived benefits of individualized instruction. The use of peers or older pupils as tutors represented an economical means of achieving more individualization of teaching.

So What Are Peer Tutoring, Cross-Age Tutoring and Mentoring?

Damon and Phelps (1989) define peer tutoring as 'an approach in which one child instructs another child'; but they go on to say 'in material on which the first is an expert and the second is a novice'. Clearly, there are numerous successful projects where peer tutors demonstrably are not expert in the subject matter yet produce positive outcomes for tutors and tutees. (See, for example, Scruggs and Osguthorpe, 1986, and Cook et al., 1986, where studies with learning disabled tutors are described.) The earlier part of the Damon and Phelps definition will suffice for this chapter. While there is considerable literature describing the reciprocal benefits of students in further or higher education tutoring school-age pupils (e.g. Goodlad, 1995), the focus here will be on school-age tutors and mentors.

Many authors and researchers do not make a distinction between peer and cross-age tutoring. In this chapter the distinction will be applied in that peer tutoring will refer to tutors who are approximately the same age as their tutees, while cross-age tutors are older than their tutees. Topping (1987) makes reference to 'reciprocal tutoring', where peers are the same age and with similar abilities, an approach which is receiving increasing attention. A related area is that of 'peer collaboration', where children are approximately at the same competency level and collaborate on tasks to seek solutions (Damon and Phelps, 1989b). While research in this area is promising, Wood and O'Malley (1996) were concerned that observational studies show that this approach did not produce the promised benefits in the classroom. In general, therefore, when referring to both peer and cross-age tutoring, there will be a focus on curriculum areas with the tutor helping one or more tutees to learn subject matter.

Mentoring involves providing a positive role model to another and acting as an informal guide (Donaldson and Topping, 1996) sometimes with a focus particularly on life skills (Goodlad, 1995). Sometimes this role may be extended and include informal or formal *peer counselling* (Cowie and Sharp, 1996). This invariably involves mentors being provided with initial training in counselling and on-going support.

Peer and Cross-age Tutoring Programmes/Approaches

It is a virtual impossibility to synthesize the vast research literature concerning children teaching children, but in the following section an attempt has been made to give the reader a flavour of the many creative uses of peer tutors and the research outcomes.

Academic Skills

Topping's seminal book, *The Peer Tutoring Handbook* (Topping, 1988) remains an excellent introduction to and overview of research in peer tutoring. He describes many projects which involve children helping to develop literacy and numeracy skills, stressing the importance of providing tutors with some basic training but emphasizing that this need not be lengthy nor involve extensive monitoring. A preferred methodology is *paired reading* (Topping, 1986; Morgan, 1986) which is acquired rapidly and used relatively easily by tutors. Another approach frequently used in peer tutoring programmes is 'Pause, Prompt and Praise', which Wheldall and Mettem (1985) demonstrated could be used effectively by tutors after only sixty minutes of training.

Quoting the most extensive review of academic research available at that time by Sharpley and Sharpley (1981), Topping (1986) reported that reading was most frequently chosen as the subject of peer tutoring approaches, 'with varying degrees of success'. This and other reviews (e.g. Feldman et al. (1976), Goodlad (1979) and Ehly and Larsen (1980)), while generally reporting positive outcomes from peer and cross-age tutoring programmes, nevertheless raised cautions that many (indeed most) studies were poorly controlled and methodologically unsound. There was also some caution that while no studies reported negative effects, there were some which did not produce significant gains. Sharpley and Sharpley (1981), for example, reported that 27 out of the 62 studies considered had non-significant effects. Topping was therefore judiciously cautious at that time to avoid raising unrealistic expectations.

Topping also refers to a *meta-analysis*, an attempt to quantify and assimilate the research findings from many different studies, carried out by Cohen et al. (1982). The overall conclusion drawn was similar to the above, in that when the results of 52 studies were combined, the overall effect size could only be described as modest (Topping, 1988). However, within this meta-analysis some studies produced highly significant effects, with cross-age tutors tending to produce larger effect sizes. In 38 of the studies, tutors themselves improved in achievements, and in 33 of these tutors performed significantly better than controls in the curriculum areas that they had tutored.

Another leading researcher into peer and cross-age tutoring in the UK is Sinclair Goodlad, who has consistently demonstrated positive cognitive and achievement effects of using students in higher education to tutor school-age pupils (Goodlad, 1995). Goodlad and Hirst (1990) cites another meta-analysis by Cook et al. (1986) which assimilated nineteen research articles in which pupils with a range of special educational needs acted as tutors. This analysis demonstrated academic gains for both tutors and tutees compared to control subjects. Attitude to school improved for both tutors and tutees, and the behaviour ratings for tutors also improved.

Carol Fitzgibbon is the other foremost UK researcher into peer and cross-age tutoring. Comparing the outcomes of five controlled field experiments, she found that cross-age tutoring, mostly with a focus on improving maths skills, was more successful than the two peer tutoring studies (Fitzgibbon, 1990a). Important to the Valued Youth Programme described below is her conclusion that

> the cross-age tutoring role will evoke in tutors strong feelings of responsibility towards tutees, insights into the learning process, expressions of empathy with teachers, relief-from-boredom, a recognition that peer tutors may be able to assist learning and, very importantly, high levels of co-operation with their own teacher.
>
> (Fitzgibbon, 1990a: 57)

In another paper (Fitzgibbon, 1990b), she cites a meta-analysis of Levin et al. (1984) which compared cross-age tutoring with increased instructional time, reduced class sizes and computer-assisted learning and concluded that cross-age tutoring 'won hands down' (Fitzgibbon, 1990b: 262). Slavin et al. (1991) surveyed research on early intervention programmes aimed at preventing failure and came to a similar conclusion. Of nine types of intervention, which included reduced class sizes, provision of instructional aids and pre-school provision for 4-year-olds, they concluded that the most effective strategies were those which included one-to-one tutoring.

Another study with a focus on developing basic number skills (Beirne-Smith, 1991) concluded that the input from cross-aged tutors was the key factor for acquisition of basic facts, rather than the method of instruction. As with reading, the research evidence consistently shows gains for both tutors and tutees in maths skills from involvement in both peer and cross-age tutoring approaches (Damon and Phelps, 1989a; Britz et al., 1989).

While the focus here has been on studies relating to basic academic skills, it is evident that peer and cross-age tutoring is now being used in virtually every educational area, including personal and social education. Topping cites its usage in

> contraception, sexually transmitted diseases, smoking, diet and nutrition, alcohol abuse, drug abuse, drinking and driving, oral English language proficiency, violence prevention, suicide prevention, gang membership, dealing with divorce and loss, drop-out prevention, coping with chronic/terminal illness, rape awareness, sexual harassment and post-traumatic stress syndrome.
>
> (Topping, 1996: 24)

He argues that not only are peers effective in these areas, but that professional teachers would find many of these areas difficult to address.

Peer and Cross-Age Mentoring Programmes/Approaches

Mentoring schemes are established at almost all American universities, as evidenced by the number of such schemes which came up as 'hits' on an Internet search for 'peer mentoring'. There is even a phenomenon called 'cyber-mentoring', where students gain support on-line via e-mail and chat-rooms. There is growing interest in the UK in mentoring schemes to help and support students and pupils with various difficulties, in particularly those seen to be disaffected. One such in Birmingham is the KWESI project, which aims to provide black adult male mentors for African Caribbean boys at risk of exclusion. No formal evaluation is as yet available, but anecdotally KWESI mentors report successes in preventing exclusion. There is also interest in peer and cross-age mentoring and, as with tutoring, some of the research is promising.

The face validity of peer and cross-age mentoring as an approach with intrinsic merit is compelling, particularly with adolescents. Many of us can recall the powerful effect of having talked through a life problem with an adolescent peer or of receiving useful advice from such. For pupils who have difficulty forming relationships, such spontaneous counselling may not be available and may need to be engineered by teachers.

There is growing evidence that peer mentoring and counselling approaches are perceived by pupils as highly beneficial in helping them to cope with and to counter bullying (e.g. Cowie and Sharp, 1996). Sharp (1996) concludes that indeed effective intervention must involve peers. These authors advocate strongly that young people can be readily trained in counselling skills such as active listening, reflection and paraphrasing, and can put these into practice to good effect (Sharp et al., 1994).

Some studies have compared the effectiveness of girls to boys as tutors. Sharpley and Sharpley (1981), in their review, concluded that while girls produced significantly better results than boys, same sex pairings did not produce better results than opposite sex pairings. Topping and Whiteley (1993) combined the results from projects in fifteen schools. They found that male pairings worked particularly well, female pairings tended to produce better scores for tutees though not for tutors, and mixed gender combinations produced good results for tutors but not for tutees, especially where a female tutor was paired with a male tutee. However, they point out that in these studies mostly same or similar aged peers were involved, whereas a third of reported studies of cross-aged tutoring showed good results for mixed gender pairings. Ainsborough (1994) found that boys and girls were equally effective as tutors using the 'Pause, Prompt and Praise' approach, but interestingly presents some evidence that if tutees are given the choice of gender of their tutor they gain more.

In the remainder of this chapter, a detailed description is given of a programme with a strong cross-age tutoring component which has deliberately recruited disaffected pupils as tutors.

The Valued Youth Program

The Intercultural Development Research Association (IDRA) is a non-profit-making educational foundation based in San Antonio, Texas, USA. It gives as its mission statement: to improve schools for the benefit of all students. In southern Texas there is a large student population from Hispanic (Spanish-speaking) backgrounds; research carried out by IDRA in the 1980s revealed that a very high percentage of these students dropped out of school before reaching high school, and many more dropped out of high school itself (Cardenas et al., 1988). Recent studies have shown that while only 12 per cent of high school students are Hispanic, they account for 22 per cent of the drop-out population (US Census Bureau, 1997). Out of concern at these alarming statistics, IDRA has focused much of its energy and resources on reducing the drop-out rate, particularly among the Hispanic groups.

The reasons American students gave for dropping out of school varied considerably. Woods (1995) cites a comprehensive literature survey by Wells and Bechard (1989) which concluded that there appeared to be four main categories of risk factors which add up to a profile of characteristics that can lead to a student dropping out of school. These were student-related, school-related, family-related and community-related factors. As the combination of risk factors becomes more complex, the greater is the probability of the student dropping out of school.

Among the school-related factors, the strongest predictor of dropping out was poor academic performance (Hess et al., 1987; Woods, 1995) with students who repeated a grade being twice as likely to drop out. Student-related factors include substance abuse, pregnancy and behaviour difficulties related to school such as truancy, lateness and exclusion for disciplinary offences. The degree to which parents could give support to students was dependent upon factors such as the stability of the family unit, socio-economic status, membership of a minority group, single-parent household, parents' education, and English as an additional language (Horn, 1992). Crucially, of the community-related factors, poverty constituted the strongest predictor. Many students stop attending school for largely economic reasons, in many cases to supplement the family income, with the likelihood of dropping out increasing with the number of hours worked per week (Winters et al., 1988).

IDRA was concerned that traditional responses to the problem of students dropping out failed to take account of many of these factors but equally did not build on the strengths of students at risk (Robledo et al., 1986). They surveyed existing intervention programmes that had been implemented and evaluated in the USA and attempted to distil from these what might be the vital ingredients to make up a successful package to keep students in school. Ten elements were identified and can be summarized as follows:

1   the provision of bilingual instruction for limited-English-proficient students, the development of higher-order thinking skills and provision of accelerated learning for disadvantaged students;
2   a cross-age tutoring component which gives the role of tutor to the at-risk student;
3   activities to enrich, expand, extend and apply the content and skills learned in the classroom;
4   school–business partnerships to provide financial resources, job opportunities and role models;
5   reinforcement of student accomplishments, talents, leadership and participation;
6   parent participation in meaningful activities which contribute to their empowerment;
7   formative evaluation of the programme to develop and improve the programme;
8   co-operative staff development with campus activities to take account of curriculum and student needs;
9   strong programme leadership to reinforce success and establish educational goals;
10   the development of a curriculum incorporating self-paced, individualized instruction using co-operative learning and whole language approaches.

(Cardenas et al., 1992)

These elements were incorporated in the IDRA 's 'Coca-Cola Valued Youth Program' (VYP), so named after the principal sponsor and funding agent. The programme is established in 91 separate school sites in a number of states in the United States of America. The programme is comprehensively evaluated in each school site with invariably highly positive outcomes for participating students (IDRA, 1996).

A comparison study between a group of Valued Youth (VY) Tutors (N = 101) and a control group (N = 93) matched for limited English proficiency and reading level was carried out between 1988 (baseline) and 1990 (Cardenas et al., 1992). Both VY tutors and control group students were from the same pool of at-risk students. At baseline there were no differences between the groups on age, ethnicity, grade retention, average grade in reading, Quality of School Life (QSL) (Epstein and McPartland, 1978) and self-esteem (Piers and Harris, 1969) scores. There was, however, a statistically significant difference between the groups in terms of eligibility for free or assisted school lunches, indicating that the VY tutor group were significantly lower in socio-economic status. Since Winters et al. (1988) concluded that poverty was the strongest of the community-related predictors of dropping out, it is possible that the VY group may, if anything, have been more at risk than the controls.

The results of the two-year study showed that only one VY tutor (i.e. 1

per cent) dropped out of school, compared to 11 (12 per cent) of the control group. The VY tutors also had significantly higher gains in reading. After the first year of their involvement in the VYP, the tutor group had significantly higher self-concept scores, and this difference was sustained by the end of the second year. The same pattern emerged for the attitude to schools as measured by the QSL. As we have seen, these results are consistent with the findings of many other studies on the beneficial effects of peer and cross-age tutoring. What was unique at the time about this study was that the target group was seriously at risk of dropping out of school. Not only did the programme bring success for the tutors as outlined above, but the indications were that these effects were being maintained over time.

The Valued Youth Programme in Birmingham, England

Impressed with these results, the unusual combination of programme features, the high-risk target group and the highly positive orientation of the approach, the present author became interested in the Coca-Cola VYP and established regular correspondence with IDRA. There was considerable concern in Birmingham at the increasing numbers of pupils being excluded from school, and in particular the over-representation of boys of African Caribbean origin in the exclusion statistics. Shortly after his appointment in 1993 as Chief Education Officer, Professor Tim Brighouse commissioned Ted Wragg (Professor of Education, Exeter University) to report on areas of concern within Birmingham and to recommend courses of action the City might consider to address such problems as the exclusion rates. Wragg challenged Birmingham to seek innovative approaches to the phenomena of under-achievement and widespread disaffection of African Caribbean students. The parallels with the Hispanic students in the USA were apparent to the author, who renewed his resolve to research the VYP further and in particular to seek funding to attend the annual VYP conference in San Antonio.

In early 1996, a new charity, Second City; Second Chance (SCSC), was established in Birmingham, dedicated to reducing exclusions by promoting and extending the use of adult mentors in helping to motivate disaffected pupils from different cultures. The VYP, with its emphasis on training at-risk middle school students to become tutors for younger elementary school pupils, seemed consistent with the basic aims of SCSC, which raised funds from local industry to enable a fact-finding group to visit San Antonio to participate in the VYP Annual Conference, to see the VYP in action in Texan schools, and to discuss with IDRA the possibility of transplanting the programme to Birmingham, recognizing the very different educational contexts of the two cultures. Impressed with the organization of the programme and the high commitment of teachers, students and IDRA staff, the group set about devising a pilot programme to attempt to replicate the VYP as closely as possible within the British school context.

So what is the VYP?

As the title of the programme suggests, the philosophy of VYP is that all students are regarded as valuable and no student is expendable. VYP sets about finding ways of conveying this sense of being valued to the selected students, virtually all of whom may well have developed negative self-perceptions, seeing themselves as trouble-makers or educational failures.

As stated above, there are a number of interesting features in the VYP, some of which have evolved since the early programmes, but at its core is a cross-age tutoring programme where students aged 12 and over, who have been identified as at risk of dropping out or being excluded from school, are trained to act as tutors to younger pupils. Following two weeks' initial training, the VY tutors are allocated up to three pupils (tutees) in a class at a nearby elementary school, whose education they support under the direction of the class teacher. There is always a four-year gap in terms of attainment between tutor and tutee to ensure the former has a sufficient educational basis for the task of tutoring. Tutors who themselves are behind educationally may therefore be allocated pupils as young as kindergarten age to preserve the four-year gap.

Typically, tutors provide a session of up to an hour per day for four days each week during the programme. On the fifth day, they meet together as a group led by the 'teacher co-ordinator' of the programme for on-going training, preparation, basic skills support work, peer support and debriefing. There are many reinforcers built into the programme but, most particularly, tutors earn a stipend for their work, often equivalent to the state minimum hourly wage, which they receive in a fortnightly pay packet. At its best, the VYP programme provides students with peer and adult support, engendering group solidarity and teamwork. Many American educators are convinced, and the research tends to support them (Cardenas et al., 1992), that the VYP provides young people with a positive alternative to street gang culture.

The Birmingham Valued Youth Programme

Seven secondary schools opted to join a hastily constructed pilot programme commencing in October 1996 to run through until July 1997. The basic aim of this pilot was to examine the feasibility of operating the VYP, given the constraints of the British educational system. IDRA was contracted to provide training, materials and their standard evaluation, all of which was felt necessary to ensure the programme met IDRA's minimum standards. SCSC was already committed to the use of adult mentors, and it was intended from the outset to compare the outcomes for pupils who became Valued Youth tutors with those who had mentors only and with those who had both. Although initially pupils were assigned to one or other of these conditions, pragmatic decisions by teacher co-ordinators (TCs), often for ethical considerations, resulted in pupils being transferred to another condition, most usually from mentor only to VYP. Thus the intended comparison was not possible.

A separate strand of this programme relates to the Behaviour Support Service (BSS). From January 1997, three BSS Centres which provide education for permanently excluded pupils recruited a number of pupils to train as VY tutors. These were all either year 10 or year 11 pupils, and hence the aims of involving them in the VYP were to increase their motivation to remain within the education system, to increase their self-esteem, to provide them with additional worthwhile experiences to the three sessions they received per week in the Centres, and to enhance their Records of Achievement.

Adaptations to the Coca-Cola VYP

Criteria

Criteria were adapted for the British context from the American programme to identify target groups of pupils. An essential criterion was given as

> Higher than average disciplinary referrals: for example, at least one fixed term exclusion in the last year; two or more referrals to senior staff in the past term; high 'at risk of permanent exclusion' rating from two or more senior staff.

In addition, at least two of the following were required:

- higher than average (for the school) absentee rate;
- non-participation in extra-curricular activities;
- two or more National Curriculum levels below year average;
- lack of career orientation;
- low socio-economic level (e.g. free school meals).

Group Size

Up to eight pupils meeting these criteria in each school were invited to take part in the programme. This group size is smaller than those in the American programme, where typically whole tutor groups of up to eighteen pupils would be usually involved on a single school site. The smaller numbers for this pilot programme were suggested (a) on the assumption that this would be more manageable for TCs, and (b) as potentially providing a modest sample for comparison. As will be seen below, both these assumptions proved to be false.

Teacher Co-ordinators

Typically in the USA, teacher co-ordinators (TCs) are released for significant periods of time from their curriculum duties to enable them to undertake the many tasks demanded in the pure programme. This was simply not possible in all our schools, particularly since timetables had already been fixed prior to the pilot being agreed. In virtually all cases, the TC – usually a year tutor or deputy head – fitted in as many of the tasks as possible on top of their regular commitments. This had significant consequences for the programme and particularly the evaluation, as will be seen below.

Time for Tutoring

As stated above, typically American VY tutors spend up to an hour a day for four days per week tutoring their group. Our National Curriculum has much less flexibility, and as a compromise tutors worked for a minimum thirty minutes per day on three days of the week. This was deemed acceptable by IDRA. Also, American tutors have a weekly group preparation/debriefing session which was not usually possible here due to timetabling difficulties. However, TCs did provide back-up support in almost all cases, in the form of individual or small group sessions to prepare VY tutors and offer them advice. However, this is seen by the author as a serious weakness in the pilot which will need to be addressed in future years.

Rewards

The main rewards for American VY tutors take the form of stipends equivalent to the state minimum hourly wage (currently about $4.75, or approximately £3.00) which they receive in fortnightly wage packets. After much consultation and deliberation, it was decided to reward Birmingham VY tutors with tokens which had a nominal monetary value but which can be saved towards a back-up reward of the tutor's choice. The tutors agree these rewards with their mentors, who ensure the reward is appropriate and in the tutor's interest. Thus the mechanics of the system are that for each thirty-minute session a tutor works, a teacher signs a record form. Each signature represents a token, worth (in the pilot year) £1.00, and a running total is kept. The tutor agrees with his/her mentor what the back-up reward will be, and at a minimum of a half-termly interval the tokens may be exchanged for the agreed reward. Some tutors opted to save for expensive back-ups which may take considerably longer than half a term to achieve. (One tutor opted for an electric guitar!) It is possible for tutors to opt for a cash reward with the agreement of their mentor. In this event, a bank account is opened for the tutor, into which earnings are paid half-termly.

Mentors

The use of volunteer, external (to the school) adult mentors is a Birmingham addition to the VYP but one which has the full support of IDRA. Integral to the American model is the use of positive role models who typically pay one-off visits to schools adopting the VYP to talk about their background and experiences. Such visits have been encouraged by SCSC, which has met some of the expenses of visitors. Mentors provide much more by giving on-going support on a fortnightly basis to VY tutors. These mentors receive basic training from SCSC: for example, on listening skills and important issues such as child protection.

Reading Is Fundamental (RIF)

This is another American import and is that country's largest children's literacy organization. RIF seeks to establish community-based, volunteer-supported literacy projects which provide books for young people to choose and own at no cost to them. It is aimed at motivating children to read for pleasure, by engaging them in planned activities involving parents, families and the whole community. SCSC is the Birmingham agent for RIF, and this provided an opportunity to reward primary schools which were prepared to accept VY tutors. In the year of the study (1998), VY tutors consequently focused on literacy skills, although in the light of their and the primary teachers' feedback, in future VY tutors will engage in whatever support pupils require during their visit and on any curriculum area.

Initial VY Tutor Training

As stated above, in American schools two weeks' preparation is given to VY tutors, which again has not been possible in our context. The amount of training has varied between schools but in all cases appears to have been both brief and relatively superficial. The author considers this another weakness which will need to be addressed in the future.

Schools

Of the seven secondary schools which originally opted to be involved in the VYP pilot programme, one school had an OFSTED inspection during the winter term and consequently delayed starting the programme. There was therefore insufficient time to judge whether or not the programme was having any effect here, as tutors were involved for less than two terms. Another school had serious difficulties conforming to the minimum requirements of the programme and ultimately abandoned it. One of the remaining schools was in the inner city, while all others were on the outer ring, predominantly in areas of economic deprivation. In addition, another secondary school approached SCSC with a request to include one girl pupil who was causing serious concern, and this was accepted as a goodwill gesture. Seven primary schools hosted VY tutors. Our experience of San Antonio was that elementary (primary) schools were on the same campus as the middle (secondary) schools, whereas all but one of our primaries were some distance away, requiring a bus ride for the tutors in most cases. In one instance, the primary school was several miles away, which proved ultimately unsatisfactory.

Pupils

In all, 43 pupils – 31 boys and 12 girls – commenced the programme in one or other of the conditions. The ethnic distribution was as follows: 21 white European, 15 African Caribbean, 2 Asian and 5 mixed race. Tutors visited their nearest host primary schools and were allocated to classrooms in pairs, working with up to three tutees each.

The pilot programme had serious difficulties in data retrieval from schools in this pilot year, due to a number of factors which have been addressed for a full trial run which is nearing completion at the time of writing.

General Conclusions from the Pilot

It has not been possible to compare outcomes for VY tutors with those who had mentor only and with those who had both, and this kind of comparison has for the moment been abandoned. Teachers invariably argued that the at-risk pupils identified should be given access to whatever support was available and that it would be unethical to limit them to one condition only.

In this pilot phase, five schools successfully implemented the programme for two terms, and 31 tutors were involved. As stated above, a further school requested one pupil to be involved, making a total of 32 tutors. Five tutors dropped out of the programme quite quickly for a variety of reasons, some finding tutoring too stressful, others simply finding it unrewarding. One other pupil was withdrawn from the programme for a positive reason, in that an alternative programme became available which more closely matched his needs. Three pupils were taken off the programme due to poor attendance and one for disciplinary reasons. It should be noted that the support for tutors in this pilot fell well short of the American model, and this is one of several limitations.

Thus, of the 32 tutors starting the programme, 22 (68 per cent) completed it successfully, with reported gains from teachers in self-esteem, social skills, disciplinary record and attitude to school. Although this percentage is lower than one would have hoped, given the population and the programme limitations it represented a positive beginning for the VYP in the UK.

Anecdotally, several successes were remarkable, in that several pupils deemed to be on the brink of exclusion not only completed the programme but were now expected to remain in school.

Following this crude pilot, seven secondary schools opted to implement the programme and adhere to the minimum programme requirements set by IDRA. Data collection and analysis is incomplete, so it is not possible here to report on the outcomes. However, what is apparent already is that the vast majority of pupils meeting the at-risk criteria and who were deemed by their schools as likely to be excluded have 'survived' their year on the programme. All schools remain enthusiastic about the programme and are committed to continuing with it – and, indeed, making it available to more pupils. All receiving primary schools also wish to continue with help from VY tutors and report anecdotally that tutees are benefiting from the input they receive. By word of mouth, several other secondary schools have heard of the programme and wish to adopt it on the strength of recommendation from their colleagues, and at the time of writing five other LEAs are negotiating with IDRA and SCSC to commence VY programmes in selected schools.

Final Thoughts

Nationally, there is major concern about the rising number of pupils being excluded from school. In addition, there are unacceptable numbers of pupils who are dropping out of school and are lost to the education system. Paradoxically, with this level of exclusion and self-exclusion, many teachers and educationalists have embraced the rhetoric of *inclusion*, but while there are demonstrable successes of schools including pupils with learning, communication, physical and sensory difficulties in mainstream, pupils who present challenging behaviour are an exception to the inclusive trend.

The VYP in the United States was recognized by the National Diffusion Network as a programme which works to counter dropping out. As such, it was recommended to schools throughout the country, and consequently was favourably regarded for funding at federal and state level. Apart from the genuine humanitarian concerns of IDRA, it is clear that the sponsorship of the VYP by a company such as Coca-Cola brings with it economic considerations. Coca-Cola clearly wishes to be associated with a successful programme. However, the federal and state governments are aware of the huge economic and social costs of pupil failure in terms of crime and the penal system, and hence there is a mutual interest of the state and private enterprise in co-operating to support programmes of this kind. Investment in preventive programmes which work makes social *and* economic sense. In the UK, we cannot afford to ignore the success of such a programme if we wish to be truly inclusive and embrace a philosophy that 'All pupils are valuable, no pupil is expendable'.

The early, admittedly soft indicators are that the VYP can be transplanted to our system and can make an impact with suitable local modifications, prime among which is the additional component of mentoring with which our American colleagues are extremely impressed. This author is committed to rigorous evaluation of the VYP, and will be presenting future papers which it is hoped will add to the impressive volume of work on the benefits of children teaching and helping other children.

References

Ainsborough, S.E. (1994) 'The peer tutoring of reading using Pause, Prompt and Praise: a study examining the differential effects of gender pairings'. Unpublished MEd thesis, School of Education, University of Birmingham.

Beirne-Smith, M. (1991) 'Peer tutoring in arithmetic for children with learning difficulties', *Exceptional Children*, 57, 330–7.

Bell, A. (1797) *An Experiment in Education Made at the Male Asylum of Madras: Suggesting a System by which a School or Family may Teach Itself under the Superintendence of the Master or Parent*. London, Cadell and Davis.

Britz, M.W., Dixon, J. and McLauchlin, T.F. (1989) 'The effects of peer tutoring on mathematics performance: a recent review', *British Columbia Journal of Special Education*, 13(1), 17–33.

Cardenas, J.A., Robledo, M.R. and Waggoner, D. (1988) *The Under-Education of American Youth*. San Antonio, TX: Intercultural Development Research Association.

Cardenas, J.A., Montecel, M.R., Supik, J.D. and Harris, R.J. (1992) 'The Coca-Cola Valued Youth Program – dropout prevention strategies for at-risk students', *Texas Researcher*, 3, 111–30.

Cohen, P.A., Kulik, J.A. and Kulik, C-L.C. (1982) 'Educational outcomes of tutoring: a meta-analysis of findings', *American Educational Research Journal*, 19(2), 237–48.

Cook, S.B., Scruggs, T.E., Mastropieri, M.A. and Casto, G.C. (1986) 'Handicapped students as tutors', *Journal of Special Education*, 19(4), 483–92.

Cowie, H. and Sharp, S. (eds) (1996) *Peer Counselling in Schools – A Time to Listen*. London: Fulton.

Damon, W. and Phelps, E. (1989a) 'Critical distinctions among three approaches', in N.M. Webb (ed.) *Peer Interaction, Problem-Solving and Cognition: Multidisciplinary Perspectives*. NY: Pergamon Press.

Damon, W. and Phelps, E. (1989b) 'Strategic uses of peer learning in children's education', in T.J. Berndt and G.W. Ladd (eds) *Peer Relationships in Child Development*. NY: Wiley.

Donaldson, A.J.M. and Topping, K.J. (1996) *Promoting Peer Assisted Learning amongst Students in Higher and Further Education*. Birmingham: SEDA.

Ehly, S.W. and Larsen, S.C. (1980) *Peer tutoring for Individualised Instruction*. Boston: Allyn and Bacon.

Epstein, J. and McPartland, J. M. (1978) *The Quality of School Life Scale*. Boston, MA: Houghton Mifflin Co.

Feldman, R.S., Devin-Sheehan, L. and Allen, V.L. (1976) 'Children tutoring children: a critical review of research', in V.L. Allen (ed.) *Children as Teachers: Theory and Research on Tutoring.* NY: Academic Press.

Fitzgibbon, C.T. (1983) 'Peer tutoring: a possible method for multi-ethnic education', *New Community*, 11(12), 160–6.

Fitzgibbon, C.T. (1990a) 'Success and failure in peer tutoring experiments', *Explorations in Peer Tutoring*, CEM Publication 52. Newcastle: Curriculum, Evaluation and Management Centre.

Fitzgibbon, C.T. (1990b) *Empower and Monitor: The EM Algorithm for the Creation of Effective Schools*, CEM Publication 16. Newcastle: Curriculum, Evaluation and Management Centre.

Goodlad, S. (1979) *Learning by Teaching: An Introduction to Tutoring.* London: Community Service Volunteers

Goodlad, S. (1995) 'Students as tutors and mentors', in S. Goodlad (ed.) *Students as Tutors and Mentors.* London: Kogan Page.

Goodlad, S. and Hirst, B. (1989) *Peer Tutoring: A Guide to Learning by Teaching.* London: Kogan Page.

Goodlad, S. and Hirst, B. (1990) *Explorations in Peer Tutoring.* Oxford: Blackwell.

Greenwood, C.R., Delquardi, J.C. and Hall, R.V. (1989) 'Longitudinal effects of classwide peer tutoring', *Journal of Educational Psychology*, 81(3), 371–83.

Hess, G.A., Well, E., Prindle, C., Liffman, P. and Kaplan, B. (1987) 'Where Room 187? How schools can reduce their dropout problem', *Education and Urban Society*, 19(3), 330–55.

Horn, L. (1992) *A Profile of Parents of Eighth Graders: National Education Longitudinal Study of 1988. Statistical Analysis Report.* Washington, DC: National Center for Educational Statistics, Office of Education Research and Improvement, US Department of Education.

IDRA (1996) *Coca-Cola Valued Youth Program – 1995–1996 Stewardship Report.* San Antonio, TX: IDRA.

Jenkins, J.R. and Jenkins, L.M. (1987) 'Making peer tutoring work', *Educational Leadership*, 44(6), 64–8.

Lancaster, J. (1803) *Improvements in Education as it Respects the Industrious Classes of the Community, Containing, among Other Important Particulars, an Account of the Institution for the Education of One Thousand Poor Children, Borough Road, Southwark; and of the New System of Education on which it is Conducted.* London: Darton and Harvey.

Lieberman, D.J. (1989) 'Peer counselling in the elementary school: promoting personal and academic growth through positive relationships'. Unpublished paper, Nova University, Florida (ED323449).

Morgan, R.T.T. (1986) *Helping Children Read – The Paired Reading Handbook.* London: Methuen.

Piers, E.V. and Harris, D.B. (1969) *The Piers–Harris Children's Self Concept Scale.* Los Angeles: Western Psychological Services.

Robledo, M.R., Cardenas, J.A. and Supik, J.D. (1986) *The Texas School Dropout Survey Project: A Survey of Findings.* San Antonio, TX: IDRA.

Scruggs, T.E. and Osguthorpe, R.T. (1986) 'Tutoring interventions within special educational settings: a comparison of cross-age and peer tutoring', *Psychology in the Schools*, 23, 187–93.

Seaborne, M. (1966) *Education: The History of Modern Britain.* London: Studio Vista.

Sharp, S. (1996) 'The role of peers in tackling bullying in schools', *Educational Psychology in Practice*, 11(4), 17–22.

Sharp, S., Sellors, A. and Cowie, H. (1994) 'Time to listen: setting up a peer counselling service to help tackle the problem of bullying in schools', *Pastoral Care in Education*, 12(2), 3–6.

Sharpley, A.M. and Sharpley, C.F. (1981) 'Peer tutoring: a comparison of cross-age and peer tutoring', *Collected Original Resources in Education (CORE)*, 5(3), 7–C11 (fiche 7 and 8).

Slavin, R.E., Karweit, N.L. and Wasik, B.A. (1991) *Preventing Early School Failure: What Works?* Report no. 26. Baltimore, MD: Centre for Research on Effective Schooling for Disadvantaged Students.

Topping, K. (1986) *The Kirklees Paired Reading Training Pack* (second edition). Huddersfield: Kirklees Directorate of Educational Services.

Topping, K. (1987) 'Children as teachers', *Special Children*, 14, 6–8.

Topping, K. (1988) *The Peer Tutoring Handbook*. Beckenham: Croom Helm.

Topping, K. (1996) 'Reaching where adults cannot', *Educational Psychology in Practice*, 11(4), 23–9.

Topping, K. and Whiteley, M. (1993) 'Sex differences in the effectiveness of peer tutoring', *School Psychology International*, 14(57), 57–67.

US Census Bureau (1997) *School Enrolment – Social and Economic Characteristics of Students: October 1995*. Washington, DC: US Census Bureau.

Wheldall, K. and Mettem, P. (1985) 'Behavioural peer tutoring: training 16-year-old tutors to employ the "Pause, Prompt and Praise Method" with 12-year-old remedial readers', *Educational Psychology*, 5(1), 27–44.

Winters, K.C., Rubinstein, M. and Winters, R.A. (1988) *An Investigation of Education Options for Youth at Risk, Ages 9–15: Demographics, Legislation and Model Programs. Research Report no. 88–10*. Washington, DC: National Commission for Employment Policy (DOL).

Wood, D. and O'Malley, C. (1996) 'Collaborative learning between peers', *Educational Psychology in Practice*, 11(4), 4–9.

Woods, E.G. (1995) *Reducing the Dropout Rate. School Improvement Research Series*. Washington, DC: Office of Education Research and Improvement (OERI), Northwest Regional Educational Laboratory.

Section 4

Pressure Groups

13 Parents' Organizations

Single Interest or Common Good?

Jane Martin

It has long been acknowledged that parents play a key role in the education of their children with special educational needs. Current government policy has reinforced the importance of a positive relationship between parents and schools, and with the local education authorities who have the statutory responsibility to make appropriate educational provision. In seeking to create a 'partnership' between parents and local authorities, the government is clearly intending to counter the increasingly confrontational relationship which was the experience for many parents as they struggled to ensure proper educational provision for their child during a time of shrinking resources. In the same way as 'mainstream' parents exercise their rights over choice of school, parents of children with SEN also want to ensure a proper standard of education for their child, but their influence on the system, either as individuals or in self-supporting 'lobby' groups, has been weak. This chapter will explore the particular issues for parents of children with SEN as the government develops an integrated system and encourages a closer partnership between parents as individuals, teachers, support groups and the local education authority. It will be suggested that public policy has accentuated tensions between individual rights and interests, and collective justice and equity. In this context, more 'advantaged' groups of parents have been able to assert their interests at the expense of others, in a system which has been concerned with the distribution of limited resources. A more socially just system – which encourages diverse parental interest groups to 'voice' their claims, in a partnership with professionals, to achieve shared agreements about provision for special educational needs – will be more likely to be truly inclusive.

The Policy Context : Choice, Entitlement and Partnership

In the 1997 Green Paper (DfEE, 1997) the Secretary of State for Education emphasized the important role of parents of children with SEN as one of the six themes of the document:

> We want all parents of children with SEN to get effective support from the full range of local services and voluntary agencies, to have a real say in decisions about their child's education, and to be empowered to contribute themselves to their child's development. Some parents need to be helped to gain access to these opportunities.
>
> (DfEE, 1997: 5)

The planned programme for action during the lifetime of the parliament, then, includes specifically; 'working with a group of LEAs, schools and voluntary bodies representing parents, to promote effective arrangements for parent partnership' (p. 7).

The subsequent *Programme for Action* (DfEE, 1998) confirms the government's commitment to (among other things) 'Working with parents to achieve excellence for all' (p. 10). In his foreword, the Secretary of State again reiterates the importance of parents in the context of a more inclusive system:

> We recognise the case for more inclusion where parents want it and appropriate support can be provided.... We firmly support the vital role that parents play within a child's education and the need to strengthen the partnership between parents and professionals. ... We are determined to see continuing real improvements. But these will only come about through on-going commitment at all levels, and even greater partnership between parents and professionals.
>
> (p. 3)

In this document it is confirmed that, following consultation, parents' main concerns are fourfold:

- more emphasis on early identification of difficulties and appropriate intervention to tackle them;
- effective support, including access to independent advice, from the earliest stage at which their child's special educational needs are identified;
- a powerful say in the way their child is educated;
- greater certainty about what they have a right to expect.

(p. 11)

In setting the policy agenda, the Green Paper in many respects mirrors the increased role for parents in mainstream education – it highlights:

- choice,
- entitlement, and
- partnership.

Parental choice of school has been a major development in the 'quasi-market' in education established in the 1980s which cast parents in the role of 'consumer' (e.g. Munn, 1994). Enshrined in a neo-liberal rights-based ideology, this policy development has been shown to be wanting, since it enabled some groups to exploit competition to their own advantage (e.g. Glatter et al., 1997; Ball et al., 1995). The evidence suggests that this system is also disadvantaging pupils with SEN who wish to attend the mainstream school of their choice. (Armstrong and Galloway, 1994; Lunt and Evans, 1994.) As Riddell has said, its effect has been to 'discourage schools from welcoming pupils with social and emotional difficulties and learning difficulties who may be perceived as making significant demands on resources whilst having a negative effect on the school's public image and performance' (Riddell et al., 1994: 329).

Corbett and Norwich (1997) also discuss the tension between a quasi-market system which encourages self-interest, and an inclusive system which encourages co-existence: 'If the market allows for choice, this may result in a general impetus to remove difficult and disruptive children from mainstream schooling, strongly supported by teachers' unions, parent groups and political parties' (p. 385).

They refer to the coverage given by the popular press to parents who campaign *against* certain individual pupils attending their own child's school, and suggest that the increasing rates of exclusion from schools only serve to underline the dilemmas experienced by many teachers in the face of such tension.

And yet the government clearly intends to strengthen the rights of parents of pupils with SEN to choice of school, and is currently reviewing statutory provisions:

> Section 316 of the Education Act 1996 provides that children with statements should normally be educated in mainstream schools unless their parents wish otherwise subject to certain conditions being met. Some believe the conditions – relating to the needs of the child, those of peer children, and the use of resources – operate, either in principle or in the way they are interpreted, as barriers to inclusion.
>
> (DfEE 1998: 24)

An integral part of the parental choice policy is the provision of public information on school performance 'league tables' and other information for parents about the school and their child's progress. The policy is designed to give parents the information they need to exercise initial choice of school (and to 'exit' from one school to another as necessary throughout their child's career) rather than to collaborate with the school to secure the best education of their child. Thus, an *entitlement* to information throughout their child's education has also been established. Since the Code of Practice for SEN was introduced in 1994, there has been an increased emphasis on the need for schools to notify parents at an early stage of identification and to keep them informed of progress. It has also been a requirement that the govern- ing body publish details of SEN provision in the Annual Report to Parents. Under the *Programme for Action*, the government now intends that parents have information from LEAs about how SEN provision will be resourced.

The language of *partnership* with parents has had a distinguished if some- what messy history since the Plowden Report first established parental involvement in their child's education as good practice. It is a term much favoured by politicians, policy-makers and practitioners, although quite what 'partnership' means for different people in different contexts is unclear. Certainly, the research establishing parents as the primary educators of their child and the importance given to good home–school relations in the school effectiveness literature has given the term some credibility. And yet, many have raised questions about the reality of partnership, given the unequal distribution of power between parents and professionals (Armstrong, 1995) and suggest that, even given the necessarily closer relationship parents of pupils with SEN have with professionals, there is little evidence of partner- ship. Vincent and Tomlinson (1997) (referring to the work of Goacher et al., 1988 and Galloway et al., 1994) explain:

> Those parents with children identified as having special educational needs severe enough to warrant assessment and statementing under the 1993 Education Act (and previously the 1981 Act) may find themselves in a quantitatively and qualitatively different relationship with educa- tion professionals from other parents. They are likely to have more and sustained contact with the children's teachers and a range of other professionals. They are asked to contribute their views of their child's social and educational needs and progress. Yet research suggests that professionals involved in special education are actually no more likely than others to involve parents in significant decision-making.
>
> (Vincent and Tomlinson, 1997: 370)

Although there are constraints, the potential for partnership nevertheless exists. The Warnock Report (DES, 1978) first referred to parents of SEN pupils as partners, and the SEN Code of Practice (DfE, 1994) continued the theme:

> Children's progress will be diminished if their parents are not seen as partners in the educational process with unique knowledge and informa- tion to impart. Professional help can seldom be wholly effective unless it builds upon parents' capacity to be involved and unless parents consider that professionals take account of what they say and treat their views and anxieties as intrinsically important.
>
> (para 2.28)

In an SEN context, partnership as a supportive mechanism has been formalized with parent partnership schemes in each LEA which, among other things, provides Named Persons (now termed Independent Parental Supporters (IPS) under the Programme of Action) to act as advocates and advisers to parents.[1] In their evaluation of these schemes, Wolfendale and Cook (1997) are optimistic that partnership with parents is possible but yet to be fully realized:

> the majority view of those PPOs, LEA professionals and parents who were interviewed in the course of the research is that partnership between parents, LEAs, schools and voluntary bodies is 'on the way' to be being realised, but there were few instances of respondents being unequivocal that the partnership goals, in the spirit of the Code of Practice, have been achieved.
>
> (Wolfendale and Cook, 1997: iii–iv)

Towards an Inclusive System: Tensions to be Resolved

This summary of government policy suggests a tension in the role of parents between a *consumer–individualist* perspective and a *collaborative–partnership* perspective. How this tension is to be resolved, and the strategies employed for doing so within a quasi-market, will inevitably have an effect on the success of an integrated and inclusive system.

Several commentators have already raised some of the dilemmas. Corbett and Norwich (1997) have noted that within the context of rights and choice, 'some parents are adept at exploiting the possibilities for privileged services and are using a special needs diagnosis to improve the quality of their children's schooling' (p. 380). They summarize the changing policy context for special education:

> The role of special education has traditionally been concerned with the needs of the minority as they relate to majority interests. In the late 1990s, this is now set within a context of increased competition between schools, anxiety about educational attainments and standards of pupil behaviour. The politics of special educational needs is reflected in increasing tensions between the medical model of disability and the social model, in which the voices of disabled people themselves are heard to challenge the effects of special schooling and social discrimination.
>
> (Corbett and Norwich, 1997: 380)

The point surely, here, is that special educational needs have increasingly become a *political issue* which affects the role that parents play. To what extent this has already become a middle-class affair is being increasingly explored. Evans and Vincent (1997) draw upon Ball's work (Ball et al.,

1995) to suggest that those parents who 'operate effectively as a consumer' are those 'most frequently associated with membership of the professional middle class' and that 'parents of children experiencing difficulties in learning might be automatically positioned as less effective, less powerful consumers' (p. 107).

Not only is a market system necessarily one which results from aggregated individual needs, it is also socially biased. As Ranson (1992) notes:

> The market is formally neutral, yet substantively interested ... Yet of course the market masks its social bias. It elides but also reproduces the inequalities which consumers bring to the market place. Under the guise of neutrality, the institution of the market actively confirms and reinforces the pre-existing social order of wealth, privilege and prejudice. The market, let it be clear, is a crude mechanism of social selection and is intended as such.
>
> (p. 72)

Alongside tensions connected with parental choice, there are equal tensions around rights and entitlement, particularly concerning resource allocation where middle-class parents, once again, may be most effective in making use of the system to obtain special services and additional resourcing: for example, the dyslexia lobby. (See Duffield et al., 1995; Slee, 1995.) Research by Riddell et al. (1994) clearly showed that it was middle-class parents (assisted by the local dyslexia association) who were more likely to use private tuition to supplement state provision for the child with SEN. They also suggested that middle-class parents were able to secure 'a disproportionate share of additional provision within the state sector' (p. 338). The role of parent groups, or alliances between parents and disability lobby groups, is clearly a critical factor in helping parents to articulate their concerns and find solutions. Such alliances have most often come about to represent and defend the *interests* of parents, in a bid to win adequate resources for SEN, in an environment where the professionals were cast as guardians of a limited resource. An integrated and inclusive system, while clearly still resource-dependent, will require the interests of groups within special education and the interests of mainstream parents and pupils, to be accommodated within a context of shared values which are socially just.

Traditional conceptions of social justice (cf. Rawls, 1971; Harvey, 1973; Nosick, 1974) have offered different mechanisms for regulating our social arrangements in the fairest way for the benefit of all. They have tended to polarize around the processes of redistribution and production – Nozik, for example, defends market-individualism, and privileges production where Rawls accentuates the importance of redistribution. The contested nature of social justice, as Rizvi and Lingard (1996) point out, is relevant for special education, not least because integrated systems are legitimated from a very narrow social justice agenda. However, all conceptions of social justice which concentrate only on the equal distribution of resources have failed to recognize the significance of 'voice' in representing different cultural and material interests to establish a just system.

This view is asserted by those theorists who wish to reconcile equality and difference. Young (1990), for example, highlights not only the social injustice of formal institutional structures but also the day-to-day practices which result in subordination or exclusion. From this position, democratic political processes which enable different voices to be heard are central to social justice. She asserts:

> Instead of a fictional contract, we require real participatory structures in which actual people, with their geographical, ethnic, gender and occupational differences, assert their perspectives on social issues within institutions that encourage the representation of their distinct voices.
>
> (Young, 1990: 16)

The success of the government's policy to develop an inclusive education system for pupils with special educational needs will be the extent to which resources are distributed fairly according to need. This will, in turn, require shared agreements among parents about collective well-being and educational provision, rather than one group disadvantaging others as they privilege their own needs. This tension is underpinned by issues of power. Partnership requires power sharing, but if the partners are unwilling or unable to share power, partnership will be no more than rhetoric. Power sharing will only be possible if it is informed by values which are socially just and which enable the 'voices' of all the partners to be heard. The strategies parents employ to articulate 'voice', either individually or collectively, in defence of their interests, are therefore a central concern. This is not just a question of the parental 'voice' but the accommodation of different parental 'voices'.

Parental Voice

The concept of 'voice' focuses the relationship between the school and its parents upon deliberation and debate. It is a political concept used by Hirschman (1970) to describe client or member participation as a potential antidote to the economic concept of consumer 'exit'.[2] In the context of special educational needs, therefore, 'voice' is paramount, because it is the ability to be able to *change* an objectionable state of affairs rather than *escape* from it which is the key issue for parents of pupils with SEN. For many of them, a notion of school choice (either mainstream or special) may well be extremely limited, often for very practical reasons in connection with the facilities on offer. Nixon et al. (1996) have already highlighted the importance of voice in the school context, with particular significance for countering 'estrange-ment' and 'disaffection'. However, there are barriers to the articulation of voice which are also relevant in an SEN context.

First, as many researchers have suggested, the power differential between parents and professionals is too great to allow for an equal partnership. Armstrong (1995) suggests that parents do little more than legitimate the decisions taken by professionals and are often not given the information they need about the assessment process or their rights. He says:

> At face value the 1981 Education Act establishes a co-operative frame-work. In practice, the bureaucratization of the multi-disciplinary assessment procedures may lead to a situation in which the main outcome of parental involvement in an assessment is the legitimation of decisions taken by professionals. Moreover, a sharp contrast can be detected between the view of professionals that assessments involve a high degree of consensus, and the view expressed by parents that their agreement with decisions taken by professionals stems from a belief that no other choice is possible or realistic.
>
> (Armstrong, 1995: 43)

He goes on to suggest that these situations frustrate parents, such that they adopt strategies which work around and are independent of official procedures to further their case. This is where parent support groups and the voluntary associations play an important role in helping parents find and articulate their voice.

Second, as Evans and Vincent (1997) point out, 'the special education system is based on the identification and "treatment" of individual pupils who are perceived to deviate from the norm' (p. 103). It is, of course, self-evidently the case that parents play a role when their child is assessed for special educational need on an individualistic basis, since the process is designed to meet the particular learning needs of that child. Armstrong (1995) highlights this aspect:

> The 1980s and 1990s have been characterized by an increasing atomiza-tion of needs as they have come, once more, to be represented in terms of individual deficits, failures and personal tragedies. Separated from forms of collective action and decision-making, social disadvantage has been reconstructed as individual despair and responses to that despair have been made dependent upon the outcome of individual negotiation.
>
> (Armstrong, 1995: 25)

This situation is only made worse by the market system dominated by consumer individualism, as suggested above. Corbett and Norwich (1997) describe the shift from a caring (and ultimately patronising) model of special needs to a rights-led demand from individuals. Limited resources are now up for grabs from those who can fight for them.... The concepts of empowerment and entitlement have fostered a climate in which those who are alert to opportunities are able to gain resources.

(p. 384)

They go on to cite examples of individual parents whose stories have hit the headlines as they fight for the rights of their child to 'mainstream' provision through expensive litigation.

The power differential between parents and professionals, which can prevent parents from finding and articulating a constructive 'voice' with which to generate partnership, could be challenged through collective action. As Armstrong (1995) suggests:

For children and their parents the outcome of partnership may, in practice, amount to disempowerment by consensus. In these circumstances, the most effective partnership may be that which is forged through the strength of collective action outside the structures of the state and against the impositions of needs by the state.

(Armstrong, 1995: 150)

The role of parents' groups has already been established as a support for individual parents as they fight their corner, but does their role as pressure groups on behalf of competing interests promote the strong collective voice which could be so important in an integrated system?

Parents' Groups in Special Education

It has already been acknowledged (for example, Wolfendale, 1989) that there has been a significant growth in parents' groups since the Education Act 1981. As Vincent and Tomlinson (1997) point out, the existence of groups is haphazard around the country and some of them are short-lived, such that it is difficult to assess the success of such groups on a nationwide basis, particularly since so many of them work locally and without much publicity. Nevertheless, their existence is an important demonstration of parental voice.

We see these groups as important because of their exceptionality, when set against the otherwise limited tradition of public participation in public sector institutions, including education. Their existence seems to challenge the easy assumption of a passive polity in relation to education. They provide forums for collective participation and action by parents, a channel for their collective voice(s).

(Vincent and Tomlinson: 1997: 371)

Mostly these groups were formed as local alliances when parents were concerned about provision in their LEA and were often regarded as militant. However, as Wolfendale (1989) points out: 'Early confrontation has led, in some instances, to constructive dialogue and shared activities, such as day conferences for parents and professionals' (p. 112). This has clearly led to what Vincent and Tomlinson (1997: 371) have called the 'culture of communication' which, they suggest is a recognition by LEAs of the presence and the strategic importance of such groups. Paige-Smith (1997) points out that although there was a small lobby for parental rights at the time of the Warnock Report in 1978, the impetus for the proliferation of local groups stemmed from the 1981 Education Act, which did not give parents any rights to challenge LEA decisions, and because individual parents needed advice and support about the new arrangements which they found difficult to understand. Groups have therefore tended to coalesce around local interests to campaign for the rights of parents in a particular LEA.

Parents for Inclusion (formerly Parents in Partnership), for example, was a London-based group set up in 1984 to campaign for integrated education. Since the break-up of the Inner London Education Authority it has included all the London boroughs. While this group continues to be primarily a lobbying group for integrated education, it also offers advice and support to any parent with a pupil with SEN. The work of this group, as reported in Paige-Smith (1997), shows how support groups can empower parents. One of their workers describes the difficulties facing parents as a 'deficit view of disability' rather than a 'social model of disability which accepts all children'. Paige-Smith reports how this woman 'empowers' parents:

> There's a range of things, accessibility on the telephone, people can phone us and get from us a range of information, just basic, what people's rights are, what the legislation actually means, whether the professionals or the people they are surrounded by are actually doing it according to the book.
>
> (Paige-Smith, 1997: 47)

This group also acts as a network for smaller localized groups in the London boroughs to become pressure groups.

Network 81 was set up by one couple who realized from their own experience that parents need a lot of support through the statementing process. This organization now has charitable status and receives some funding from the DfEE, as well as Children in Need, to offer information and training for parents. The group also supports the setting up of local parent lobbying groups, and in 1996 had 67 local parent pressure groups affiliated to it. Paige-Smith (1997) reports on their style of campaigning: 'While the group does not campaign by "waving banners" according to the national co-ordinator, the group encourages parents to go out and question how LEAs respond to their requests for the provision they want for their child' (p. 49).

As Armstrong (1995) has suggested (see above), such groups provide a valuable focus for parents who need support and advice *outside* the system to further their interests. Another route is provided by groups focused on a particular disability, such as the British Dyslexia Association (BDA), which has local parent groups, although research in this area has shown that these tend to foster a largely middle-class membership (Riddell et al., 1994). A recent editorial by the Chief Executive in *Dyslexia Contact*, the official magazine of the BDA, highlights their primary campaigning role:

> Policy work and lobbying, in the experience of dyslexia associations and dyslexia people, is at the heart of our work.... In our response to draft Government guidance we called for schools where dyslexic pupils are enabled, challenged and stretched. Our voice, alongside others, had led to a DfEE rethink.... it announced that guidance on education development plans would include a new annexe on SEN and that there will be further consultation.... The BDA is calling for DfEE guidance on the prevention and management of underachievement for all children – including those with SEN. We'll also continue to lobby for improvements in teacher training and press the Government to deliver real and measurable improvements for all SEN children, especially dyslexic pupils ... Lobbying at local level is crucial. The Local Associations Board wants to support dyslexia associations in building partnerships with schools and LEAs.
>
> (BDA: 1998: 3)

This quotation signals a new style of lobbying which is potentially more collaborative but, more particularly, suggests a movement towards campaigning about the *substance* of special education within an integrated system rather than how resources are allocated. Troyna and Vincent (1996) have noted this shift:

> There are signs that parent groups active in special education are no longer obsessed simply with issues of distribution and resourcing and are increasingly assertive and confrontational as they begin to challenge the ways in which their children have been defined and categorised.
>
> (p. 141)

If this is so, it can only be welcomed. So long as individual parents or parents' groups are driven to compete with each other for resources, the possibility for a stronger, collective voice remains weak. In some localities the existence of a group has resulted in arrangements with the LEA which are close to partnership. For example, in the London Borough of Newham the LEA routinely informs parents of the Parents' Support Network, which is part of the Newham Parents' Centre (Wolfendale, 1989). Troyna and Vincent (1996) report on 'Midshire' LEA where there is a regular liaison group which consults on all aspects of LEA special education policy. Nevertheless, they remain pessimistic about the 'political clout' which parents' groups actually exert despite operating in a 'collective fashion'. They put this down to marginalization in the policy-making process:

> Despite their incursions in some localities, collective campaigns which parents have organised in this sphere of education remain structurally peripheral to and marginalised by the direction and nature of decision and policy-making processes in special education.
>
> (Troyna and Vincent, 1996: 142)

This suggests that parent groups should rethink their approach in order to be more effective for the common cause of special education within an inclusive system. Indeed, this must surely be the focus in order that the inclusion of pupils with SEN into mainstream education does not result, in political terms, in their 'disappearance'. The aim should surely be for the special needs lobby to persuade the mainstream parent lobby of the strength of their arguments for meeting the learning needs of all children adequately and effectively.

Lessons might be learned from other 'user' groups. Writing about such groups in the area of mental health services and disabled people, Barnes (1999) (drawing upon theories of new social movements and citizenship) raises two important issues:

> the significance of identity as a factor defining both motivation to act collectively and the objectives pursued by such groups; and changes within local governance which have provided space in which user groups can act but which have prioritized the identity of service users as consumers rather than citizens.
>
> (Barnes, 1999: 76)

Drawing upon Melucci (1985) and Phillips (1993), Barnes suggests that the need now is for such groups to acknowledge pluralism and emphasize the agency of actors who have 'shared identities' and 'common interests'. A quote from Phillips highlights the difference between identity groups and interest groups:

> The new pluralism homes in on identity rather than interest groups: not those gathered together around some temporary unifying concern – to define their neighbourhood against a major road development, to lobby their representatives against some proposed new law – but those linked

by a common culture, a common experience, a common language. These links are often intensely felt, and, more important still, are often felt as opposition and exclusion. Identity groups frequently secure their identity precisely around their opposition to some 'other', focussing on a past experience of being excluded, and sometimes formulating a present determination to exclude.

(Phillips, 1993: 78)

Such a debate is pertinent now for parents' groups in special education. How inclusive can they be in order to build strong alliances and networks within an inclusive system of education for their children? This raises questions about the term 'pressure group' and their legitimation as powerful players. Organized groups in special education, as elsewhere, may be seen as self-interested and even unrepresentative of the 'unorganized' users of the system. There is always the danger that formalized groups, while still seeking to represent, become detached from the grassroots. As Barnes suggests:

Organising within user movements can create the conditions in which it is possible for people to act as 'genuine' representatives of communities of identity, but it can also be used to undermine the legitimacy of such representations by constructing them as expressions of self-interest in the context of pressure group activity.

(Barnes, 1999: 79)

She also raises questions about the connotations of 'pressure' for different people and suggests that it could be seen as resistance (very necessary in attempting to remove barriers and change attitudes). As the special education needs' lobbies become part of a more integrated system, should their work now be seen in a more positive light? And how can they accommodate both different identities and different interests?

Conclusion

And what of social justice? As previously suggested, so long as a deficit model of special education persists within a system which is oriented to reject those with special educational needs – and within a quasi-market there is no evidence to reassure us that this will not continue to be the case – there is little hope for a socially just model which embraces and encourages special education, in all its forms, in a truly inclusive system. So long as this situation continues, the role of parents' groups will be vital to maintain the strongest possible 'voice' – that of the collective – in defence of the interests of all pupils with SEN. They will also need to persuade mainstream parents and reach shared agreements with them about what an inclusive education system means and how it should operate. This is a matter of acknowledging and accommodating difference.

Corbett and Norwich (1997) have already pointed out the importance of an 'inclusive ideology' in order that an inclusive education system can flourish. So long as there is a market system in education, they suggest, 'the values of choice and diversity (market values) come into conflict with those of equality and social cohesion (inclusion values)' (p. 385).

Individual self-interest must, therefore, be informed by collective interests. This will not necessarily result in a consensus around a 'common good', but will result in common goals based on the values of social cohesion. This will require individuals and groups (both within special education and more widely) to come together to form shared agreements and to acknowledge mutual needs and interests. Parents' groups in special education would have a significant role to play in shaping such a process. There must be an accommodation between more powerful groups of parents who are able to shift resources in favour of their children, as Riddell et al. (1994) suggest, and those with fewer resources who are likely to come off worse. Research has already highlighted the importance of the 'independent' strategies some parents and parent groups have used to effect institutional change, but as Vincent and Tomlinson (1997) point out; 'Is it possible that these groups can create a new model for parental participation in the education system – one that is neither that of passive partner nor individual consumer?' (p. 373). For this is surely the way forward. In 1987, Dessent suggested that a parent-led organization was required to 'embrace the needs or rights of all pupils with learning difficulties' (Dessent 1987: 46). Surely this would be a 'voice' to be reckoned with?

Notes

1   GEST funding has been available for parent partnership schemes following the introduction of the Code of Practice in 1994. From 1999 the government expects all LEAs to have such a scheme and, if necessary, will legislate to make this a requirement. (See the *Programme for Action*, DfEE, 1998.)

2   Hirschman (1970) defines 'voice' as:

> To resort to voice, rather than exit, is for the customer or member to make an attempt at changing the practices, policies and outputs of the firm from which one buys or the organization to which one belongs. Voice here is defined as any attempt at all to change rather than escape from an objectionable state of affairs, whether through individual or collective petition.
>
> (p. 30)

References

Armstrong, D. (1995) *Power and Partnership in Education*. London: Routledge.

Armstrong, D. and Galloway, D. (1994) 'Special educational needs and problem behaviour: making policy in the classroom', in S. Riddell and S. Brown (eds) *Special Educational Needs Policies in the 1990s: Warnock in the Market Place*. London: Routledge.

Ball, S., Bowe, R. and Gewirtz, S. (1995) 'Circuits of schooling: a sociological exploration of parental choice in social class contexts', *Sociological Review*, 43(1), 52–78.

Barnes, M. (1999) 'Users as citizens: collective action and the local governance of welfare', *Social Policy and Administration*, 33(1), 73–90.

Barry, B. (1989) *Theories of Social Justice*. London: Harvester Wheatsheaf.

BDA (British Dyslexia Association) (1998) *Dyslexia Contact*, 17 (September), 3.

Corbett, J. and Norwich, B. (1997) 'Special needs and client rights: the changing social and political context of special educational research', *British Education Research Journal*, 23(3), 379–89.

Department for Education (1994) *Code of Practice on the Identification and Assessment of Special Educational Needs*. London: HMSO.

Department for Education and Employment (1997) *Excellence for All Children: Meeting Special Education Needs*. London: HMSO.

Department for Education and Employment (1998) *Meeting Special Education Needs: A Programme for Action*. London: The Stationery Office.

Department for Education and Science (1978) *Special Educational Needs* (The Warnock Report). London: HMSO.

Dessent, T. (1987) *Making the Ordinary School Special*. Lewes: Falmer Press.

Duffield, J., Riddell, S. and Brown, S. (1995) *Policy, Practice and Provision for Children with Specific Learning Difficulties*. Aldershot: Avebury.

Evans, J. and Vincent, C. (1997) 'Parental choice and special education', in R. Glatter, P. Woods and C. Bagley (eds) *Choice and Diversity in Schooling: Perspectives and Prospects*. London: Routledge.

Galloway, D., Armstrong, D. and Tomlinson, S. (1994) *The Assessment of Special Educational Needs*. London: Longman.

Glatter, R., Woods, P. and Bagley, C. (1997) *Choice and Diversity in Schooling: Perspectives and Prospects*. London: Routledge.

Goacher, B., Evans, J., Walton, J. and Wedell, K. (1988) *Policy and Provision for Special Needs*. London: Cassell.

Harvey, D. (1973) 'Social justice, postmodernism and the city', *International Journal of Urban and Regional Regeneration*, 16, 588–601.

Hirschman, A.O. (1970) *Exit, Voice and Loyalty: Responses to Decline in Firms, Organisations and States*. London: Cambridge University Press.

Lunt, I. and Evans, J. (1994) 'Dilemmas of special educational needs; some effects of local management of schools', in S. Riddell and S. Brown (eds) *Special Educational Needs Policies in the 1990s: Warnock in the Market Place*. London: Routledge.

Melucci, A. (1985) 'The symbolic challenge of contemporary movements', *Social Research*, 52(4), 789–816.

Munn, P. (ed.) (1994) *Partners, Customers or Managers?*. London: Routledge.

Nixon, J., Martin, J., McKeown, P. and Ranson, S. (1996) *Encouraging Learning*. Buckingham: Open University Press.

Nosick, R. (1974) *Anarchy, State and Utopia*. New York: Basic Books.

Paige-Smith, A. (1997) 'The rise and impact of the parental lobby; including voluntary groups and the education of children with learning difficulties or disabilities', in S. Wolfendale (ed.) *Working with Parents of SEN Children after the Code of Practice*. London: David Fulton.

Phillips, A. (1993) *Democracy and Difference*. Cambridge: Polity Press.

Ranson, S. (1992) 'Towards the learning society', *Educational Management and Administration*, 20(2), 68–79.

Rawls, J. (1971) *A Theory of Justice*. Oxford: Clarendon Press.

Riddell, S., Brown, S. and Duffield, J. (1994) 'Parental power and special education needs: the case of specific learning difficulties', *British Education Research Journal*, 20(3), 327–44.

Rizvi, F. and Lingard, B. (1996) 'Disability, education and the discourse of justice', in C. Christensen and F. Rizvi (eds) *Disability and the Dilemmas of Education and Justice*. Buckingham: Open University Press.

Slee, R. (1995) *Changing Theories and Practices of Discipline*. London: Falmer.

Tomlinson, S. (1982) *A Sociology of Special Education*. London: Routledge.

Troyna, B. and Vincent, C. (1996) 'The ideology of expertism: the framing of special education and racial quality policies in the local state', in C. Christensen and F. Rizvi (eds) *Disability and the Dilemmas of Education and Justice*. Buckingham: Open University Press.

Vincent, C. and Tomlinson, S. (1997) 'Home–school relationship: the swarming of disciplinary mechanisms?' *British Educational Research Journal*, 23(3), 361–77.

Wolfendale, S. (1989) 'Parental-involvement and power-sharing in special needs', in S. Wolfendale (ed.) *Parental Involvement: Development Networks between School, Home and Community*. London: Cassell.

Wolfendale, S. and Cook, G. (1997) 'Evaluation of special education needs parent partnership schemes', *DfEE Research Report RR34*. London: HMSO.

Young, I.M. (1990) *Justice and the Politics of Difference*. Princeton, NJ: Princeton University Press.

14 Inclusion and the Role of the Voluntary Sector

Olga Miller

Introduction

In any examination of the development of a more inclusive society there is inevitably a need to focus not only on the individual but also on the infrastructures, which support the individual in society. In terms of education, such infrastructures include the context of schooling as well as the mechanisms which facilitate the process of education itself. In recent years, central government has played an increasing part in moulding both the context and the process of education. This overt involvement in education by government has, in many instances, triggered a reaction from the voluntary sector. The voluntary sector has always played an important role in providing a counterbalance to state control. Successive governments have recognized the need for an active voluntary sector and have encouraged (if not always valued) its intervention in support of minority need or alternative forms of policy and provision. In the field of education, children with special needs have, therefore, traditionally been a focus for voluntary sector involvement.

Recent legislation has reinforced what is often described as a partnership between statutory provision and the voluntary sector, though how much equity actually exists between the 'partners' is open to much discussion. In England the 1997 Green Paper, *Excellence for All Children: Meeting Special Educational Needs*, gave particular emphasis to multi-agency planning and service delivery. Indeed, in his foreword to the Green Paper the Secretary of State indicates that:

> we want all parents of children with SEN to get effective support from the full range of local services and voluntary agencies, to have a real say in decisions about their child's education, and to be empowered to contribute themselves to their child's development.
>
> (DfEE, 1997: 5)

The equivalent discussion paper in Scotland *Special Educational Needs in Scotland* (Scottish Office, 1998) goes further by including a specific section on the role of the voluntary sector and in listing a number of areas in which the voluntary sector can contribute to an improvement in provision for children and young people with special educational needs. Some of the areas identified in the Paper can be seen as complementary to statutory services, while others overlap and some may eventually challenge statutory service provision. These include:

- offering advice and guidance to parents and young persons;
- providing advocacy services, e.g. through the provision of Named Persons;
- providing local authorities with a range of staff training and development opportunities;
- supporting early identification and informing the assessment process for SEN;
- advising parents and schools in the increasingly important area of special educational needs technology;
- undertaking special educational needs research and applying it to provide examples of good practice.

In line with government policy, much recent legislation has been concerned to foster more inclusive practices within education. This emphasis on inclusion in government rhetoric is combined with underpinning exhortations for ongoing collaboration between voluntary and statutory sectors. However, tensions emerge from the implicit assumption that the voluntary sector and central government share a common view of inclusive practice. There is also a further tension, which arises from a notion that the voluntary sector in its many forms will display a unity of purpose.

Assumptions made by central government do not recognize the diversity of the voluntary sector. In order to explore how the disparate areas of activity within the sector may impact on concepts of inclusion, it is useful to look closely at a sector which is described by its critics as an anachronism, still embedded within its Victorian philanthropic roots, and by its supporters as at the cutting edge of contemporary service provision.

The Voluntary Sector

The voluntary sector has come to play an increasingly important part in society, not only in providing a safety net for the disadvantaged but also as an active partner with central government in decision-making and service delivery. It is therefore extremely difficult to use a single definition of this sector to adequately describe its diverse, dynamic and complex interactions with everyday life. Low (1998) gives a broad definition of voluntary sector activity as 'one of the oldest and most basic forms of social activity – the voluntary coming together of individuals to engage in undertakings for the common good' (p. 116).

The Report of the Commission on the Future of the Voluntary Sector (1996: 15) also emphasizes the historical aspects of a sector which brought individuals together for mutual benefit. However, unlike other areas of activity within a capitalist society, the voluntary sector was not dependent upon the market place. This distinct 'not-for-profit' feature of the sector remains its determining characteristic, and it is this which has given it a freedom to comment often denied other sectors. Beyond the commonality of this 'not-for-profit' approach, voluntary sector organizations are diverse and individual in their structures and mandates. Indeed, this is one of the great strengths of the sector and helps to maintain its flexibility and independence.

The voluntary sector is large. There are over 40,000 organizations in the UK, which relate to the sector as a whole. But this figure does not include many small local initiatives. Were these to be included, this figure would probably rise to well over a million (Halfpenny, 1996). Not all voluntary bodies are registered as charities. There are under 100,000 registered charities in England and Wales (Low, 1998). However, the number registered is growing, probably as an outcome of the increasing wariness of funders to support organizations not registered as charities. Government tax incentives have also increased the desirability of charity registration.

Handy (1990) identifies five overlapping types of voluntary organizations; his list includes direct service providers, self-help groups and those concerned with research, advocacy or leisure. Knight (1993) expands this view by defining six categories of voluntary organizations. In Knight's categorization of the voluntary sector service philanthropy remains the dominant form of action. In this model 'the helper is often socially distant from the helped' (Knight, 1993: 45). Knight goes on to identify what many consumers of services provided by the voluntary sector often see as a more acceptable model, that of social solidarity. This category assumes a commonality of interest and need arising from mutual experience.

Not all voluntary bodies are devoted to a specific interest group or 'cause'. Some maintain an overarching concern for the sector itself. Knight describes these bodies as intermediaries. Intermediaries respond to the needs of other voluntary bodies and provide important links between organizations as well as a range of services and representation. They can also provide a conduit for aspects of joint action. A notable example of the role of intermediaries within education was the National Council for Disabled Children's function in supporting the work of the Special Education Consortium during the passage of the 1993 Education Act, and its involvement in the subsequent development of the 1994 Code of Practice. The role of the intermediary in this instance was to provide a ready-made forum through which specific lobbying could take place. Out of the forum a consortium developed, with a commonality of interest and specific terms of reference. The consortium was then able to function independently of its host intermediary body.

Knight's final three categories do much to highlight the less tangible qualities of the voluntary sector. In these aspects Knight points to two of its most publicly recognized components and one more subtle and personalized aspect. The first of these is generally understood to be the focus of the voluntary sector overall. This aspect is concerned with changing the attitudes and behaviour of others. Inextricably linked to this first aspect is the need to fundraise and find volunteers. It is often at this point that the general public first become aware of and involved in the work of a particular charity.

Knight's third descriptor of the voluntary sector highlights what is often deeply embedded within much of the work of self-help or mutual support groups and is often implicit rather than explicit. It is a more complex and creative aspect which focuses on a general wish of those deeply involved in an issue to find others who share their beliefs or experiences. Although this final aspect can be seen as a vital starting point for the development of effective lobbying, it is often fraught with potential conflict. Such deep personal involvement with a specific cause is often linked with an antagonism towards those who do not share the same ideals. Direct action may take the place of lobbying and allegiances formed with political activists. Thus, there is sometimes a narrow division between direct action and politicization. This is an important distinction because charity law precludes organizations considered to be politically motivated. Large established charities are therefore nervous of being seen to be too radical in their dealings with central government.

The discomfort of charitable bodies in relation to areas of political activity has both advantages and disadvantages. Advantages rest with the ease of negotiation with central government and its agencies experienced by most large charities. This is regardless of the political complexion of the government in power. Disadvantages lie in the suspicion of the larger charities felt by smaller voluntary bodies often representing the same client group. These smaller groups tend to see themselves as offering mutual support, and are sometimes excluded from decision-making on the basis of their direct action. Criticisms of more established bodies therefore emerge on the basis that their compromises with government are too great and consumer interests have given way to political expediency.

The relationship between different aspects of the voluntary sector is complex. In order to gain a more cohesive view of the sector it is possible to sub-divide it under the terms 'broad' and 'narrow'. In this distinction the 'broad' sector includes a wide range of organizations. These organizations may not readily be associated with the voluntary sector, but nevertheless are included on the basis of their not-for-profit status. Such organizations include trade unions and professional associations. The 'narrow' sector, however, relates to a more traditional concept of charitable bodies, which are essentially seen as philanthropic (Leat, 1993).

The inherent pluralism within the sector as a whole is emphasized in a definition of the charitable sector given by the Charity Commission in its evidence to the Commission on the Future of the Voluntary Sector (Commission on the Future of the Voluntary Sector, 1996: 19–20). In its evidence, the Charity Commission focused on the fine distinctions between charitable and voluntary sectors and concluded that the charitable sector can be considered as a subset of the voluntary sector. However, the voluntary sector, while embracing the charitable sector, functions within a separate organizing principle.

Thus, many voluntary organizations straddle several areas of activity and it is not unusual to find, for instance, that one organization may offer direct services on a basis of income generation and in addition engage in activities such as advocacy and campaigning. Nor do voluntary organizations necessarily remain fixed in their primary focus or role, but adapt and change in response to the current demands and values of society.

User Involvement in the Voluntary Sector

Much of what is still a traditional view of the voluntary sector derives from perceptions of nineteenth-century service philanthropy and is bound up in what are seen as paternalistic attitudes. Within education there is a strong tradition of voluntary sector involvement in the creation of school provision for those seen as disadvantaged by social exclusion as a result of poverty, neglect or disability. Victorian philanthropists recognized that the outcome of any one aspect of social exclusion formed an inevitable link with others, the interaction between all components thus creating and recreating the cycle of disadvantage and disaffection. Nor were the disadvantaged the only recipients of schooling provided by the voluntary sector. Even today, private schooling for the socially advantaged maintains charitable status.

At its best, the work of Victorian philanthropists built on the awareness of eighteenth-century writers such as Diderot, who in a letter of 1774 had recognized some of the potential difficulties arising from blindness and in an elegant plea for better treatment concluded: 'We must be wretches indeed if we can grudge either labour or expense in procuring them every source of entertainment which, when procured, remains in their own power and yields what may be in some measure termed self-derived enjoyment' (RNIB archive).

A more widely held perception of Victorian philanthropy derives from what Handy (1976: 184) and others have described as a power culture which is often based on charismatic authority (Weber, 1924). Therefore, at its worst, Victorian patronage in the form of charity is seen as excluding, controlling and disempowering the individuals identified as those in need, while feeding self-aggrandizement on the part of the benefactor. Drake (1992) expands this view by a reflection on the conceptual relationship between power and participation and the need to avoid tokenism. Participation,

Drake argues, is dependent on three preconditions in order to be meaningful:

1 that consumers must have the capacity to actually exercise power;
2 that consumers must occupy roles in which power can be exercised – they must have authority – and
3 that the role must be situated within links and networks such that the exercise of power is effective – that it achieves its purpose.

(Drake, 1992: 271)

Drake is keen to emphasize that all three preconditions must be present if full and meaningful participation is to take place. It therefore follows within Drake's model that those wishing to participate must have the necessary levels of functioning, including sufficient reflexivity, to be able to do so. This view tends to exclude some of the most needy and deprived individuals on the grounds of severe intellectual impairment or diminished responsibility. Drake's model highlights the problems children face in their struggle for participation. Even those organizations which claim to represent the views of the child do so by assuming the role of consumer 'on behalf' of the child. One outcome of the limited participation of children and young people in voluntary sector decision-making is that policy initiatives are most commonly directed towards parents or those acting in the role of significant other, and do not adequately reflect the views of children as direct service consumers.

The rise within the voluntary sector of demands for a move away from service philanthropy towards a more proactive concept of social solidarity has been particularly strong within the disability movement. Campbell and Oliver (1996) offer a rationale for focusing on disability organizations. This rationale is based on a division between historical and current concepts of the voluntary sector. In particular they (p. 42) cite the split between 'traditional organizations for the disabled and the newer more democratic organizations run by disabled people themselves'. This seeming division between organizations *of* as opposed to organizations *for* has led to much soul-searching within disability-focused charities and the development of new approaches in the provision of services. For instance, those charities which still provide direct services such as special schools are now planning the development of more indirect services, where resources are targeted towards supporting children with disabilities within local mainstream provision. Low gives an example from the field of disabilities of sight and cites the role of the Royal National Institute for the Blind (RNIB):

> In the last twenty years or so, the emphasis has increasingly shifted to the provision of 'indirect' services – information, advice and pressure directed at 'mainstream' service providers like hospitals, local education

authorities or the social services. This pressure is designed to improve the services which the providers offer to blind people, because RNIB has recognized that blind people are mostly going to be using these 'mainstream' agencies already established within the community.

(Low, 1998: 132)

Other charities with a specific childcare brief, such as Barnardos, have closed children's homes and moved into more community-focused projects aimed at working to keep families together and supporting children within their home environment. An example of such an initiative is quoted in the Green Paper: 'The parent partnership scheme in Bradford is based on a three-way partnership between the LEA, Parent Link (a network of local parents and parent support groups) and Barnardos' (DfEE, 1997: 27).

While there have been many benefits arising from the disability movement's challenges to the voluntary establishment, there are also subtle ironies at play. Potentially lost within the emphasis on disability-related issues is a greater awareness of what social solidarity might mean to other groups marginalized by society but with little or no organized support within the voluntary sector. Dyson (1997: 154) suggests that we have lost sight of the relationship between 'children's difficulties in school and wider patterns of socio-economic disadvantage and inequality'. Dyson goes on to warn that an increasing emphasis on disability shifts the more broadly based argument in relation to inclusion towards the more specific one of the inclusion of children with disabilities into mainstream schools. This emphasis on disability is not only true of the discourse around mainstream provision. For instance, as LEAs seek to rationalize special school provision there is an increasing tendency to combine specialist provision for those with sensory impairments, moderate learning difficulties or severe learning disabilities under a label of learning disability. While this provides the necessary economies of scale and potentially facilitates a shift in resourcing towards inclusion, it potentially ignores the implications of subsuming sensory and other needs under a label of learning disability.

This imbalance can easily be attributed to the success of what Dyson describes as 'a highly politicised and articulate disability movement' (1997: 155). It can also be argued that a further spin-off from the success of disability rights campaigners is the emergence of what Dyson terms the new disabilities of dyslexia, dyspraxia and attention deficit disorder, among others. There is ample evidence from surveys of expenditure conducted by the then DES and subsequently by the DfE and DfEE from the early 1990s onwards that teacher training expenditure in the newer disabilities has grown disproportionately to expenditure in other areas of SEN, such as emotional and behavioural difficulties or moderate learning difficulties. This is supported by figures from the Teacher Training Agency (1997). Non-disability categories of SEN have long been over-represented by those from ethnic minorities and other sectors considered socially or economically deprived or disadvantaged.

While it could be argued that it is the very 'newness' and recent identification of some areas of SEN – such as attention deficit disorder – which force LEA pump priming in relation to teacher training, this begs the question of the relationship between short-term funding and long-term planning. While there is need for flexibility, there is a danger in reacting to issues solely in response to lobbyists. Each new disability, in order to reach prominence, tends to be championed by well-organized, single-issue pressure groups, which rapidly develop into successful organizations able to maximize central government's wish for partnership with the voluntary sector.

Most of these single-issue disability groups develop from the concerns of a small core of parents. Well informed and articulate, such parents exhibit skill in mobilizing pressure groups in order to lobby for change. These parents are usually white and middle class. Such success in advocacy has not been the case for areas of special educational need such as emotional and behavioural difficulties, where parents from ethnic minorities and other socially disadvantaged groups tend to predominate. Parents are often suspicious of authority and confused by the complexity of the education system. If voluntary sector action exists, it is often through the domain of service philanthropy rather than social solidarity. Evidence from groups representing those from ethnic minorities (NCVO, 1996) such as SIA (the national development agency for the black voluntary sector) has emphasized the importance of the black perspective and the depth of the problems faced by black and minority members of society. There is a general feeling that, although the ethnic minority sector is very active at a generic level, there is insufficient support available for the specific requirements of the large number of different groups involved.

Accountability and the Voluntary Sector

'Performance is the ultimate test for any institution. Every non-profit institution exists for the sake of performance in changing people and society' (Drucker, 1990: 81).

The voluntary sector, in its breadth and diversity, covers many institutions as well as small mutual support groups which rise and fall according to the needs of their constituents. Accountability in small groups usually relates only to their membership, and since many such organizations exist in pursuit of a single issue then performance is easily measured. But with the growth of what is often termed 'social marketing' (Bruce, 1994) when combined with the involvement of many aspects of the voluntary sector within a contract culture, issues around accountability have become more complex. While there has been a significant increase in collaborative working between voluntary and statutory sectors, this has also been coupled with radical changes in the structure and ethos of central government. This change is highlighted in the 'Efficiency Scrutiny' of the funding of voluntary organizations carried out by the Home Office in 1990. The National Council for Voluntary Organisations (NCVO) notes the main conclusions of the scrutiny: 'Departments should establish clear policy objectives for any core or project grant or scheme, relating to objectives in departments' planning processes. Grants or schemes, which no longer relate to such objectives, should be phased out' (NCVO, 1996: 47).

While it is laudable that expenditure within the voluntary sector should be monitored, careful budgeting is not the only outcome of the change from grants to contracts. By ensuring that only policy objectives supported by central or local government receive funding, the independence of the sector is potentially compromised. Emphasis also shifts towards measures of accountability, which can be applied to both voluntary and private sectors. Competition for funding is therefore extended not only among voluntary bodies, but also between voluntary bodies, the for-profit sector and statutory providers. In education this move has been reflected in some LEAs by the creation of small business units to deliver SEN support services. The voluntary sector has thus found itself in the difficult position of bidding for contracts to provide aspects of support service provision while at the same time offering advocacy for those disadvantaged by the competitive contract culture.

As the voluntary sector is increasingly faced with meeting the demands set by a system based on competition, it must be very clear about its policy objectives from the outset. Involvement in the formulation and implementation of government policy is integral to the work of most established voluntary bodies. Funding relationships with central or local government have made policy work more difficult. Many sophisticated techniques are thus used by the voluntary sector to maintain its involvement in the policy cycle, the most obvious of these being orchestrated lobbying. This route is available to even the smallest organization. Other techniques require access to Ministers as well as ongoing liaison with government departments. Most large charities now employ parliamentary officers who operate as professional lobbyists.

One of the features of the Green Paper was the role played by the National Advisory Group on Special Educational Needs (NAGSEN). A quick look down the membership list of this group indicates the extent of the links with the voluntary sector, which are considerable. However, there are dangers that too close an involvement with policy formulation can hamper objectivity. A delicate balance has to be struck by the voluntary sector in how far it allows itself to be sucked into the policy process and how much distance it maintains. This is particularly important during the stages of policy implementation where unwelcome and unexpected outcomes of policy may have great significance for minority groups.

Inclusion

The role of the voluntary sector in the promotion of a more inclusive society is as complex as the sector itself. Although it is generally true that the disability rights movement has led the way in politicizing the issues facing those with disabilities, there is by no means agreement among disabled people about what inclusion might mean. Colin Low highlights this tension when he writes of the difference between 'inclusion' and 'inclusivism':

> 'Inclusion' or 'full inclusion' as it is often termed, means more than the simple inclusion of disabled people in mainstream society ... 'Inclusivism' is the idea, which is rapidly gaining in popularity, that we should not be creating special services and environments for disabled people.
>
> (Low 1997: 72)

The fundamental differences in perception around the concept of inclusion displayed by the voluntary sector can often be seen as an emphasis on the pragmatic rather than the ideal. However, that is not the only explanation. There is no one view predominant throughout the voluntary sector about what inclusion might mean to those concerned. Within education the debate has tended to focus on the split between special and mainstream provision and is often portrayed as more an issue of resourcing rather than attitudinal or behavioural change. It is worth noting that the Green Paper in its examination of practical steps towards greater inclusion bases three out of its seven proposals specifically on financial incentives:

- direct increased levels of capital support to extend the existing Schools Access Initiative;
- target specific grants towards measures which would enhance mainstream schools' ability to include pupils with SEN;
- give some priority for capital support where possible to planned school reorganisations which would enhance SEN provision in mainstream schools.

> (DfEE, 1997: 47)

That the voluntary sector does not speak with one voice on the subject of inclusion is evidenced by the fact that government policy is also rather equivocal. The reluctance of central government to insist on the closure of special schools derives largely from the mixed messages given by lobbyists. On the one hand is the hard-line stance taken by disability rights activists who take issue not only against the current range of provision available to them but also to the traditional voluntary sector itself. Oliver writes:

> The continued presence and influence of ... traditional organizations is now positively harmful both in terms of the images they promote and

the scarce resources they use up. The time has now come for them to get out of the way. Disabled people and other minority groups are now empowering themselves and this process could be far more effective without the dead hand of a hundred years of charity weighing them down.

(Oliver, 1996: 10)

On the other hand is the reality that a myriad of small mutual support organizations exist in order to promote what they consider to be the very specific needs of their constituents. Within education these groups tend to be concerned with the newer or very low incidence areas of disability, although organizations such as CASE (Campaign for the Advancement of State Education) have more global concerns. There is no doubt that Oliver's strength of feeling is echoed by many disability activists. If the large traditional charities were the only players, then abolishing them would certainly promote significant change. But it would be hard to predict the nature of such change. For instance, it could be argued that the biggest barrier to the closure of specialist provision is parental choice. Many activists within the large traditional voluntary sector are disabled, or parents and carers of those with disabilities. There is an enormous variety of stakeholders involved. Among the many questions to be asked is whether the discourse around power and participation is in tune with the future. For instance, who will meet the needs of those with complex and profound disabilities or the increasing number of elderly, frail and disorientated members of society? Such groups are currently major consumers of specialist services. If all areas of provision were equally well resourced, then inclusivism would work. To assume that this is likely is idealistic at the very least. It therefore seems neither possible nor desirable that specialist provision should entirely disappear. Can government, for instance, guarantee that a sufficient range of specific services be available to abused and emotionally damaged children and their families without the support of the voluntary sector? Does any government really want to make such a commitment? All evidence to date points to the contrary.

Although much of the rhetoric around the voluntary sector and inclusion is concerned with disability, there are wider issues to be considered. Facing the voluntary sector in the next millennium are challenges arising from fundamental changes within society. Some of the most important of these are identified in *Meeting the Challenge of Change*, the second volume of the Report of the Commission on the Future of the Voluntary Sector (Commission on the Future of the Voluntary Sector, 1996: 119). How these changes evolve may lessen or increase the need for an independent voluntary sector. Such changes include the role of the state and any subsequent changes in the systems involved in providing welfare, as well as the changing nature of employment, in terms of both availability and the status of the unemployed.

It is unlikely that all inequalities will be removed, and discrimination may well persist in relation to any number of factors, both traditional – such as race or gender – and emerging – such as ageism. As far as the voluntary sector and children are concerned, changes within the structure and composition of the family are likely to impact significantly on its role in society. There are also questions to ask, for instance, in relation to society as a whole. Will a sense of community persist in the wake of ever-greater mobility? Will a greater balance be struck between rights and responsibilities? And how will the needs of the individual fare when in conflict with the demands of multi-national corporations? There have already been massive changes as a result of new technologies: where will these lead in the future – to greater equality or increased control?

Conclusion

Inclusion is a multi-dimensional concept embedded within individual rights and responsibilities as well as those of society as a whole. The voluntary sector continues to argue vigorously for the individual but is not always so clear about finding a match between individual and community needs. There are worrying dilemmas facing the sector, one of the most significant being the increasing role of voluntary bodies in the provision of statutory services. In relation to support services provided by LEAs for children with special needs, voluntary bodies tend to operate within the remit of particular disabilities. While this can successfully safeguard provision for some children, in the future this approach could militate against a more cohesive and inclusive view of service development.

Children and young people with special educational needs have provided a focus for much activity by the voluntary sector. This is for many reasons, both historical and contemporary. Much of the emphasis of the voluntary sector tends to be disability-related. Disability was an early concern for Victorian philanthropists, not least because many of them had personal experience of disability within their own families. Deafness and blindness are no strangers, even to the aristocracy. There is still a general perception of disability as 'a good cause' when donating to charity. Disability-focused organizations, therefore, remain relatively wealthy in an increasingly difficult and competitive financial climate. They have little of the social stigma attached to charities supporting those without homes or with mental health problems.

Lobbyists within the voluntary sector have often worked with very different and conflicting agenda. But where efforts have been concerted there have been many undoubted benefits as a result of close working relationships between government agencies and the sector. For example, the development of an enhanced dialogue between consumers represented by the voluntary sector and policymakers has resulted in better-informed policy-making. However, it can also be argued that the impact of the disability rights movement has been lessened by the conflicting voices within the voluntary sector, just as the success of the disability rights movement has in turn possibly lessened the attention paid to the more general impact of social disadvantage and deprivation. This is not a simple divide between traditional, monolithic and hierarchical charities as opposed to newer paradigms based on social solidarity, but the result of a pluralistic sector responding to the competing demands of its many stakeholders. It is unlikely that the future will bring an end to the voluntary sector. Even if a more inclusive society evolves, this is unlikely to diminish the need or the wish for individual action. Like-minded people will continue to meet together. Ironically, a more inclusive society may well promote an increase in the voluntary sector as individuals become more aware of the needs of each other.

References

Bruce, I. (1994) *Meeting Need – Successful Charity Marketing.* Hertfordshire: ICSA.

Campbell, J. and Oliver, M. (1996) *Understanding Our Past, Changing Our Future.* London: Routledge.

Commission on the Future of the Voluntary Sector (1996) *Meeting the Challenge of Change: Voluntary Action into the 21st Century.* London: NCVO Publications.

Corbett, J. and Norwich, B. (1997) 'Special educational needs and client rights: the changing social and political context of special educational research', *British Educational Research Journal*, 23(3), 379–90.

Department for Education (1993) *Code of Practice on the Identification and Assessment of Special Educational Needs.* London: HMSO.

Department for Education and Employment (1996) *The Code of Practice Two Years On*, report of national conferences held in London and York. London: DfEE.

Department for Education and Employment (1997) *Excellence for All Children: Meeting Special Educational Needs.* London: The Stationery Office.

Drake, R.F. (1992) 'Consumer participation: the voluntary sector and the concept of power', *Disability, Handicap and Society*, 7(3), 267–78.

Drake, R.F. (1994) 'The exclusion of disabled people from positions of power in British voluntary organisations', *Disability and Society*, 9(4), 461–80.

Drucker, P.F. (1990) *Managing the Non-profit Organisation.* London: Butterworth-Heinemann.

Dyson, A. (1997) 'Social and educational disadvantage: reconnecting special needs education', *British Journal of Special Education*, 24, 152–7.

Florian, L. (1998) 'An examination of the practical problems associated with the implementation of the inclusive education policies', *British Journal of Special Education*, 13, 105–8.

Halfpenny, P. (1996) 'Future developments in funding for the voluntary sector', *Meeting the Challenge of Change: Voluntary Action into the 21st Century.* London: NCVO.

Handy, C. (1976) *Understanding Organizations.* Harmondsworth: Penguin.

Handy, C. (1990) *Understanding Voluntary Organisations.* Harmondsworth: Penguin.

Knight, B. (1993) *Voluntary Action.* Edinburgh: CENTRIS.

Knight, B. (1995) 'Voluntary Action and Community Development'. Paper for the Scottish Community Development Centre.

Leat, D. (1993) *Managing Across Sectors*. London: City Business School.

Low, C. (1998) 'Is inclusivism possible?' *European Journal of Special Needs*, 12(1), 71–9.

Oliver, M. (1996) 'User involvement in the voluntary sector – a view from the disability movement', in National Council of Voluntary Organisations *Meeting the Challenge of Change: Voluntary Action into the 21st Century*. London: NCVO.

Scottish Office (1998) *Special Educational Needs in Scotland – A Discussion Paper*. Edinburgh: The Stationery Office.

Special Educational Needs Training Consortium (1996) *Professional Development to Meet Special Educational Needs*. Staffordshire County Council: SENTC. Copies available from Flash Ley Resource Centre, Hawksmoor Road, ST17 9DR.

Teacher Training Agency (1997) 'Training of SEN specialist teachers – next steps'. Unpublished discussion document, Teacher Training Agency.

Thomas, G. (1997) 'Inclusive schools for an inclusive society', *British Journal of Special Education*, 24, 103–7.

Weber, M. (1924) 'Legitimate authority and bureaucracy', in D.S. Pugh *Organisational Theory – Selected Readings*. Harmondsworth: Penguin.

15 Parents, Legislation and Inclusion

Katy Simmons

Whatever models of inclusive practice are debated by education professionals, there still remains a significant group of children and young people who never gain access to a mainstream school or classroom, despite the preference for mainstream expressed by their parents. These children may become the subject of appeals to the Special Educational Needs Tribunal, or even to the High Court. Often their cases become *causes célèbres* locally. Some parents are ultimately successful in their appeals and eventually their children become mainstream pupils, though they have missed significant amounts of education. Other would-be mainstream pupils remain permanently out of school.

Special education legislation currently does not offer children an unqualified individual right to a mainstream place. Nor does it offer a parent the unqualified right to have a child educated in 'a school which is not a special school'. For individual families, the lack of such rights leads to compulsory segregation and to situations where children, in the words of the Directors of the Centre for Studies in Inclusive Education 'are forced into separate special schools against the family's wishes' (Vaughan and Shaw, personal communication). Though current legislation creates presumptions in favour of mainstream education and in favour of parental choice, it lacks the force, in practice, to prevent the compulsory segregation of a significant number of young people.

Inclusion and the Law

Since the enactment of the 1981 Education Act, in 1983, local education authorities have had a qualified legal duty to place children with special educational needs in mainstream schools. In practice the effect of this qualified duty is that LEAs must place children in mainstream schools unless a number of criteria cannot be met. If an LEA wishes to place pupils in a special school, then it must bring forward sufficient evidence to overcome the presumption in favour of mainstream. An LEA's legal duty is currently set out in Section 316 of the 1996 Education Act. Since so much debate focuses on this Section and it has been the source of such difficulty for many families, it is worth setting it out in full at the start of this chapter.

Section 316 reads as follows:

(1) Any person exercising any functions under this part in respect of a child with special educational needs who should be educated in school shall secure that, if the conditions mentioned in sub-section (2) are satisfied, the child is educated in a school which is not a special school unless that is incompatible with the wishes of his parent.

(2) The conditions are that educating the child in a school which is not a special school is compatible with:
    (a) his receiving the special educational provision which his learning difficulty calls for,
    (b) the provision of efficient education for the children with whom he will be educated, and
    (c) the efficient use of resources.

What does this Section mean in practice? Simply, that those empowered to make decisions about placement, whether they are LEA officers, Tribunal panels or High Court judges, can legitimately block a mainstream placement by invoking one or more of these conditions (generally referred to as 'the caveats'). Further to Section 316, Schedule 27 to the Act gives parents the right to express a preference for a particular school, which LEAs must honour, again subject to the three caveats. But once an initial decision not to make a mainstream placement has been made under Section 316, the expression of such a preference carries no force. In this way, parents who want a mainstream place can find themselves, as far as the law is concerned, on a less than level playing field, since their parental preference carries no weight once one or more of the caveats in Section 316 has been invoked.

Crucially, although LEAs always have a general duty to use their resources 'efficiently', the mainstream/special decision is the only decision in the area of special education where relative costs can be invoked as a defining part of the decision-making process. Many parents, having established that the mainstream school they prefer could meet their child's needs, find themselves unable to counter the argument that it would cost more to send their child there. Section 316 provides no impetus for change in LEAs where custom and practice have established segregated provision as the norm. So, for example, in LEAs which historically have invested in special school provision, and where there is no political will for change, it is particularly difficult for parents to counter the resource argument. Figures published regularly by CSIE show that it continues to matter where you live (Norwich, 1997). For parents, access to mainstream education may depend on which county you live in, what age your child is and what kind of special needs your child has. For example, Stephanie Lorenz, writing in 1995, was able to point to areas of England and Wales where the majority of children with Down's syndrome attended their local school and no parent had needed to use the appeal procedure to secure a mainstream place. At the same time, she commented, 'there are still some LEAs where no children with Down's syndrome have been placed in their local school' (Lorenz, 1995: 18). The Alliance for Inclusive Education reported the story of the Clarke family, who moved from Northumberland to Calderdale in order to secure a mainstream place for their hearing impaired child (Mason, 1998). Parents in Devon have reported that 'though it is now easy to secure a mainstream place for a child with Down's syndrome in Plymouth, it is still almost impossible to transfer to mainstream secondary provision' (Network 81, 1998: 21).

Section 316, therefore, has allowed the continuation of a patchy national picture, where placement depends not only on a child's age, where they live and what kind of special needs they have, but also on parental energy and commitment, as well as willingness to face possible prosecution (Brandon, 1997; IPSEA, 1994). For a few families, the refusal to accept a segregated placement for their child has led to court appearances and, in the case of Gail McKibben in Northern Ireland, a one-year suspended sentence for her refusal to send her son David to a special school (Mason, 1998).

The Legal Framework

In offering no guaranteed right to mainstream placement where parents prefer it, Section 316 is the weak link in a legislative framework which, in its totality, offers children with special educational needs quite robust protection. This framework guarantees a child with special educational needs access to entitlement to assessment and provision which is on offer to no other part of the community. The same piece of legislation, the 1981 Education Act, which included what was to become Section 316, also created a situation where children with special educational needs have a right in law to have their needs identified, to have them met by provision and to have them regularly reviewed. These entitlements are created through a series of interlocking legal duties placed on LEAs and reinforced in subsequent legislation. These duties are owed personally to the child and are non-delegable. The statement is the mechanism by which the legal entitlement is delivered.

No child is entitled to 'the best': no LEA should use their resources inefficiently. But children with special educational needs are entitled to have their needs met, whatever policies are adopted by their LEA. As a point of principle, Parliament decided that this small group of children should have a protected entitlement to the provision which meets their needs.

This protected legal status makes children with special educational needs very different in law from, for example, disabled adults or the elderly who require Care in the Community. For disabled adults or for the elderly there is no such entitlement. Though they may be entitled to assessment, they are not entitled to provision. What they get depends on what their local authority can, or will, spend: locally developed 'criteria' can be drawn so stringently that few qualify for provision, though the authority may well be aware of unmet need. Such a situation cannot arise with children with special educational needs: once need is established through assessment and set out in the statement, then the LEA must provide for that need: they cannot lawfully argue that they do not have the resources to meet the child's needs. Significantly, following the Law Lords' ruling in the Tandy case, even where a child does not have a statement, it is need, not local resources or policies, which must determine provision (Ruebain, 1998).

So overall the framework of the law pertaining to children with special educational needs is a robust one, in that it forges a direct link between need and provision and lays on LEAs a direct duty to meet individual need. In times of financial stringency in LEAs, such a protected area is likely to be an obvious target for cuts. Weakening such a framework in order to replace legal obligation with local discretion is, from an LEA perspective, a desirable aim of government.

And so it was in October 1997 when the New Labour government introduced its Green Paper, *Excellence for All Children: Meeting Special Educational Needs* (DfEE, 1997).

The SEN Green Paper and Inclusion

Many people thought the Green Paper was simply about inclusion. Indeed, what previous government document had declared its support for the Salamanca Statement (UNESCO, 1994)? What previous government policy statement had promised to 'promote' inclusion wherever possible? What previous Secretary of State had personal experience of segregated schooling, which, he felt, had left him unprepared for life? Yet, as Estelle Morris, the Minister with responsibility for the Green Paper said to the Select Committee, inclusion 'was not the reason for having produced the Green Paper ... it is not all that is in the Green Paper' (*Hansard*, 9 December 1997).

Why the Green Paper was produced, its contents and implications, have been discussed at length elsewhere (Simmons, 1998). From the viewpoint of many voluntary organizations, the focus on inclusion had to be viewed quite separately from the rest of the document. What the document was primarily about was the 'capping' of statementing. It was an attempt to remove the link between need and provision, weaken a child's right to detailed and specified provision and remove individual need as the pivot of provision. Goodwill and discretion were to become substitutes for legal duty and children's entitlement.

Many voluntary organizations and parents, while welcoming the focus on inclusion, reacted strenuously to the threat it posed to the legal framework. RADAR, for example, a national voluntary organization working for and with adults with disabilities, was quick to see that the proposals in the Green Paper would slide children in the general direction of LEA discretion and away from statutory entitlement, so that their position would mirror that of RADAR's own (adult) client group. RADAR's press release, issued at the time of the publication of the Green Paper, was clear about what it considered to be the real focus of the document:

> RADAR is deeply concerned that by reducing the statementing process the allocation of resources will become a lottery, decided by those parents and schools that are the most vociferous. RADAR is also deeply worried by the proposal that some individual local education authorities can consider resources when considering a child's needs. The needs of a disabled child must come first and not be superseded by financial implications.
>
> (RADAR, 1997)

The voluntary sector – and parents – were not convinced that the way to promote inclusion was by the reduction of legal right to provision. A number of national and local voluntary organizations, some of them direct campaigners for inclusion, formed an alliance on this central issue of legal entitlement. The group, Action on Entitlement, wrote to Secretary of State David Blunkett:

> The Government has announced that it means to shift resources from statemented to non-statemented children ... a shift from provision protected by statute to provision which is discretionary and variable. The organizations we represent have no confidence that the discretion or goodwill of local authorities will deliver the necessary support. It is the force of law alone that protects these vulnerable children's interests.
>
> (Action on Entitlement, 1997)

The groups that formed Action on Entitlement had direct contact with parents: many of them were directly engaged in case work. Unlike some more theoretically based commentators, they could see that it was the detail in statements that in many cases actually ensured a mainstream placement for many children. In its response to the Green Paper, the Independent Panel for Special Education Advice (IPSEA), made this point and cited one of their cases as an example:

> Under current law, a child whose needs cannot be met by the resources available to their school has their right to special educational provision secured by means of a statement of special educational needs. The statement should list all the child's needs and should specify the educational

provision required to meet them (S324 (1) EA1996). In our view, when LEAs fulfil their duties under the law, statements are effective guarantees of provision. The real problem is LEA failure to detail provision as the law intends.

Children with special educational needs who are included in mainstream schools have a particular need for statements written in a way that is consistent with the law. IPSEA's experience is that particularly for children with a number of needs, such as those with Down's syndrome or cerebral palsy, the detail of the statement is the key to a successful mainstream placement. Where provision has not been specified, or where it is dependent on 'discretion' or 'goodwill' then breakdown of the placement becomes more likely, particularly for secondary age children. Conversely, in our experience, a detailed statement which sets out all the child's needs in the way the law intends, matching each one with the necessary provision, can turn an initially reluctant school into the child's most active advocate.

Take, for example, the case of Kavita, aged 10, who lives in a London Borough. She has cerebral palsy, spastic quadriplegia with athetoid movements and mild epilepsy controlled by medication. She communicates through eye pointing. There is considerable evidence that her cognitive skills are age appropriate and her parents wished her to attend a local primary school. The LEA refused and her parents appealed to the SEN Tribunal.

At the hearing the LEA agreed to name the school the parents preferred. A detailed statement was drafted at the hearing with the agreement of both parties. In due course, Kavita became a pupil at the school.

The result has been an unqualified success story. Kavita is doing well, she has been accepted by her peers and by school staff and pupils. The success of the placement is largely due to the detailed statement which made completely clear what Kavita was to have and who was to provide it. Her parents are convinced that without that detailed statement, the placement would never have had a chance of success.

(IPSEA, 1997a: 13)

By yoking its proposals on inclusion so firmly to its proposals to weaken the law, the Green Paper suggested, in a way that might be seen as disingenuous or at best naive, that in some way the legal framework established by the 1981 Education Act prevented inclusion. As can be seen from IPSEA's response, that was not the perception of those agencies who advise individual parents. For those organizations who joined Action on Entitlement, it was entitlement to, for example, detail on statements, that actually kept many children in mainstream schools.

The experience of many parents seeking an inclusive place is that the root of the problem is not the statement itself. Rather, it is the caveats in Section 316 which enable LEAs to block mainstream placement. And on this area the government remained adamant that no changes were possible. So, paradoxically, having put out a Green Paper that appeared committed to inclusion, when asked at a parents' meeting about the removal of the caveats, Estelle Morris stated that they would not be removing them. She justified her position by saying that '[the government] didn't want to see children in situations where they were not welcome'. She added that 'everything possible would be done to overcome this kind of prejudice', but did not say how this could be achieved (Network 81, 1998: 22).

The SEN Action Plan

The consultation period had led to overwhelming numbers of responses from parents, petitions, demonstrations, parliamentary questions and intense lobbying from the voluntary sector. When, on 5 November 1998, the government released its long-awaited Action Plan, the follow-up to its consultation process on the Green Paper, its main concern was to reassure parents that, whatever its initial plans had been, it no longer intended to make changes to the fundamental legal structure which guaranteed provision to children with special educational needs. Estelle Morris went further and pledged that not only would the government not be making changes of this kind, but that 'it never would'.

'No change in legislation', while being good news for those who had feared the end of legal entitlement, was a disappointment for those (many of them the same people) who had hoped for an end to the caveats in Section 316. While the Action Plan was being developed, there had been considerable lobbying around Section 316, both by the voluntary sector and in Parliament during the passage of the Schools Standards Bill. The proposal being put forward, which gradually appeared to be gaining ground with the government, was that the caveats in Section 316 would go, leaving Schedule 27 intact. The effect of such a change would be that no parent would be categorically denied a mainstream place for their child. However, they would not be guaranteed a particular place in a named school. The LEA would have to offer the child a mainstream place but not necessarily in the school for which the parent had expressed a preference. This position had earned the support of a consensus of interested parties, who recognized that on a practical level it might be some time before every local school would be sufficiently well resourced to meet the needs of every child and that such a proposal would represent a significant step forward from the current situation. As

Lady Darcy de Knayth pointed out in the House of Lords, 'There will be no compulsory placement in a special school, but equally there will be no automatic right to the preferred school either. For the parent who prefers a special school placement that choice is left intact' (*Hansard*, 8 June 1998: col. 825).

As the debate around this Section continued, it appeared that the government was being persuaded towards the removal of the caveats, though there was repeated reference to lack of parliamentary time and the need to avoid pre-empting the deliberations of the Disability Rights Task Force.

The Action Plan, when it came, promised only 'a review' of the statutory framework for inclusion, in conjunction with the work of the Task Force. There were other proposals: for example, from 1999, LEAs would be required to publish information about their policy on inclusion in their Education Development Plans. Additional funding was promised to promote inclusion, as well as additional money through the Schools Access Initiative. There were to be no targets set for increased inclusion in particular authorities. In brief, the law remained as it had been since 1983, and individual parents seeking mainstream placements were left in an all-too-familiar situation.

Securing a Mainstream Place

For parents wishing to challenge a placement in a special school and secure a mainstream place, the caveats remain a barrier. To a limited extent these parents have been assisted by the creation, through the 1993 Education Act, of the Special Educational Needs Tribunal, which replaced the old local appeal system. The brief of the SENT is to consider the child's needs on the day of the Tribunal, and it makes its decisions based on the evidence before it. It is therefore the parent's responsibility to build up a case and to present evidence which will counter whichever conditions of subsection (2) of Section 316 have been cited by the LEA. So parents may have to demonstrate that their child's needs could be met in the mainstream school they prefer, that other children will not be adversely affected and that it will not be an inefficient use of the LEA's resources. Generally, it is the first and third of the caveats which are cited by LEAs and these are the hardest for parents to counter.

Parents' difficulties at Tribunals have been explored elsewhere (Simmons, 1997): it can be very difficult for them, for example, to find a teacher who knows the child well and who is willing to speak in support of a placement that does not have LEA approval. There is a good deal of informal evidence that teachers have pressure to put on them to support their LEA's line at Tribunals. Consequently, parents need to find an independent professional witness who could provide evidence that the preferred school could indeed meet the child's needs. Finding such witnesses can be a great difficulty for parents, particularly when they cannot afford to pay for independent assessments.

Similarly, it can be difficult to argue against inefficient use of resources without access to extensive financial information. Much of this can be made available to parents, but they would need to use the Tribunal Regulations which allow disclosure of documents: again, less confident or less educated parents may be at a disadvantage.

But, where parents have had good advice, or where they have themselves been able to organize their arguments and evidence, the Tribunal process has prevented some LEAs from simply citing the caveats without supporting their decision with evidence. Particularly in the area of 'efficient use of resources', LEA arguments have been put under scrutiny. Once obliged to present evidence, for many LEAs the case for the special school has become less robust.

Significant Cases

Importantly, the Tribunal has questioned, for the first time in a legal forum, what 'efficient use of resources' might mean, and showed that it might not necessarily mean 'cheapest'. Although Tribunal cases do not set legal precedents, some of its judgments have offered useful starting points for other parents.

Such a case was that of K, a 5-year-old girl with severe learning difficulties. Following assessment, her LEA issued a Statement naming a special school, despite the parents' preference for a place at K's local mainstream primary school. The LEA argued that the mainstream placement would not be able to meet K's special educational needs and that it would represent an inefficient use of resources.

The Tribunal initially addressed the first caveat and asked itself the question 'Could the mainstream school meet K's needs?' Its judgment was as follows:

> We do not consider it realistic to expect K's skillbase to increase to a level where she can take full advantage of all that there is to offer in a mainstream setting. Nevertheless, at the present time we do accept that there are potential opportunities where K could greatly benefit, i.e. from the role models around her, particularly in the area of language and speech development to which she is not having access in her present environment. It would also have the added benefit that [the primary school] being a local school would enable K and her family to establish more community-based links, particularly with other children.
>
> (IPSEA 1996: 12)

Then, since the LEA had not cited the second caveat in its refusal of the mainstream place, the Tribunal went on to consider the third caveat, 'efficient use of resources':

> As far as resources are concerned, the cost of a place at [the primary school] with the special school's assistant would be £10,067 p.a. compared to a cost of a place at [the special school] of £5,894.13, but [the special school] figure also needs to have added transport costs of some £4,180, making a total of £10,074. At present K is transported to [the special school] but this would not be necessary were she to be placed at [the primary school]. A true comparison therefore between [the special school] and [the primary school] is £10,074 as against £10,067. In these circumstances, we do consider that a placement at [the primary school] is an efficient use of the LEA's resources.
>
> (ibid.)

The Tribunal further set aside the argument that costly adaptations would need to be made to the primary school:

> As far as the costs of adapting [the primary school] are concerned, we do not believe that these are costs that should be solely attached to K's placement. We accept the argument that provision of ramps and disabled toilet are facilities that might well be installed in any event.
>
> (ibid.)

In K's case, careful presentation of detailed evidence ultimately succeeded in persuading the Tribunal that the caveats should not be seen as a barrier to an inclusive place and that 'efficiency' was not simply a question of cost.

The Crane case, which failed before the Tribunal, but which went to appeal in the High Court, established further ground rules in the 'resources' argument (*C.* v. *Lancashire County Council*, 1997). The judge ruled that, when an LEA or Tribunal considered whether a child's placement in a mainstream school represented an efficient use of resources, they had to employ a two-stage decision process. They should first calculate the additional expenditure involved, then, second, consider the additional benefit that this extra expenditure might bring. This ruling prevents LEAs from simply citing resources as a reason for denying a mainstream place – as a result of the Crane ruling, LEAs must argue their case, not simply assert the resources caveat.

Another Tribunal case concerning resources has been recently appealed to the High Court (*B.* v. *London Borough of Harrow and the Special Needs Tribunal*, 1998). In this case, the parent was seeking an out-of-borough placement for the child. The court held that in considering parental preference and the efficient use of resources, the Tribunal should look at the use of resources of both authorities. They were not entitled to take account only of the cost to the sending authority, but should look at public resources generally. This judgment widened the interpretation of 'efficiency' and has enabled other parents successfully to seek out-of-borough placements.

Case Studies

While for individual children the intervention of the SENT has been effective and radical, for others, in particular those of secondary age, its outcomes have been inconsistent. The interpretation of Section 316 has varied and appeals to the High Court have failed to bring clarification. In addition, the situation for families wishing to challenge Tribunal decisions has been made extremely difficult because of the Legal Aid ruling, which, because parents, not children, are parties to Tribunal cases, means that only the very poorest or very richest of families can instigate legal actions. Two cases which attracted national publicity were those of Niki Crane, then aged 12, from Lancashire and Joanne Spendiff, aged 13, from North Tyneside. Niki was described in his Statement as having severe learning difficulties and 'varying degrees of delay in all areas of development'. Joanne has Down's syndrome. Both young people had been educated in mainstream schools at primary and, in Joanne's case, at middle school level. For both, secondary transfer proved the point at which their LEAs insisted on a special school placement.

Niki Crane's case has been fully documented in Stewart Brandon's book *The Invisible Wall* (1997), which details the background to the case as well as the appeal to the Special Educational Needs Tribunal. John Wright, in a review of this book, commented, 'Stewart observed the two-day Tribunal appeal and his record must be unique, to date, in documenting the cut and thrust (and fudge and evasion) of the SEN Tribunal proceedings' (IPSEA, 1997b: 12–13).

Niki's parents wanted him to attend Tarleton High School, his local secondary school. After protracted negotiation, the LEA had agreed to a placement at Tarleton but then, at the last minute, changed their minds. Their decision to name the special school was upheld by the Tribunal, though the LEA consistently refused to give information about the grounds on which they had based their sudden change of direction. At the Tribunal, the LEA representative and witnesses refused to say who made the decision or when it was made – and certainly not why. Further, the Tribunal steadfastly refused to press the LEA on these questions. Niki's parents appealed against the Tribunal's decision to the High Court, on the grounds that the way the decision had been made, by people who were not professionally involved with Niki (the school staff associations and the governors of Tarleton High), had a direct bearing on the correctness of the resulting decision. Their appeal did not succeed: as John Wright comments, 'Reading this account, it is difficult to avoid the conclusion that the law on inclusion does not work' (ibid.).

A similar conclusion might have been drawn in Joanne Spendiff's case.

When transfer to secondary education was imminent, the Spendiffs expressed a preference for their local Catholic high school. Instead, their LEA named a special school, on the grounds that the preferred school could not meet Joanne's needs, her placement at the school would be detrimental to the education of their children and that it would be an inefficient use of resources. In short, all three caveats were invoked. An independent psychologist assessed Joanne and visited her school. This psychologist later wrote a detailed report, strongly supportive of a mainstream placement for Joanne.

Under the Regulation which allows disclosure of documents, the family had shown that the LEA had not even consulted the preferred school. In the family's view, the LEA had no evidence at all that the school could not meet Joanne's needs, that her placement there would be detrimental to others or that it would be an inefficient use of resources. The family presented evidence in all three areas.

The result, a decision which dismissed the Spendiff's appeal and upheld the LEA decision, was not only deeply disappointing but, potentially, legally flawed. A review of the decision was requested from the Tribunal. Meanwhile the family sought legal advice, though it was likely that the Legal Aid ruling would prevent them from taking action. When the request for a review was turned down, legal action remained the only route open – but where was the money to come from?

A campaign followed to raise national awareness of the problem and to try to raise the money to support both the Spendiffs and the Cranes. Eventually the Barrow Cadbury Trust, interested in social issues and particularly struck by the injustice in these cases, agreed to underwrite the legal action. The case came to the High Court but failed again. The judge upheld the LEA and the Tribunal's decision to prevent Joanne attending a mainstream school without the school itself having been consulted. For Joanne, however, the High Court action was not the end of the story. Although the case had been lost, her LEA eventually offered an alternative mainstream place in a school in a neighbouring LEA, a school which she continues to attend successfully and happily.

The Way Forward

The law governing inclusion, viewed from the perspective of parents, is thus one of the less reliable areas of special education law. The introduction of the Special Educational Needs Tribunal has been helpful for some parents, particularly those with primary age children. But despite the efforts of parents such as the Cranes and Spendiffs, Tribunal and High Court judgments in relation to secondary age pupils have been less predictable. Despite the best efforts of their legal advisers, acting *pro bono*, these families have found that test cases have on the whole delivered little clarification of what proper implementation of Section 316 should involve.

It may be that clarification will come once the recommendations of the Disability Task Force have been translated into legislation. Until then, families will do the best they can to secure mainstream placements. Some will abandon the process of law altogether and rely on direct action to change local opinions. Others will arrange 'education otherwise' for their children. Sadly, it may be some time before legislation measures up to rhetoric.

References

Action on Entitlement (1997) 'Good will "not enough for disabled children" says group of national charities'. Press release, 22 December 1998.

B. v. *London Borough of Harrow and the Special Educational Needs Tribunal* (1998). CA 98 4 ELR 351.

Brandon, S. (1997) *The Invisible Wall: Niki's Fight to be Included*. Hesketh Bank, Lancs.: Parents with Attitude.

C. v. *Lancashire County Council* (1997) 4 ELR 377.

Department for Education and Employment (1997) *Excellence for All Children*. London: The Stationery Office.

House of Commons Official Report (*Hansard*) (1997) Education and Employment Committee: Minutes of Evidence. Tuesday 9 December, Question 4.

House of Lords Official Report (*Hansard*) (1998) 'Children with special educational needs in ordinary schools'. 8 June, col. 825.

IPSEA (Independent Panel for Special Education Advice) (1994) *Integration on Trial*, Special Edition, January, 1–3.

IPSEA (Independent Panel for Special Education Advice) (1996) *Inclusion Decisions*, Special Edition, September.

IPSEA (Independent Panel for Special Education Advice) (1997a) 'Rights at Risk?' Submission to Department for Education and Employment during consultation on Green Paper, December.

IPSEA (Independent Panel for Special Education Advice) (1997b) *Niki Crane – The Struggle Continues*, Special Edition, September, 12–13.

Lorenz, S. (1995) 'The placement of pupils with Down's syndrome: a survey of one northern LEA', *British Journal of Special Education*, 22(1), 16–19.

Mason, M. (1998) *Forced Apart*. London: The Alliance for Inclusive Education.

Network 81 (1998) *Network 81 News*, Summer Term.

Norwich, B. (1997) *A Trend towards Inclusion: Statistics on Special School Placements and Pupils with Statements in Ordinary School England 1992–96*. Bristol: CSIE.

RADAR (1997) 'Government proposals on special education sound alarm bells for disability organisations'. Press release, 22 October.

Ruebain, D. (1998) '*R. v. East Sussex County Council ex parte T*,' *Network 81 News*, Autumn, 14–15.

Simmons, K. (1997) 'What parents need to know', in S. Wolfendale (ed.) *Partnership with Parents in Action*. London: NASEN, 35–40.

Simmons, K. (1998) 'Rights at risk: a response to the Green Paper,' *British Journal of Special Education*, 25(1), 9–12.

UNESCO (United Nations Educational, Scientific and Cultural Organisation) (1994) Salamanca Statement. Paris: UNESCO.

Notes on Contributors

Mel Ainscow is Professor and Dean of the Research and Graduate School in the Faculty of Education, University of Manchester. His recent publications include *Understanding the Development of Inclusive Schools* (Falmer) and *From Them to Us: An International Study of Inclusion in Education* (Routledge).

Angela Creese researches and teaches at the Institute of Education. She has wide interests in the sociology of language. Her interests are in language diversity in education and the policies and practices of managers, teachers and students as they play out in school and university classrooms. Collaborative structures and systems which work with diversity and difference are of special interest.

Harry Daniels is Professor of Special Education and Educational Psychology at the University of Birmingham, where he is also Deputy Head of School (Research). His research interests include gender and attainment in junior schools, peer support for teachers, emotional and behavioural difficulty, and mental health. He has taught in mainstream and special schools and is president of the Association of Workers for Children with Emotional and Behavioural Difficulties and the European Association for Special Education.

Lesley Dee is a lecturer in Inclusive Education at the School of Education, University of Cambridge. She is currently researching the experiences of young people with special educational needs and their families during their transition from school.

Alan Dyson is Professor of Special Needs Education, Co-Director of the Special Needs Research Centre and Director for Research in the Department of Education, University of Newcastle upon Tyne. Before moving to Newcastle University in 1988, he spent thirteen years as a teacher in special and mainstream schools in Newcastle and the north-east of England. He has published and researched widely in the field of special needs education, and is a member of the National Advisory Group on Special Educational Needs which is working on the implementation of the SEN Green Paper. His recent publications with colleagues at Newcastle include *New Directions in Special Needs* (Cassell, 1997) and *Theorising Special Education* (Routledge, 1998).

Peter Evans completed his PhD in mental handicap at the University of Manchester after taking a degree in psychology and anthropology at the University of London. In 1976 he returned to the University of London, to the department of special education at the Institute of Education, where he ran courses for teachers of children with learning difficulties. In 1989 he moved to the OECD in Paris, France, where he has responsibility for the work carried out at the Centre for Educational Research and Innovation on disability and exclusion. He has published some twenty books and many articles and chapters, and has travelled extensively, studying special education systems in both OECD and non-OECD countries.

Valerie Hey is a senior researcher in the academic group Culture, Communication and Societies, Institute of Education, University of London. She was a teacher in secondary, further and adult education for ten years. She has published widely in the field of gender, education, social policy and methodology, and has a particular interest in questions of social difference and feminist post-structuralism. She has recently published a well-received ethnographic study of schoolgirl friendship, *The Company She Keeps* (1997), and is currently co-directing an ESRC-funded study, 'Learning and Gender: a study of underachievement in junior schools'.

Jesper Holst is working as Associate Professor at the Royal Danish School of Educational Studies. From 1988 to 1997 he was a member of a cross-institutional Danish group researching quality of life for persons with disabilities. During the last five years he has been working with SEN and disability matters in Romania and Mongolia.

Penny Lacey is a lecturer at the University of Birmingham. She works in the Learning Difficulties Team running courses for teachers and other staff who work in special and mainstream schools. She has a particular interest in students with profound and multiple learning disabilities and in the way in which staff work together to meet a complexity of needs. Her current research is focused on the role of learning support assistants in the inclusive learning of pupils with severe and profound learning difficulties.

Diana Leonard is Professor of Sociology of Gender and Education and

Director of the Centre for Research and Education on Gender at the Institute of Education, University of London. She has published extensively on the sociology of gender and the family and has recently completed two ESRC-funded research projects on 'Gender and SEN in mainstream junior schooling' and 'Family work of young people, their educational achievement and post-16 careers'. Since October 1997 she and colleagues at the Institute and the University of Birmingham have been working on special needs and violence in schools. Her other interests include differences between the experiences of women and men, and home and overseas doctoral students.

Geoff Lindsay is Director of the Psychology and Special Needs Research Unit, Institute of Education, University of Warwick. He was previously Principal Psychologist, Sheffield LEA. He has been developing and researching approaches to the early identification of children's special educational needs for over twenty years. His main current research interests are baseline assessment, services for children with specific speech and language difficulties, and ethical dilemmas of psychologists and psychotherapists. He is the editor, with David Thompson, of *Values into Practice in Special Education* (1997) and the author, with Martin Desforges, of *Baseline Assessment: Practice, Problems and Possibilities* (1998).

Francis Mallon was born and went to school in Newry, Northern Ireland. He graduated from the University of Birmingham in Psychology and Sociology, and after gaining his PGCE went on to teach in secondary and primary schools in Birmingham before completing professional training in educational psychology. He has worked with the Birmingham Education Department since 1977, and has been a principal psychologist since 1986. He is currently undertaking doctoral research evaluating the impact of the Valued Youth Programme in Birmingham schools.

Jane Martin is a research fellow in the School of Education at the University of Birmingham where her research interests are the role of parents and governors in schools. She has worked on a range of projects for a variety of sponsors, including the Department for Education and Employment and the Organisation for Economic Co-operation and Development, and her current research on parental voice is funded by the Economic and Social Research Council.

Olga Miller is UK Development Officer: Services for Children and Young People with Multiple Disabilities for the Royal National Institute for the Blind and Research Associate at the Institute of Education: University of London.

Brahm Norwich has worked as a teacher in mainstream and special schools and as an educational psychologist. He is Professor of Special Needs Education at the Institute of Education, London University.

Katy Simmons is a former teacher and lecturer in higher education who for the last six years has been the co-ordinator of IPSEA (The Independent Panel for Special Education Advice), a national advocacy group which advises parents of children with special educational needs. Following the 1997 Green Paper on SEN, she led IPSEA's 'Rights at Risk' campaign and founded Action on Entitlement, a consortium of voluntary organizations formed to defend children's entitlement in law to the provision which meets their needs.

Marjorie Smith has taught throughout the age range including higher education. Her main interests are in the areas of special educational needs and gender, and she has been involved in research activities and school-based projects in these fields. She is currently an educational psychologist in the London borough of Newham.

Paul Timmins is a professional and academic tutor to the professional training course in educational psychology in the School of Education at the University of Birmingham. He also works as a senior educational psychologist in Solihull LEA. He has researched and written on the topics of collaboration approaches to research and development for school improvement and group processes and learning.

Index

Note: Figures and tables are indicated by italic type, e.g. 27*f* 23*t*. Bibliographic references at the ends of chapters are indicated by bold type, e.g. **152**